THE
MESS
WE'RE
IN

Other books by Bernard Keane

Surveillance
A Short History of Stupid (with Helen Razer)
War on the Internet (ebook)

THE MESS WE'RE IN

HOW OUR POLITICS WENT TO HELL AND DRAGGED US WITH IT

BERNARD KEANE

ALLEN&UNWIN

SYDNEY · MELBOURNE · AUCKLAND · LONDON

First published in 2018

Allen & Unwin
83 Alexander Street
Crows Nest NSW 2065
Australia
Phone: (61 2) 8425 0100
Email: info@allenandunwin.com
Web: www.allenandunwin.com

 A catalogue record for this
book is available from the
National Library of Australia

ISBN 978 1 76063 250 2

Set in 13/27 pt Bembo by Midland Typesetters, Australia
Printed and bound in Australia by Griffin Press

10 9 8 7 6 5 4 3 2 1

The paper in this book is FSC® certified.
FSC® promotes environmentally responsible,
socially beneficial and economically viable
management of the world's forests.

For Lincoln

We were not aware that civilisation was a thin and precarious crust erected by the personality and the will of a very few and only maintained by rules and conventions skilfully put across and guilefully preserved.

John Maynard Keynes

CONTENTS

INTRODUCTION

If you're under the age of 70 and live in the Western world, you've never really experienced firsthand what happens when civilisations lose their way. You're too young to remember the conflagration of World War II. The Great Depression is something you read about in textbooks; the rise of fascism is the subject of black and white documentaries. That's not to say major events haven't occurred in the years since. The Cold War was an epochal conflict that almost saw much of the world incinerated. The social fabric of the United States and European countries seriously frayed in the 1960s. There were recessions every decade from the 1970s on, sending millions into unemployment. But even when things seemed about to go seriously wrong, we managed to stay on course.

Then there was 2016, 2017 and 2018.

Those years didn't see a world war or a depression, of course (well, at least, not by the time of writing). But they gave us a startling sense that things had gotten dangerously out of control, that as a civilisation we'd lost our way, that the things we thought we knew were merely convenient illusions. In particular, it made us feel there was something seriously wrong in our societies, that a lot of our fellow citizens were very different people to what we'd assumed—they were people who deeply alarmed us.

These years have been terrible for progressives. In Australia, we saw the return of an old disease that many had believed the body politic cured of, with Pauline Hanson elected to the Senate with three (and nearly four) colleagues. Donald Trump became US president, and turned out to be an even more awful leader than expected. The United Kingdom voted to leave the European Union, then voted in an incompetent minority Tory government to implement it. In Europe, far-right parties enjoyed electoral success unseen since the 1930s.

But it wasn't much better for many conservatives. In Australia, the return of Pauline Hanson set alarm bells ringing in the Liberal and National parties. A Coalition government re-embraced protectionism of the kind last seen here in the 1970s, while its incompetence left even supporters speechless. Both Brexit and Trump represented a kind of populism that many on the Right are deeply uncomfortable with. Trump is openly hostile to free trade and blew out the US budget deficit. In the United Kingdom, over 40 per cent of Tory voters backed Remain, especially in wealthy areas in the south-east of England, while Jeremy Corbyn, a figure dismissed as a kind of joking reference to the ideological silliness of the 1970s, suddenly became a credible alternative prime minister. In central and eastern Europe, the monster of anti-Semitism appeared once again.

A new kind of terrorism arose: the elaborately planned mass-casualty events of the early years of the War on Terror gave way to cruder attacks, 'inspired' by Islamic State, that took hundreds of lives in Europe, the United States, the United Kingdom and Australia. Right-wing terrorism grew more common: a fascist murdered a British MP; a neo-Nazi murdered a protester in Charlottesville; Muslims were murdered by white terrorists in London and in Canada. Mass murders by angry males, motivated by misogyny, racism or homophobia became a recurring phenomenon. The United States endured mass shootings, often in schools, with numbing regularity; in 2017, Las Vegas was the site of one of the worst massacres since the wars against native Americans when a single gunman slaughtered 58 people and left hundreds wounded. Meanwhile, mass murder and war crimes occurred regularly in Syria, Yemen and Burma, to the general indifference of Western governments, except to the extent that those conflicts threatened to send new waves of refugees towards them.

Most pervasively, the overall tone of public debate plummeted. Hate speech, misogyny, complete indifference to facts, incoherence and stupidity were now acceptable discourse, on the basis that they were somehow 'authentic'. Even in Australia women, Muslims and LGBTI people were vilified by politicians and commentators.

What's transpired since 2016 has sometimes felt like a horrible interlude in the slow betterment of society; other times, like a mask has been pulled off to reveal our real diseased face. To determine which one is true, we must investigate what has driven these events in Australia and across the West in the last couple of years, and what underlying causes have interacted to produce the kind of dislocation and political upheaval we've witnessed. Our first step is to sort through the turmoil of 2016–18 and identify the issues beneath each event: to analyse it, categorise it, work out how it all fits together. Only once we've done that can we begin to examine the causes, and that'll be the task of Parts 2 through 4, where we'll explore three long-term forces of disruption that have engendered this turmoil. And at the end, I'm going to suggest some possible ways to repair the thin and precarious crust of civilisation that Keynes—who has a walk-on role in many of these chapters—warned us needed protecting.

Methodological note

A recurring aspect of my day job as a political writer for Crikey is people approaching me to ask, 'Why are you so cranky?'

I have little to be cranky about. I'm a middle-class white male living in a wealthy Western country that even now panders to people like me as a matter of course. My life is free of discrimination, censorship or oppression of any kind. But yes, I'm still prone to crankiness, though usually not on behalf of myself.

On whose behalf, then? *Why* exactly am I so cranky?

Well, I guess, as silly as it sounds, on behalf of facts. If there's one thing that infuriates me, it's lies, hypocrisy, inconsistency. Everything summed up by the marvellous word 'bullshit'. If someone lies in public debate, it irrationally enrages me. I can't help it. And I've ended up in the one profession where I'm exposed to little *but* lies: public debate is riddled with them, like the microbes that swarm over and within our bodies. At least most microbes serve a particular purpose, and may even be of use to the host. Lies, however, only serve the interests of those who utter them. Perhaps 'lies' is the wrong word. What we're talking about are not merely lies but deceptions: the half-truth, the twisted or incomplete fact, the wilful misinterpretation, the self-serving inconsistency, pushed with an agenda of misrepresentation.

Increasingly, though, blatant lies *are* the currency of public debate, and not just in the United States where there is a Liar-In-Chief in the Oval Office, but in Australia as well. Over the ten years I've been fortunate enough to be paid to watch politics, I've also become less and less tolerant of hypocrisy in public life. For a long while, I saw hypocrisy as a proper part of the political process, a kind of grease that kept the machine moving—oppositions that railed against outrageous practices became governments that behaved exactly the same way, using the same excuses, before savaging such practices again after the next election loss.

I understood the rationale, too. When the Rudd government tried to break from the more egregious political customs that both sides had previously engaged in, such as appointing people from both political sides to key appointments and making government more transparent and accountable and less partisan, it got exactly zero credit from either the public or the media. Understandably, Labor subsequently abandoned such a ridiculous commitment to better government. It was all downside for them.

But eventually, I came to see hypocrisy as a kind of gateway drug, a ready-to-hand double standard that enabled bigger lies and greater cynicism. Tolerating it was extending the benefit of the doubt to politicians who didn't deserve it. Not that it was confined to politicians, of course. Many in the media participate in this trashing of rationality and civil discourse. But politicians are supposed to be a bit better than that, which makes them more culpable. And if a government doesn't get credit for doing the right thing, well, bad luck—you're not in public life to get applause.

Much of this book, then, is about the contrast between what powerful people claim, and the truth. Because for all that we supposedly live in a post-truth world in which anything goes, truth still has a thorny quality that eventually ensnares even those who glibly reject it.

So now, to work: I'm going to adopt the guise of a grumpy Virgil and take you on a tour of the horrors of the past three years.

PART I

SYMPTOMS OF CHAOS: A THEMATIC HISTORY OF 2016–2018

So, things are appalling. The world's gone mad. You check the news each morning with a weird combination of terror and schadenfreude. You can barely bring yourself to follow domestic political news because it's all so abysmal. If you see your favourite musician or actor trending on Twitter, it's probably because they died, or were revealed to be a sexual predator. There is so much death and misery, so constantly from any number of places around the world, you start to feel numb.

Tell me about it. One of the challenges of writing this book has been keeping up with the constant stream of bad news, and stories of stupidity, incompetence or malice. At the time of writing, it was genuinely hard to say whether Donald Trump might still be president at the end of 2018 or Malcolm Turnbull prime minister of Australia or Theresa May prime minister of the United Kingdom, such is the fragility of the structures left teetering after the events of recent years.

It's easy to feel overwhelmed by the sheer horror of it all. But there's some good news: you can at least get a grip on all this instead of feeling like you're constantly about to be smacked in the face by a wave of sewage. One of the things that will emerge from this book, hopefully, is the realisation that while we confront a long list of problems, in some important ways the world is actually a better place than it has ever been, that part of the problem is that we're far more exposed to the bad bits than we have ever been before, and we're therefore losing sight of what's good. Another is that we're not helpless: these problems can be broken down and linked to specific causes— causes that we can actually address as intelligent citizens. So the first step in combating the feeling of being overwhelmed is to put what's been happening in recent years into some sort of order and start looking for the patterns behind it. That won't fix any problems, but it will give us a greater sense that what's going on isn't a chaotic set of disasters without rhyme or reason, but the logical consequence of things that we can fix. Once we've regained our balance and stopped feeling so overwhelmed, then we can think about what's gone wrong and how to repair it. So let's look at the last few years—not as a chronology, but through a series of themes—to see what underlying causes we can identify.

The death of trust

At the 2016 federal election in Australia, well over a million people simply didn't bother voting, leading to an unprecedented two-percentage point fall in turnout to 91 per cent—the lowest ever recorded under compulsory voting. Voters stayed away in droves. And support for the major political parties was also at an historical low, with more than one in five voters opting to back candidates from outside the mainstream Labor–Coalition nexus.

Australians, it appeared, have a problem with their democracy. Survey results confirm this. 'Australians' trust in politicians hits two-decade low', reported a University of Canberra survey in 2016. An Australian National University survey a month later revealed 'trust falls to lowest level ever recorded'. Australians aren't unusual on this. The 2017 Edelman Trust Barometer—the longest-running global trust survey—recorded the largest-ever drop in trust in politicians in the United Kingdom, and showed that Canadians' trust in their politicians had 'plummeted'. Another survey in Ireland found just 21 per cent of people trusted politicians. In the United States, Gallup found that Americans' level of trust in their political leaders fell to a new low in 2016, before Donald Trump became, in record time, the least popular president ever.

These results aren't so much about partisan anger—there will always be a substantial proportion of the electorate antipathetic toward the incumbent government in any democracy—as about how citizens of democracies, regardless of what they think of the party currently in power, view their entire governmental system. The most recent Edelman poll early in 2018 showed something even more unsettling. Many Western governments either plumbed new depths of voter distrust or continued at historic lows, but trust in the world's worst dictatorship, the Chinese government, had surged to a new high: 84 per cent of Chinese respondents trusted their government compared to 35 per cent of Australians who trusted theirs, 46 per cent of Canadians, 33 per cent of Frenchmen and women, 33 per cent of Americans and 36 per cent of Britons. Lest you think the Chinese government had worked to influence the poll, 51 per cent of Turks trusted the autocratic Erdoğan regime; 65 per cent of Singaporeans trusted their authoritarian government; even 44 per cent of Russians trusted the monstrous Vladimir Putin. The survey came out shortly before Chinese premier Xi Jinping revealed he would be abolishing China's constitutional term limit in order to remain in power permanently.

How could people living under tyranny trust their government more than citizens of democracies? That wasn't how it was supposed to work. Back in the 1990s, we had blithely assumed liberal democracy would spread around the world, with tyrannies quaking and ultimately falling in the face of people-power.

That was before Trump. Before Brexit. Before voters in country after country seemingly began to reject democratic business as usual. Suddenly, democracy began to feel like a political philosophy under siege from within and without. And leading that siege were the

Fake populists

Donald Trump ran for president as, and in office has continued to claim the status of, an outsider who would shake up an ossified US political system and put American workers first. In fact, Trump is the ultimate insider: a multimillionaire (if not the billionaire he claims to be) born into the American elite

4

and with all concomitant advantages—most particularly the ability to litigate or buy his way out of responsibility for any misconduct or criminal activity. Most of his policies reflect his membership of the conservative elite: tax cuts for large corporations and the rich; healthcare 'reform' that would deprive millions of Americans of coverage; climate change denialism: and repeal of environmental regulation. His claim that he would pursue a radically less interventionist foreign policy proved as fake as his claim that he had opposed the Iraq war. Far from being an unprecedented or radical intruder into the US political process, Trump is something we've seen before many times—indeed, it's a political archetype in the American south: the capitalist who uses racism to distract his victims from the fact that he is exploiting them.

This faux populism is a piece of anti-establishment fakery shared by similar figures elsewhere. Boris Johnson, who opportunistically paraded as a tribune of working-class *ressentiment* in campaigning against migration and threats to British sovereignty during Brexit, was educated at Eton and Balliol College, Oxford, and is a multimillionaire and former TV personality. Like Trump, Johnson is an Establishment figure who has exploited populism to give himself power, even if neither have proved competent enough to wield that power effectively. Johnson's fellow Brexiteer Nigel Farage is also a millionaire (from his career in that traditional target of populism, banking). Courtesy of riches inherited by her father, far-right French presidential candidate Marine Le Pen enjoys wealth and privilege far beyond the circumstances of the working-class French voters she purports to represent. These wealthy people pose as outsiders determined to take on the establishment that spawned them, tails that would eat their own snake.

Here, Tony Abbott is the same: the child of Sydney North Shore privilege—the finest Catholic education, Sydney University and Oxford—who embraces ever more populist positions, such as opposing immigration (despite being a migrant himself), in order to cause trouble for his successor Malcolm Turnbull. Even Barnaby Joyce, the former Nationals deputy prime minister forced out by his affair with a staff member, fits the profile: educated, like Abbott, at one of Sydney's most exclusive Catholic private schools, Riverview, the former accountant Joyce boasted that he understood the 'weatherboard and iron' people of regional Australia better than anyone because he was just like them.

These are people who, at best, haven't had any grasp of what it's like to be working class for a very long time, and more likely never, but who claim to somehow channel the beliefs and values of ordinary voters in order to garner their support.

A recurring issue in elections involving populists was

Fake news and denialism

You've heard the phrase 'fake news' endlessly in recent years. But as it turns out there are three types of fake news. The original was the kind of clickbait that exploited Google's advertising algorithms, churned out by websites such as those based in the Macedonian town of Veles: near-nonsensical stories that attracted clicks because they were so outlandish, generating remarkable revenue from Google ads. There was no political agenda to these fictions—they were simply stories intended to gull the stupid and credulous into delivering traffic to sites that could monetise it, using social-media platforms like Facebook to distribute the content. But as it turned out, the best kind of viral stories were ones that appealed to the stupidity and credulity of Donald Trump supporters.

This led to a far more overtly political kind of fake news that was strongly pro-Trump, anti-Hillary Clinton and pandered to conspiracy theorists. It also exploited a serious failing of Facebook's 'news feed': it promoted 'news' stories without regard to their accuracy or source, with credible mainstream media and eastern European fake news sites readily jumbled together. And once this phenomenon of viral pro-Trump propaganda was christened 'fake news', conservative and reactionary figures like Trump, Nigel Farage, Pauline Hanson and even Malcolm Turnbull in Australia seized on the term and used it to describe *any* news story they didn't like, regardless of accuracy. Trump went even further, with his administration claiming it had 'alternative facts' when verifiable evidence was against them, such as Trump's insistence his poorly attended inauguration was the most popular ever. The Putin regime, meanwhile, used Twitter to help Donald Trump's election: thousands of Twitter bots—automated accounts created by Russians—retweeted Trump around 470,000 times and circulated pro-Trump coverage, as part of a coordinated campaign to boost Trump and Bernie Sanders.

But this is not a phenomenon confined to the far Right. The far Left has its own fake-news agents. Western left-wing extremists, who see Syrian mass murderer Bashar al-Assad as some sort of socialist anti-American hero, enthusiastically peddle propaganda for his regime, attempting to discredit the overwhelming evidence of that dictator's mass slaughter of his own people, including with chemical weapons, and smear credible independent and anti-regime sources. And these efforts, too, are supported by Russian trolls and bots.

The irony here is that this Russian effort to create fake supporters for particular causes replicates a US military operation, revealed by journalist Barrett Brown in 2011. That project spent millions on 'online persona management' software that would allow the United States to influence online debates in other countries via fake personas pushing an agenda favoured by the US military. The Russians used exactly the same idea on the Americans themselves. On the internet, more than anywhere else, what goes around comes around.

What, then, is real online? Is that pro-Trump Twitter follower real? Is that story on Facebook about immigrants raping local women true? Is a negative story about Trump from a respected outlet true? The less certain you are of what is true, the harder it is for the people who are supposed to hold governments to account—the media, civil society bodies and opposition parties—to do so.

And fake news isn't going away. Algorithms can now seamlessly lip-sync any audio to the video of any speaker. Creating completely fake but authentic-looking lip-synced footage of a political figure saying words culled from their previous statements will soon be a technique of propagandists and fake-news peddlers. The resulting footage doesn't have to be good enough to pass forensic examination—it just needs to be good enough to look convincing on a Facebook page. The possibilities for creating chaos are limitless. Imagine Trump appearing to declare war on North Korea, or declaring martial law. Or Putin declaring the annexation of Ukraine. Or Xi Jinping announcing that the renegade province of Taiwan was to be returned to the motherland. All intended to fool online viewers, perhaps goad them into taking to the streets, or aimed at crashing stock markets (or boosting the share prices of certain companies). It's possible that in coming years, the fake news of the 2016 election will look positively innocuous.

But to what extent did such manipulation help elect Trump? Almost certainly not a great deal. More damaging was the Russian hack of the Democratic National Committee's emails, which were then passed via a third party to WikiLeaks and used to undermine the Clinton campaign. But even this wasn't particularly significant. It was Hillary Clinton's and the Democrats' incompetence that lost the election. The problem was the audience for fake news, not the creation of it. The problem was the deep alienation in the US electorate fake news played to, not the Russian government-funded trolls of the Internet Research Agency. The sort of people who believed fake news were probably never going to vote for Clinton anyway.

The flip side of a willingness to believe fictional 'news' is rampant denialism—not merely a lack of interest in, but an active hostility to, evidence that doesn't accord with people's preferred narrative, whether on Clinton versus Trump, the economic consequences of leaving the European Union, the alleged threat of sharia law, or vaccination or climate change. This refusal to accept facts that don't suit people's political views seems to go hand in hand with a willingness to accept lies, no matter how implausible, that do.

Like the rise of fake news, this outbreak of mass hostility to facts has had journalists, media commentators and academics agonising over where it came from. Psychologists are pressed to explain why so many people are now so averse to evidence, especially on things as well documented as vaccination or climate change. One argument, advanced in a psychology thesis by Swedish doctoral candidate Kirsti M. Jylhä, is that conservative white males are the people most likely to be climate denialists, because they are more likely to benefit from the preservation of the status quo, less likely to be empathetic and more likely to have 'social dominance orientation'—to think in terms of rigid hierarchies, with themselves at the top and everyone else, including the environment, below them.

But one problem with this argument is that denialism isn't confined to old white men. While climate denialism is primarily the province of white, conservative, right-wing males (like Holocaust denialism, which appears to exist almost exclusively among right-wing males), vaccination denialism has a far wider demographic distribution. In Australia, it extends to both affluent middle-class women in metropolitan areas and alternative lifestylers in regional communities; in the United States, anti-vaxxers range from affluent and well-educated communities to middle-income conservatives. Western supporters of Assad who reject all evidence of atrocities by that regime in Syria include academics and highly educated, affluent left-wingers. While it is true that denialism appears to be a particularly *white* phenomenon, and often occurs among older people, it occurs too frequently across different groups to be linked simply to demographics.

If fake news and denialism didn't play as big a role in political events as some have maintained, there's no doubt that another form of bias did:

Xenophobia and bigotry

Australia's 2016 election saw the return of Pauline Hanson to the political stage, eighteen years after she had last demeaned it with her presence. Hanson (who has grown wealthy via election funding over the last two decades, garnering public funding payments estimated at $6 million) was elected to the Senate with another Queensland senator, a New South Wales senator and a Western Australian senator, and came within a few votes of getting a Tasmanian senator as well. Hanson's political model is based on bigotry, although she has mostly relinquished the original target of her racism in the 1990s— immigrants from China and Southeast Asia—in favour of calling for a ban on Muslim immigration, banning the burqa (she wore one in the Senate as a stunt) and even the internment of Muslims. One of Hanson's senators (among several who left or lost their seats) also peddled old myths of international financial conspiracies and frequently singled out the Rothschild family as a sinister force in world affairs.

Hanson had benefited from the decision of the Seven television network to give her, in effect, free advertising in the lead-up to the 2016 election via a regular morning breakfast television slot (the same network, incidentally, that in 2018 gave a neo-Nazi a platform to vilify Sudanese migrants in Victoria).

Not that racism and bigotry are confined to One Nation in Australian politics; members of the Liberal and Liberal National parties frequently use similar language about Muslims. In early 2018, former prime minister Tony Abbott called for a massive cut in immigration until migrants had better integrated into Australian society. Turnbull and his immigration minister tried to whip up panic about violence by Sudanese immigrants in Victoria. The Senate, with the support of the government, conducted an 'inquiry' into halal certification. One Liberal senator circulated social-media posts by Britain First, the racist group linked to the murder of British MP Jo Cox and the Finsbury Park terror attack. Even the Labor Party was embarrassed by an ad promising to protect workers that featured almost entirely white faces.

Xenophobia was on the march elsewhere as well. Donald Trump famously began his campaign for the presidency by singling out Mexicans, whom he declared were rapists and murderers, then endlessly claimed he would 'build a wall', paid for by Mexico, to stop illegal immigration. The wall—which was later sometimes called a fence and perhaps, by the time you read this, will have been reduced to a sturdy hedge—remains unbuilt and Mexicans unbilled. Trump also has it in for Muslims, promising to prevent them from entering the United States, and with sufficient bluntness that successive courts struck down his entry ban, despite the best efforts of his administration to pretend it wasn't religion-specific.[1] Trump also caused controversy, even within his own White House, when he defended Nazis who converged on Charlottesville in August 2017 as 'fine people'.

Unsurprisingly, Trump is the most racially polarising presidential candidate for over a generation. He received just 8 per cent of the African–American vote in November 2016, 28 per cent of the Hispanic vote and 27 per cent of the Asian–American vote. But he performed spectacularly well among working-class white voters, where he thrashed Hillary Clinton. And not just working-class white males, either: more than half of white female voters were prepared to overlook Trump's boasts of sexual assault, the many women who alleged

---

1   Six months after taking office, Trump finally got the US Supreme Court to allow a highly modified version of it.

sexual harassment by him, his call for women to be punished for having abortions, and his misogynistic abuse of female journalists, and vote for him over Clinton.

Race also played a fundamental role in the success of Brexit in the United Kingdom in 2016. Leave campaigners returned time and again to the issue of immigration and the lack of controls over the entry of European workers into the United Kingdom. As in the United States after Trump's election, there was a surge of hate speech in the United Kingdom after Brexit, and not merely at predictable targets such as Muslims, but at European people as well.

In France, Marine Le Pen campaigned hard with a blatantly Islamophobic message, but also returned to that hardy perennial of the French Catholic Right, anti-Semitism—calling for bans on Israeli–French dual nationality and the public wearing of the kippah. And while she has never been as open about denying the Holocaust as her father Jean-Marie, she suggested during the 2017 French election campaign that France bore no responsibility for Holocaust-related events that occurred in that country during World War II.

Open bigotry remains a clear and present danger among right-wing politicians elsewhere in Europe. The Hungarian government of Viktor Orbán is increasingly autocratic and has begun recycling anti-Semitic tropes from the 1930s, praising Hungary's World War II Nazi collaborators and indulging calls for anti-Semitic policies. Poland's right-wing government has likewise encouraged anti-Semitism, criminalised the publication of any suggestion Poles played a role in the Holocaust, attacked women's groups and domestic-violence agencies and adopted increasingly authoritarian policies. Norbert Hofer, who was only narrowly defeated in 2016 in the Austrian presidential election, said bluntly, 'Islam has no place in Austria.' In late 2017, his far-right party, the *Freiheitliche Partei Österreichs* (Freedom Party of Austria), joined the Austrian government, with Hofer taking a senior portfolio. Just to the north, the far-right *Alternative für Deutschland* (Alternative for Germany) became the third-largest party in Germany in the September 2017 federal election.

However, the persistent theme across different countries isn't merely xenophobia, Islamophobia or other forms of religious bigotry, but

Taking back control

While there's a specifically Islamophobic and anti-Semitic strain to the parties of the European Right, One Nation and Trump, much of the racial debate in Europe has centred around flows of refugees from Syria and elsewhere in the Middle East, and illegal immigrants, primarily from Africa, entering Europe via Italy. Leave sentiment in the Brexit referendum reflected concerns about the inability of the British government, under EU rules, to prevent the free movement of EU citizens into the United Kingdom and the sense that British workers were no longer being put first. So, too, in the United States, where the promise to build a wall exploited concerns about uncontrolled illegal immigration via the United States' southern border. Right-wing parties in Italy speak of '*degrado*' ('decay'), the supposed damage caused by unchecked immigration, especially of Africans.

This reflects the Australian experience, where a widespread electoral reaction against refugees has spiked when there's been a surge of maritime asylum seekers and illegal immigrants

(Australia has been the target of numbers of Chinese and Tamil illegal immigrants, as well as genuine asylum seekers) and then lapsed when there are few boat arrivals. Otherwise, Australia's high level of immigration—more than half of all Australians were either born overseas or have a parent who was born overseas—and high per capita refugee resettlement program, has traditionally proceeded without overly concerning voters.

It is the perception that borders are uncontrolled, that anyone can come in, that appears to alarm voters in an otherwise high-immigration society like Australia. And this plays to fears of invasion by some vast Other, people not so much of a different race—although that's bad enough—but a different culture, with different values to our own (as the recurrence of the idea of 'integration with our values' suggests). Those fears are triggered far more easily among white people than among other races and cultures—consider the vast numbers of Syrian refugees that the people of Lebanon (over one million refugees), Jordan (650,000) and Turkey (3.4 million) have hosted, not happily by any means, but with greater willingness than that of many Australians to accept far smaller numbers of asylum seekers.

The concept of control is crucial to the fake populists. 'Take back control!' Boris Johnson urged Britons during the Brexit debate. 'We are transferring power from Washington, DC, and giving it back to you, the people,' Trump said in his inaugural speech. Marine Le Pen, too, promised to 'take back control' of France's borders and economy. They all feed on a potent sense of disempowerment felt by many citizens in their countries, and offer to restore a past in which, at least in the minds of those citizens, people like themselves were in control, and decided who should enter the country.

The Australian experience throughout the twentieth century has been of successive waves of Others who, in time, have been embraced as a core part of the Australian community: Irish Catholics were originally judged to be anti-British republican papists who owed allegiance to a foreign power in the Vatican; Italians, Greeks and other Europeans were deemed 'wogs' with strange customs and peculiar food; Vietnamese refugees were slighted as criminals and drug dealers who wouldn't assimilate, along with other generic 'Asians'; and now Muslims—lumped together as a sinister monolith despite the wide variety of countries and cultures they hail from—are, like all newcomers before them, held to be not only unassimilable but even unwilling to assimilate, because of their uniquely anti-Western religion. And already, Sudanese migrants are becoming the new Other.

In the historical long view, this process of alienation to affection, repeated over and over for different waves of immigrants, might be mistaken for a charming demonstration of the Aussie myth of the 'fair go'. For those who lived through it, and endured the abuse, assaults and discrimination, it was very different.

Australia's particular obsession with its maritime borders adds a different kind of xenophobia on top of this, one that prompts us to divide people into two groups—law-abiding immigrants prepared to Do the Right Thing, to wait their turn, to come to Australia 'properly', and lawless invaders unwilling to do the right thing, who want to, to use a phrase long employed in Australia, 'Jump the queue'. The rich irony of that mindset is that Australia, as a colonial settler society, was founded by the ultimate queue jumpers: invaders and occupiers who dispossessed and killed the original inhabitants of

Australia and stole their land. No wonder we're so hypersensitive about unauthorised maritime arrivals: they remind us of the very foundations of white Australian society and the fact that we remain occupiers of Aboriginal and Torres Strait Islander lands.

But if xenophobia is such an important characteristic of recent years, we need to resolve how it interacts with

Employment and economics

Many on the Left argue that it wasn't racism that drove so many white working-class Americans to vote for Trump, but liberal economics and resentment of declining manufacturing employment. African-Americans mock this echo of Marxist thinking as delusional, and given Trump's blatant white supremacism as president, it's hard to see how they don't have the better of the argument. African-Americans are three times more likely to be shot by police than white Americans and six times more likely to be incarcerated. White Americans are far more likely to walk away free when they kill African-Americans than the other way around. And overlooked in the economic argument is that African-Americans had even greater economic reason to reject a business-as-usual presidential candidate like Clinton and embrace Trump, and did not do so: for example, unemployment among African-Americans in November 2016, at 8 per cent, was still around twice that of white Americans despite years of strong growth under Barack Obama.

In Australia, too, it's hard to see how economics trumps racism. It has been wealthy politicians who have called for bans on Muslim migration and the internment of Muslims. Conservative commentators and major corporate-funded lobby groups, like the Institute of Public Affairs, openly oppose recognition of Aboriginal and Torres Strait Islander people in Australia's constitution. These things have nothing to do with economics. The wealthy think tank head or the prominent commentator who declares that there's nothing 'special' about Australia's First Peoples is not reflecting the economic fragility of a globalised world, but their own privilege as (invariably) powerful white males.

But with racism and economics, it's not an either/or: you don't have to line up with the identity-politics brigade to feel that white racism was an important element in Donald Trump's victory, but nor do you have to adhere to a Marxist 'culture is mere superstructure and capitalism is intrinsically racist' view of the world to see that economics and globalisation were key factors in the xenophobia on display around the Western world in 2016 and 2017, along with outright racism.

Leave sentiment in the Brexit debate in the United Kingdom wasn't merely hostile toward citizens from elsewhere in the European Union (especially poorer eastern European countries) but also based on concerns about the displacement of British workers by workers from elsewhere in Europe. 'British jobs for British workers', as Farage put it. Hostility to refugees in Australia is highest in suburban areas of major cities, where poor infrastructure and soaring house prices engender the bumper sticker sentiment 'Fuck off, we're full'. In many regional communities, conversely, refugees are welcomed, bringing much-needed labour and population growth to towns dealing with the complex economics of rural production and demographic decline—where Australia's production and exports have surged while the number of workers in agriculture has fallen significantly. Meanwhile, there's strong evidence that business exploits foreign workers—there has been revelation after revelation of major franchise retailers exploiting foreign workers on temporary employment or student visas, and it's well established that employers in the construction sector use sham contracting arrangements to underpay foreign workers, which both undercuts Australian workers' wages and reduces safety on construction sites.

The return of protectionism has been the primary issue in which the question of racism versus economic vulnerability has played out.

Free trade has always had a mixed reputation. Its benefits are diffuse, if very real; its disadvantages limited but concentrated. But at the moment, free trade is widely reviled. It's not merely, as previously discussed, that open borders for *people* are seen as the problem—open borders for goods, services and investment are a problem as well. Donald Trump has attacked trade agreements, imposed tariffs on steel and aluminium, and sparked a trade war with China; the British are leaving the world's largest free market; Australia has re-embraced industrial protectionism and market interventionism; everywhere, parties of both the Left and the Right are offering interventionist solutions to placate electorates.

Trump's focus is primarily on the shift of US jobs, especially manufacturing jobs, to other countries—one issue that aligns Trump much more with unionists and Democrats than with many Republicans. But it overlooks the interests of US consumers, who might benefit from buying cheaper products made in other countries, and workers in other industries disadvantaged by tariffs. The number of steel workers who will benefit from the tariffs imposed by Trump in that sector in early 2018, at around 140,000, is dwarfed by the millions of employees in industries that face higher input costs as a result of the tariffs, potentially driving their employers to reduce their workforces.

Across the Atlantic, the UK government has to address a serious contradiction around Brexit. Because Brexit was driven by hostility to foreign workers and, to a lesser extent, claims that British taxpayers were subsidising the rest of the European Union, Leavers and the Tory government have to pretend that the United Kingdom will be able to retain all the economic benefits of membership of the world's largest trade group without any of the responsibilities—a paradox that Leavers have consistently failed to coherently address, especially given the lack of expertise in trade negotiations (or, really, anything else) within the UK government. Britain is now trawling the world for 'free trade' partners, having just declared it was leaving the planet's largest free-trade zone; the chlorine-washed chicken meat of US farmers may be on British plates before 2020.

In Australia, Pauline Hanson shares this focus on local jobs and wants to withdraw from *all* trade agreements. 'One Nation is strongly opposed to the "free trade" economic policies which, over the years, have led to the gradual destruction of the Australian manufacturing industry. With the resulting loss of hundreds of thousands of Australians jobs, there is an increasing dependence on the import of foreign goods to satisfy basic local demands,' her party's platform reads, reflecting a kind of autarky thinking that sees *any* consumption of foreign products as somehow unAustralian (ironic given One Nation steals its many conspiracy theories from overseas). In

Hanson's world, it's better to live poor but self-reliant, rather than richer but with the filthy handiwork of foreign workers.

But other, less extreme, political figures in Australia also reject free trade—Nick Xenophon, who created a potent independent political force in Australia's most protectionist state, South Australia, is definitely old school when it comes to protecting manufacturing, while sharing none of the xenophobia and race hate that Hanson represents. And the Labor Party has long retained an industrial protectionist element within its ranks, which has survived the long winter of economic rationalism and is now enjoying a new spring of political fashionability.

In the last two years in Australia, as elsewhere, protectionism has also become a much greater concern for voters. This has partly manifested in regard to temporary workers. In 2013, a desperate Labor tried to use the issue of 457 visa temporary workers to portray itself as pro-Aussie workers in the run-up to that year's election, but failed to get traction. At the 2016 election, however, Labor ran a highly successful anti-457 visa campaign in Queensland, where it helped deliver them several seats. Labor continued to press the campaign following the election, and the Coalition—long a champion of skilled migration and expanding temporary-worker schemes to help business keep wages down—was forced to shift dramatically, announcing the 'abolition' of the 457 visa altogether (it has been replaced with a similar, slightly more limited and renamed, visa).

Australians also have a particular problem with foreign investment. Having always depended on foreign capital to fund our economic development, we are a superb example of the benefits of foreign investment. But we have a long-standing strain of economic nationalism that sees foreign investment as a threat, rather than an opportunity, especially in agriculture and resources projects. This is particularly directed at Asian investors. Australian agriculture has historically enjoyed very high levels of foreign ownership, primarily by British and American firms. As former Liberal trade minister Andrew Robb used to point out to protectionists, no one ever expressed concerns about white, English-speaking foreigners owning large swathes of our arable land—but it's terrible if Chinese investors do the same thing. Japanese investors and companies in the 1980s similarly faced hostility (now forgotten in the wake of Japan's Lost Decades, but extraordinarily virulent at the time, especially in Queensland). This is another form of economic nationalism that went mainstream, driven not by the Left but by the Right, with the National Party pushing hard against Chinese investment in agriculture and the Liberals against Chinese investment in real estate.

The biggest shift on protectionism was already underway by the 2016 election, and it was almost universally supported across the political spectrum. Despite ostensibly embracing 'free-trade agreements', the current Australian government, with the ardent support of the Labor opposition, has committed to spend up to $60 billion to build naval submarines and warships in Australia, rather than purchase better, cheaper vessels from other countries at, according to one estimate, around 70 per cent of the price of building the things locally. This is the ultimate in 'Paying a bit more'—a Buy Australian campaign with ten zeros. We've also committed to spending several billion dollars in an attempt to bolster Australia's defence exports via the dodgy mechanism of export financing loans, as a further fillip for this new target of government industry largesse.

Having closed our long-protected car industry, where tariffs and handouts cost around $10,000 a year per worker to generate tens of thousands of jobs, we've embraced the defence industry, where the cost is around $1 million a year per worker for a few thousand jobs. In abandoning economic rationalism for economic nationalism, we're not even doing protectionism as efficiently as we used to.

But while we've restarted the practice of handing out large amounts of money to companies to make stuff here, business has been busy

Alienating the customers

The reputation of Australian business and its leaders is dreadful. It is plagued by scandals, misconduct, tax dodging, allegations of criminality and mistreatment of workers, at even the biggest firms. 'It is not in shareholders' interests or the national interest that the relationship between banks and the community continues in this way,' said David Gonski, bank chairman and one of the country's most politically attuned business leaders, in May 2017. That was before the banking royal commission exposed some of the country's biggest companies as rapacious gougers and blatant criminals.

The royal commission was prompted by the fact that every one of the major banks in Australia has been implicated in some form of scandal in recent years. The most serious involved the Commonwealth Bank—once upon a time, government owned. Apart from tens of thousands of alleged breaches of anti-money laundering laws, its insurance arm so egregiously swindled its customers that the bank was forced to apologise, and its financial planning arm was revealed to have employed unethical and, in some cases, outright criminal financial planners who ripped millions of dollars off clients. Worse, the corporate regulator ASIC had been asleep at the wheel throughout, its failings exposed over and over as the royal commission uncovered crimes and misconduct at a level that shocked even industry veterans.

But while Australians will always hate banks, other industries also drew unwanted attention. Major retail franchise chains systematically underpaid workers. There were bribery and fraud allegations involving major mining companies. Rorts and rips-off in the vocational education industry cost taxpayers hundreds of millions of dollars. Aged-care companies gouging the elderly. Offshore environmental disasters. CEO sex scandals.

Some sectors revealed major structural problems. In the 1990s, as part of the Keating government's micro-economic reform agenda, Australia established a national (or more correctly, east coast) electricity market with what became a mix of corporatised and privatised generators, monopoly transmission and distribution providers and retailers operating in an extraordinarily complex market intended to provide least-cost, reliable power supply to both consumers and businesses. However, over the course of 2016 and 2017, it became obvious that there were three basic problems with the electricity market. First, market regulators lacked sufficient powers to prevent participants—and government-owned generators were the worst offenders—from gaming the system to force huge price rises onto customers. Second, the Liberal Party's refusal to seriously address climate change and provide a consistent framework for investors in energy infrastructure saw investment in energy fall just as the east coast's fleet of coal-fired power plants was reaching the end of their working lives. And third, the market for what was intended to be the key transitional power source, natural gas, was even more corrupt and poorly regulated than the broader electricity market, while Australia's east coast natural gas supplies were set to be connected to international markets for the first time via three new massive liquefied natural gas export facilities in Queensland.

The result was wave after wave of massive power price rises, even though the government repeatedly promised prices would fall. Worse, the closure of ancient coal-fired plants reduced supply and forced prices up, meaning consumers and industry were paying significantly more for power that was more prone to blackouts.

The much-vaunted electricity market, supposed to demonstrate the virtues of a market-based approach to providing essential services, had failed, and corporations were coining it at the expense of their customers. The application of market forces and government ineptitude to the energy sector had led to far higher prices, much lower reliability—and a surge in the sector's carbon emissions. It was an impressive threefold failure in one of the most important policy areas within the control of government.

Then there was the problem of company tax. Primarily due to the diligence of journalists like Michael West, the extraordinary extent of tax avoidance by Australia's—and some of the world's—largest companies became a greater and greater scandal with the public, who began to see the tax system as deeply skewed to benefit corporations and the wealthy. As with the banks, the government initially tried to cover the issue up,

seeking and failing to prevent laws that would require the publication of the tax details of the country's largest companies. High
profile entities, like Rupert Murdoch's News Corp, Transfield
and Qantas, were revealed to have paid no tax at all in some years,
while global tech companies like Apple paid a pittance in tax on
massive revenues, courtesy of profit-shifting arrangements.

This wasn't a purely Australian problem: the OECD
(Organisation for Economic Co-operation and Development)
and the G20 have been labouring for years on the challenge
of what is officially labelled base erosion and profit shifting, or
BEPS—the ways multinational companies game the laws of
individual countries, and use the tax havens of others, to move
money around and avoid paying tax. The United States worked
hard to stymie any international agreement that might see US
companies forced to pay something approaching a fair share of
tax in the countries where they derive revenue (US companies
like Apple had over $2 trillion in profits held offshore, beyond
the reach of any tax authorities including the United States,
until Donald Trump in effect paid them to bring it onshore
with his corporate tax cut). After initially insisting it could not
act until the OECD hammered out an international agreement, eventually the Australian government followed the lead
of the UK government and took steps to unilaterally curb the
more egregious abuses of corporate tax laws.

For the business lobby, however, the issue about tax wasn't
how they could pay their fair share, but about how their share
could be reduced: business lobbies convinced the Liberal Party
to propose a company tax cut of—at current reckoning—
around $80 billion over a decade.

What was rarely mentioned was that big business is already
paying far less than the 30 per cent nominal tax rate that

applies in Australia and which it claimed to be internationally uncompetitive. For example, the average rate of tax paid by the 120-odd members of the Business Council of Australia in 2014 and 2015 was 24.4 per cent of their profits. Thirty-eight of them paid no tax at all. Twenty-four paid the full rate of 30 per cent; another 31 paid tax at or above the 25 per cent rate proposed by the Liberals. Fifty-one companies paid less than 20 per cent, including large companies like AMP (a major target of the banking royal commission), Macquarie Bank and Fortescue Metals.

Corporations might have outraged the public with their behaviour. But were Australians themselves any better? Because it seemed like many of us were engaged in a

War on the young

According to Australia's media—which is mostly ignored by people under 25—our young people are appalling. For a start, they—like their overseas counterparts—are responsible for destroying a huge range of industries. Millennials are killing TV networks, golf, restaurant chains and department stores. They're not buying cars because they don't drive. They're leaking national security information. They 'hook up' with randoms online (or possibly they're too lazy to have as much sex as their parents' generation). They're addicted to their phones. They have no loyalty to employers. They grow silly beards. They travel overseas and pursue other self-indulgences. And of course, all that is on top of the charges levelled at every new generation: they binge drink and use the latest, scarier-than-ever drug. They also complain too much and eat food that's too expensive. The reason they can't afford housing, according to 'demographer' Bernard Salt in 2016, is because they eat 'smashed avocado with crumbled feta on five-grain toasted bread', thus condemning themselves to eternal renting, or living with their parents.

Behind the silly attacks on millennials, however, is a grim reality: our young people are set to be our most screwed-over, betrayed and exploited generation since the 1930s. They're the targets of a generational war waged by the rest of us.

Australia's tax system, which subsidises the property specu-lation of housing investors, heavily skews the property market against young people and low-income earners, in essence forcing them to compete with wealthier, and usually older, investors who can use negative gearing and capital gains tax exemptions to fund their property investment. Most of that investment has gone into the purchase of existing properties, rather than funding new housing stock. And for much of the last fifteen years, state governments, and especially the NSW government, grievously failed to drive enough housing construction in major centres. It's only been in the last three to four years, due to a long period of very low interest rates, that new dwelling stock, much of it apartments, has been created in major centres at a rate suffi-cient to match population growth. But property owners living in established suburbs in our major cities have proved adept at blocking medium-density housing development, pricing lower-income and young people out of suburbs on existing transport networks close to sources of employment—and increasing the value of their properties at the same time. NIMBYism has become another tool in our war on young people.

Unusually, in 2016 federal Labor went to an election with a tax policy that tilted the property playing field marginally back in favour of younger people and low-income earners, reversing the longstanding tendency of politicians to take the side of the more numerous, and far more politically powerful, home owners and investors. This decision by Labor was demonised as threatening the entire fabric of the Australian economy and—in one of the more amusing claims of the 2016 election campaign—that it was low-income earners themselves who mainly took advantage of negative gearing and capital gains tax exemptions.

A badly skewed property market, in which taxpayers subsidise older, wealthier home owners to compete against young people, isn't merely an issue of fairness. It is economically and socially dislocative: to access jobs and other economic opportunities, young people and low-income earners must work in areas where they can't afford to buy, meaning they rent forever or spend much of their time trapped in gridlocked infrastructure trying to get to their jobs. And services that need low- and middle-income earning employees—health care, childcare, aged care, education—struggle to attract staff because the people they would normally recruit live dozens of kilometres and 90 minutes away by car.

But we're also making it harder for young people to service a mortgage, should they get one, because we're imposing other debts on them. Instead of understanding education as an investment in the skills of Australia's next generation of workers, managers and entrepreneurs, we're imposing greater student debt on young people—debt that the Coalition has sought to significantly increase, while cutting higher education funding.[2]

---

2 Despite many Coalition ministers, who are of my generation, having benefited from either free or heavily subsidised university education.

Students and former students in Australia currently owe over $40 billion to the government, with debt expected to rise to over $180 billion by the mid 2020s. Funding has also been cut (by both sides of politics) to the higher-education sector, which has also been allowed to offer as many places as there are publicly funded takers, meaning universities have dropped standards to attract as many domestic and foreign students as possible. While this has been a boon for Australia's education 'exports'—which are third only to iron ore and coal—it has led to a serious lowering of the academic reputation of Australian universities.

Australian student debt isn't particularly high by US standards: the US$1.4 trillion student debt is the second biggest debt in that country behind mortgages, and amounts to over US$37,000 per student/former student/graduate. In 2017, UK student debt reached over £100 billion for the first time, but the per-person debt is much higher there than in the United States, at £32,000. Australians, at least, aren't compelled to start repaying their debt until their income tops $50,000, a higher figure than elsewhere in the OECD (and one the Coalition wants to reduce). Like Australians, young people in the United Kingdom also face an extraordinarily expensive property market, due to that country's apparent inability to build enough housing, perhaps explaining why Jeremy Corbyn, who promised to abolish tuition fees, has achieved folk hero status among many young people and lifted Labour's youth vote.

The combined effect of these policies is that many young Australians accrue a mid-five-figure debt even before taking on a far bigger debt to buy a home, or must live with, or borrow large amounts from, their parents.

Australia's government also has it in for our youth on climate change. Australia is the developed economy most at risk from climate change, courtesy of our tropical north, our tendency to drought, our reliance on agricultural exports and the fact that the bulk of our population lives along the coast. Australia should be a world leader in both reducing carbon emissions and in encouraging other countries to do likewise, purely out of self-interest. Instead, the government's policy is modest cuts to Australia's carbon emissions—26 to 28 per cent on 2005 levels by 2030—and (as of writing) no policy to achieve those modest cuts. Indeed, the current government removed a highly effective and cheap emissions abatement scheme, under which Australia's emissions fell significantly, and failed to replace it with any meaningful policy, causing emissions to begin rising again in 2015. We may only produce around 2 per cent of the world's carbon emissions, but we're behind only the oil theocracies of the Middle East in per capita emissions, and set a wretched example for a country that desperately needs other, bigger economies to rein in their emissions.

In the meantime the world grows hotter: 2016, 2015 and 2014 were each the world's hottest years on record. 2017 was the second hottest after 2016 and the hottest without an El Niño. Ice coverage in the Arctic has reached record lows. Extreme weather events are becoming more common and starting to have greater economic impacts.

Failure to act on climate change is intergenerational theft on a colossal scale. Future generations across the world will have lower standards of living, suffer poorer health outcomes, pay higher prices and have to deal with more climate refugees and more catastrophic weather events. The tragedy of inaction on climate change is that older generations are not even gaining a great deal from this robbery. The cost of reducing emissions is relatively low—as we saw when we had a functioning carbon-pricing scheme. (Indeed, with certainty in our climate-action policies, we might have had greater investment in our energy industry and headed off recent problems.) And the nature of climate action is such that the costs of taking action increase the longer we delay, meaning our economic gain now is limited but the future costs will continue to rise. It's a kind of malicious, self-defeating robbery where we don't even particularly benefit from what we've stolen.

It seems for many Australians, our young people are a limitless resource they can squeeze ever harder to maintain their own incomes. In 2017, there was dismay when evidence emerged that young people were abandoning private health insurance—alarming, given private health insurance basically relies on gouging younger people to subsidise the healthcare costs of older people. Given all the other ways in which our youth are being slugged, who could blame them for turning their backs on yet another rort perpetuated by people of my generation and older?

The failure to take any serious action on climate change is merely one of a long list of

Political failures

We live in an era when democratic politicians struggle to get the basics right. Sure, there are leaders like Emmanuel Macron and Justin Trudeau who have ridden a wave of popularity in office (although Trudeau's polling declined significantly in early 2018). But they appear to be exceptions to the rule that the contemporary collection of Western political leaders are, well, duds.

Let's start with the United States. Hillary Clinton managed to lose what should have been—despite the torrent of misogynistic hate directed towards her—an unlosable election against a candidate who offered political ammunition by the truckload. Her campaign had a fatal weakness: an inability to detect where the Democrat vote was weak, especially in manufacturing states, where white male working-class grievance was strongest. Having failed to detect it, she was unable to address it (or even, for that matter, campaign in those states). The vaunted Democrat ground game failed to turn out the vote when people should have been clamouring for the chance to push back against a fraud, bankrupt and self-confessed sexual predator like Trump. But part of the problem in 2016 was that, whatever her party's failings, Clinton never offered a compelling message about *why* she wanted to be president, or engaged with voters about how she would address their economic concerns. All she offered was a blithe assurance that things would continue more or less as they had, at a point when people wanted real change. If Clinton's husband had been an almost supernaturally gifted politician, she turned out to be the reverse.

But however inept Clinton was as a campaigner, you always had the sense she would have been a competent, traditional president. Donald Trump has turned out, unsurprisingly, to be wholly incompetent as president, executive and, for that matter, human being. Eighteen months since his election, hundreds of positions remain unfilled within his administration, he has sacked scores of his own senior White House officials, undermined some of the remainder by publicly criticising them, publicly feuded with former staff, presided over two government shutdowns, launched a trade war off the cuff and spent more than a quarter of his time as president at his golf resorts (even though he claimed he would have no time for golf as president because, 'I'm gonna be working for you'). Despite controlling the White House, the Senate and the House of Representatives, Republicans under Trump have so far proved unable to deliver any of his agenda except the one thing business donors paid them to produce: a huge tax cut for companies. The repeal of Obamacare, a signature policy Trump promised for 'day one', remains yet to happen. And the US budget deficit, which was slowly shrinking under Barack Obama, has increased dramatically.[3]

It's difficult to put together a highlights reel of Trump's incompetence; any random seven-day period of his administration would serve up some outrageous tweets, several blatant lies, a resignation or sacking of a Cabinet member or senior staffer (often accompanied by multiple and changing explanations), speculation about other sackings, criticism of a US ally, confusion about a major US policy, and several major leaks, usually the result of internecine wars within the White House.

Incompetence is contagious, though, and has spread across the Atlantic. It's almost forgotten that Brexit destroyed the hitherto-successful prime ministership of David Cameron, who began the referendum proposal as a ploy to head off the hardline Eurosceptics who had plagued the Conservative Party since the Thatcher years. Cameron was a reasonably competent political leader: he saw off the underrated Gordon Brown (whose handling of the financial crisis in the UK was superb) in 2010 and managed an occasionally fractious minority

---

3   Worse, it's done so at a time when unemployment in the United States was already near record lows, raising concerns about over-stimulus of the US economy.

government for five years, before defeating Ed Miliband to narrowly secure majority government (the wrong brother: if David Miliband had won the Labour leadership in 2010, British political history would now be very, very different). But with the world at his feet and his opponent a seemingly hapless Jeremy Corbyn, Cameron spectacularly blew it, turning in an indifferent performance in the Brexit campaign that left him with no alternative but to quit.

As is the pattern of these things, Cameron's departure merely opened the door to others of even less ability. Boris Johnson destroyed his own chances for the prime ministership and had to make way for Theresa May, who rapidly proved—for all the Iron Lady Redux imagery from the right-wing press—quite stupendously inept. Having promised not to call an early election, she promptly did so, bungled her way through the worst Tory campaign since the Blair years, and lost majority government. Suddenly Corbyn, who had been reviled by the political establishment and many of his own party, looked every inch the prime minister-in-waiting. May subsequently complained that her decision to call an early election had left her own party unprepared, and coughed her way through a comically awful speech to the following Tory party conference that prompted some of her own MPs to call for her to quit. She later attempted a ministerial reshuffle that came unstuck when ministers refused to move, or walked away from the ministry rather than accept different jobs.

Meanwhile, having triggered the two-year countdown to depart the European Union, Britain's exit negotiations were marked by cluelessness, chaos and a slowly dawning awareness that 40 years of economic and regulatory integration weren't to be undone in a matter of months—at least, not without basic problems like entire industries relocating from the United Kingdom to Europe, which is what began happening to the UK's economic mainstay, its finance industry. Luckily, in 2017, May received a foreign visitor well-placed to offer her advice on how to handle failure . . .

Malcolm Turnbull and the politics of disappointment

Australia's leader advised May to 'Govern like you have a hundred-seat majority', which was particularly ironic given Turnbull had a one-seat majority himself, courtesy of his own spectacular political miscalculation in also calling an early election, in 2016. Indeed, Turnbull's government has proved to be the least competent since the Whitlam years—an impressive feat given his immediate predecessors were Tony Abbott, who was so bad his own party had sacked him, and the permanent Labor brawl between Kevin Rudd and Julia Gillard. We all thought Turnbull would turn the page on years of political soap opera. How wrong we were.

Whether on policy or politics, the Turnbull government has been a disaster. The National Broadband Network—once a major nation-building project that promised to finally deliver to Australians the kinds of internet speeds most developed, and some developing, countries take for granted—was significantly downgraded, faced a massive volume of complaints about poor or no service, and blew out in cost and timing despite the downgraded service being justified as cheaper and quicker.

On Indigenous issues, we actually managed to go backwards, despite it being one of the few areas of genuine bipartisanship and goodwill. The process to recognise Australia's First Peoples in the constitution ground to a halt when the Turnbull government, having asked Indigenous communities what form recognition should take, decided it didn't like the answer—to establish an Indigenous voice in parliament and commence a process to reach a treaty between Indigenous people and non-Indigenous Australians—then wilfully misrepresented that answer for political purposes. After ten years, the Closing the Gap process to bring Indigenous people up to the health, education and economic standards enjoyed by non-Indigenous people was mostly well behind schedule, and in some cases the 'gap' was growing, not diminishing. Moreover, the government decided to seek partisan advantage in demonising proposals to move Australia's national day away from a date associated entirely with invasion and occupation.

When it came to political management, things were even worse. While Tony Abbott, within two years of being elected with a landslide and a united party behind him, was removed by his own party after losing 30 opinion polls in a row, Turnbull accomplished a still more impressive feat. Turnbull entered his prime ministership with a wave of goodwill that extended across the electorate; even Labor MPs were secretly glad he'd replaced Abbott, despite the potent electoral threat he posed to them. Within a few months, he had disappointed people's hopes of a dramatic improvement in the way politics was conducted. Within a year, he'd been reduced to near minority government. He then went on to effortlessly best Abbott's record of 30 losing opinion polls.

True, in 2016 and the first half of 2017, the Turnbull government managed merely middling incompetence. There was an illegal, later abandoned, attempt to control the

Solicitor-General, which resulted in the Attorney-General misleading parliament. There was a bungled attempt to rush through an extradition treaty with the murderous Chinese dictatorship. There was a badly flawed automated welfare 'debt recovery' process that saw thousands of Australians threatened with legal action on completely false information. The government appointed a man who had broken industrial relations law to head its new building industry watchdog. And Turnbull was routinely prevented from adopting policies by revolts from his own backbench.

But in the second half of 2017, it was as if the government's incompetence became turbocharged. First there was the citizenship crisis. It started with the Greens, two of whose senators were revealed to be dual citizens, in clear breach of the constitution. Soon, however, the crisis engulfed other minor parties, including the Nationals, the entire leadership of which was kicked out of parliament, and then to the Liberal Party itself, and finally to Labor, which had piously claimed it was untouched by the crisis. Eventually, section 44 of the constitution claimed ten MPs and senators, with others perhaps still to follow.

That proved merely a warm-up for the main event: having managed to return to parliament via a by-election, Turnbull's deputy and erstwhile New Zealander, Nationals leader Barnaby Joyce was revealed to have dumped his wife and children and moved in with a younger, pregnant former staff member who had been given jobs in other Nationals' offices. This prompted weeks of chaos, as Turnbull and Joyce publicly abused each other as 'appalling' and 'inept', before Joyce resigned amid accusations of sabotage between Liberals and Nationals.

By that stage, political journalists had run out of ways to describe how the government was tearing itself apart.

The most basic tasks of public life—doing the admin properly, delivering policy while remaining unified and keeping the confidence of the electorate—suddenly seemed beyond politicians, as did communicating effectively with voters. Trump, at least, had the excuse of being an utter neophyte to explain why his administration was a debacle from the get-go. Relatively experienced politicians like May or Turnbull had no such excuse. They appeared to have been graced with a reverse Midas touch: everything they have touched from 2016 until now has turned to shit.

Rootin' for Putin

Amid faltering democratic politicians, some pine for a strong-man like Vladimir Putin. While Donald Trump's almost worshipful admiration for the Russian thug is a matter of public record, Putin is admired by many on the Right across the world, especially in Europe, where Nigel Farage, Marine Le Pen, Norbert Hofer and others have lauded his government or even established political and financial links with his mafia-style regime. Pauline Hanson expressed this affection for tyranny best when she said of Putin that Australians 'wish we had a leader like that here'. In Hanson's mindset, the 'silent majority' that she believes she represents—but which, somehow, fails to vote her into government—hankers for a figure like Russia's murderous kleptocrat, who projects strength and untrammelled authority in dire contrast with weak Western leaders.

Admiration for the Putin regime isn't confined to the Right, of course. There remain plenty of far-left adherents who reflexively admire Russia merely because it is opposed to the United States. And as left-wingers correctly note, many of the accusations directed at Putin can also be levelled at the United States. The United States and Russia both regularly kill civilians while bombing Middle Eastern countries. Both countries assert the right to exercise a veto over who exercises influence in their own hemispheres. Both back brutal client states. And in charging Putin's regime (correctly) with interfering in the 2016 US elections, the Americans are guilty of the most gross hypocrisy, given the United States has routinely interfered in the elections of other countries for the better part of a century.

But the words that accompany praise from extremists on the Right tend to revolve around the theme of 'strength'. Putin, with his carefully confected image of physical vigour, is an archetypal strongman—a leader who gets things done, they believe, unhampered by any concerns about causing offence, or democratic niceties (like not murdering journalists).

Putin also represents nostalgia. In Russia, he offers a return to Soviet Union–style Great Power status (conveniently forgetting the economic stagnation and household misery that characterised Soviet Russia). Similarly, Trump promises to 'Make America great again'. Brexiteers ('Take back control', like 'Make America great again', is an essentially nostalgic slogan), Hanson, Le Pen and other bigots urge a return to a whiter, 'simpler', more patriarchal world that, to the extent it ever existed, was left behind in the 1970s. This childlike yearning for a past that often never existed reflects a refusal to accept the complexity of the real world, the inevitable messiness of democracy and the diversity of a healthy society. In the face of governmental incompetence and hopeless leaders, it's an abdication of responsibility to a fantasy authority figure who can only deal with problems by gaoling or killing people.

And while we're on the topic of

Political killing

2015 through 2018 saw an eruption of terrorist incidents across the West. The US University of Maryland's Global Terrorism Database records details of every single terror incident, and the numbers tell a stark story: in 2013, 46 people died in terror incidents in Western countries; in 2014, 38. But in 2015, 217 people died and 326 in 2016. The November 2015 attacks in Paris seemed the stuff of dystopian fiction. The slaughter on the streets of Nice in July 2016 was a horrific reminder that bombs and guns—or even organisation or conspiracy—aren't needed to inflict mass casualties. The number of terror-related deaths in the West fell in 2017 but incidents such as the London Bridge attacks, and the bombing of a concert audience of teenagers in Manchester, illustrated the mindless barbarity of their perpetrators.

Nor were the attacks confined to Islamist jihadists. Islam-ophobic and racist attacks by white terrorists and 'sovereign citizens' claimed lives in the United States, Canada and the United Kingdom. Australia's domestic security organisation flagged concerns about violence by white nationalists. A 2015 survey of US law enforcement agencies revealed terrorism by white supremacists and anti-government radicals was seen as a greater danger than Islamist terrorism—reflecting that white terrorists had murdered more people since 9/11 than jihad-ists in the United States. And while the US media obsessed about terrorism, America's love affair with firearms continued to claim far more lives in mass shootings than any jihadist. The world's most effective terrorist group in this period, both in terms of funding and political effectiveness, was the National Rifle Association—as it has been for decades.

But we seem to have difficulty viewing terrorism by white people as terrorism—or at least calling it that. Even after a Nazi murdered a protestor in Charlottesville, an act that even prominent Republicans called an act of terrorism, most of the media did not label it as such. In contrast, attacks involving or rumoured to involve Muslims are labelled terrorism instantaneously. Journalists describe white terrorists in ways intended to soften or even explain away their actions—they are gunmen, they are troubled loners or mentally ill—while Islamist terrorists are defined only by their professed extreme faith (no matter that they might be a violent criminal, or a hard-drinking, drug-using thug, with little knowledge of the Koran).

And, of course, our focus is only on terrorism in the West. In 2014, over 43,500 people were killed in terrorist incidents in non-Western countries. In 2015, it was over 38,000 people. In 2016, 34,500 lives were lost. Terrorism in non-Western countries is orders of magnitude worse than in the West, but receives minimal attention—unless an unlucky Westerner happens to number among the victims.

Nor are we in a particularly violent age of terrorism in the West. We're amnesiac about how bad terrorism used to be before the 'War on Terror'. In the United States, for example, the number of terrorist incidents in 2016 was still well below the average level of incidents in the 1970s, especially the early 1970s when African-American, Muslim and white supremacist groups killed and injured dozens of people. In France (a country with a rich heritage of right-wing terrorism, including repeated efforts to murder Charles De Gaulle), the number of attacks in recent years are well below the 1980s and the first half of the 1990s, when Marxist, Palestinian and separatist groups ran amok. And the United Kingdom witnessed over 3500 deaths related to the Northern Ireland conflict between the late 1960s and the late 1990s, including over 1800 civilians (and people continue to die in Northern Ireland at the hands of rogue nationalists). Australia is a contrast in this regard: the small number of terrorist incidents in the 1970s, 1980s and 1990s means that the period since the Lindt Café siege, in which five victims have been killed, represents the most violent period in terms of terrorism in Australia since the settler wars against Indigenous communities.

If we've forgotten that terrorism in most Western countries was as bad or worse 40 years ago, we've also forgotten the early years of the current War on Terror, when Al Qaeda carried out mass-casualty attacks either in the West or aimed at Westerners, in contrast to the current wave of terror in which attackers operate alone or in small groups and rely as much on knives and vehicles as on explosives and firearms. This change has lowered the death tolls from events (although not in the United States, of course, given the easy availability of firearms). Today, terrorists in the West often have violent criminal backgrounds (and, disproportionately, histories of intimate partner violence) and their links to terror groups appear tenuous or non-existent. Instead, invariably, they have 'pledged allegiance' to or been 'inspired' by the likes of Islamic State.

Bizarrely, this wave of individualist terrorism has been described as an existential threat by desperate politicians. That phrase was used about Al Qaeda's mass-casualty attacks in the 2000s, inaptly but understandably given that group's efforts to obtain weapons of mass destruction. The only truly existential threat faced by the West since World War II was the prospect of nuclear annihilation during the Cold War. That an individual with a knife, a gun or a truck could present an existential threat suggests either Western civilisation is far more fragile than we'd suspected, or that those who use the term—such as Australian Foreign Minister Julie Bishop and former Attorney-General George Brandis—don't actually understand what existential means.

That kind of rhetorical inflation, however, has been necessary to justify a suite of draconian new restrictions on civil liberties and significant expansions in the powers (and funding) of security agencies, on top of the huge increase in state powers in the 2000s. Indeed, if the rhetoric of those who incessantly push to curb civil liberties is to be believed, the harsh restrictions on basic rights imposed in the years after 9/11 were woefully inadequate to fight the current 'existential threat' of terrorism. The West managed to come through the Cold War and an extended era of domestic terrorism between the 1960s and 1990s without any such laws. But politicians remain ever vigilant for opportunities to further increase the powers of government at the expense of citizens. The result is the slow but sure construction of a surveillance state in Western countries.

Terrorism and the eagerness of some to exploit it played an important role in

The decline of civility

While Donald Trump re-opened US political debate to explicitly racist abuse, absurd smears of one's opponents, misogynist vilification and the peddling of hate, Australia was already well down its own path away from civility.

It began in Australia in the Julia Gillard years. The mere fact that a prime minister was female seemed to prompt an outpouring of misogynistic abuse. 'Witch' and 'bitch' were two of the more printable terms publicly directed at Gillard by conservative opponents. There are always people in any political movement who engage in offensive conduct, of course, but the abuse of Gillard received tacit approval from her political opponents. Coalition figures repeatedly commented on Gillard's childlessness. Tony Abbott and a coterie of shadow ministers stood in front of signs directing abuse at her. An organiser of a Coalition fundraiser devised a menu mocking Gillard's body. Australia never quite reached Trumpesque levels of hateful discourse, but we came close under Gillard— it's forgotten now that many of her enemies in the media insisted Gillard would and should be gaoled. The then-shadow Attorney-General used parliamentary privilege to call Gillard a crook and refused to provide any justification for it. It was a politer, but no more excusable version of the 'lock her up' chant we would later hear from Trump.

However, since then the quality of civil discourse in Australia has deteriorated even further. People, we were told by the nation's Attorney-General, have a right to be bigots. Racist and neo-Nazi groups are active on social media, and occasionally given a platform by mainstream media outlets, to the dismay of security agencies, who view them as a real threat. There's been an alarming increase in anti-Semitic statements, as well as vilification of Muslims. Racists like Pauline Hanson use the legitimacy of the Senate to spread their poison against Muslims. Hanson wore a burqa into the Senate in mockery of

Muslim women. In fact, to be a Muslim woman is to particularly be a target in Australia. Muslim women who dare to offer even mildly controversial opinions meet with extraordinary rage. Yassmin Abdel-Magied, whose chief crime was to be young, Muslim, female and articulate, was the target of a frightening campaign of media vilification in 2017, ostensibly for an anodyne comment about Anzac Day for which she quickly apologised (a number of white male commentators have repeatedly savaged Anzac Day as an offensive celebration of imperialism, without anyone batting an eyelid). Abdel-Magied had the rare honour of being both told by media critics to leave Australia and, when she'd had enough and did indeed decide to leave, being attacked by a media outlet saying she should 'stay and face her critics'. Another commentator 'joked' about running her over.

Australia also had to play catch up with most of the Western world in permitting marriage equality. In an absurd postal survey devised by the Turnbull government to bootstrap its way out of internal political difficulties, Australia was subjected to a bitter and deeply wounding 'debate' over an issue for which there was well-verified and widespread community support. Much of the campaign from marriage-equality opponents (almost uniformly old white males such as former conservative prime ministers Howard and Abbott, some of their hardline right-wing ministers since exiled to the backbench, former Labor Party leader-turned-far-right-ranter Mark Latham, commentators in the Murdoch press and figures in the Catholic church hierarchy) centred on efforts to link the question to unrelated or tangential issues. Worse, elements of the No campaign engaged in appalling smears, including claiming the children of same-sex parents were damaged by their parents and constituted a 'Stolen Generation'—a term profoundly offensive both to Indigenous Australians and same-sex parents—despite the huge preponderance of evidence that same-sex parenting had no impact, or even a positive impact, on children. In spite of the ultimate resounding success of the Yes campaign, the process inflicted considerable hurt on LGBTI Australians, along with vandalism, abuse and physical assaults of Yes supporters.

While racism, or homophobia, springs from readily identifiable sources, it's harder to explain the role of gender in the decline in our public discourse. A large segment of the community, including many in the media and some in politics, can *only* process public debate involving women in terms of gender: their views must be attributed to their gender, they must be judged in terms of their sexual appeal. If they offer a contrary opinion, they must be threatened with sexual violence or murder—something that routinely happens on social media to feminists like Clem Ford and Indigenous women such as Lidia Thorpe and Jacinta Price, as well as innumerable female journalists, all guilty of the crime of being female, articulate and opinionated.

This decline in civility is surely linked to another phenomenon of recent years, what we can term the

Revolt of the white men

One of the most fascinating aspects of these years has been the extent to which the anger and resentment of white men was at the centre of so many political developments. Whether fuelling Brexit via their resentment of foreign workers, or voting for Trump despite, or perhaps because of, his enthusi-asm for 'pussy-grabbing', or using pay TV shows to lash out at political correctness in Australia, angry white men made their unhappiness known.

Many white men seem hell-bent on claiming the only thing they've never had: victimhood. The privilege that white men have enjoyed for most of the last millennium, and which to a large degree we still enjoy—the privilege that means that economically, socially, culturally, being a white male gives us an advantage over everyone else—has always precluded us from being victims. White men are at the top of the hierarchy of socio-economic power and privilege in Western societies. To paraphrase a line from white men raving about terror-ism, not every white male is a powerful person, but every powerful person is a white male. But suddenly, many of us are coveting the lower rungs of the ladder, craving victimhood, anxious to possess the one thing that the less privileged have always had a more authentic claim to. We white males want *everything* other people have, including the fact that they're not white males.

This sense of victimhood has been co-opted by the broader Right because the sense of grievance and resentment at the heart of white male resentment perfectly fits the culture wars the Right pursues: it facilitates a narrative of left-wing persecution. To the culture warrior, gender or racial equality, non-discrimination toward LGBTI people, efforts to prevent domestic violence, even exercising basic civility or having regard to actual evidence, are forms of 'elite' warfare on the common sense of ordinary hardworking white males.

True, there has been mild readjustment in society. The more blatant forms of discrimination that benefited white men of

previous generations have been outlawed, and a more merito-
cratic economy means white males are a little less privileged
than they were before. But to be born a white male is still to
win the golden ticket in Western societies, and all the better
if you're heterosexual and able-bodied—it's just that it's no
longer quite as easy as it used to be.

This explains one of the key support bases for Pauline
Hanson: aggrieved, older white men who bitterly resent that
contemporary Australia fails to accord them the kind of status
they believe is appropriate to people of their gender and skin
colour. They feel disempowered, but the power they feel
they've lost is the power they believe should come from being
white and male. This is particularly the case *vis-à-vis* gender
relations. Hanson has always pushed a narrative of male victimhood in relation to family law, but in her second iteration
is doing so more than ever, demanding the abolition of the
Family Court to stop women making 'frivolous claims' against
former partners, which she claims lead to the 'frustration' that
makes men murder them. Instead, she wants a 'community'
family law system, with deterrents to women raising domestic
abuse in proceedings. Hanson would also force children to
live with abusive parents and slash child-support payments for
women. Trained professionals and experts would be removed
from the system and replaced with 'mainstream' community
members—the wisdom of ordinary folk elevated over that
of out-of-touch 'experts', just as with climate science and
vaccination.

The same bitter resentment of any female agency is a
pervasive theme of the 'men's rights movement', which
is founded on the core idea of male disempowerment and
female privilege (for example, so-called men's rights activists

make the routine, but entirely discredited, claim that one-third of domestic violence victims are men). What flows from this mindset is infantile behaviour, like boycotting movies that feature women as anything other than sexual adornments and claiming domestic violence campaigns are a middle-class feminist plot against working-class men. But it also extends to dangerous or lethal behaviour, like the targeted harassment of people perceived as opponents, threatening women with violence on social media, and in some cases, mass murders by men infuriated by their inability to attract a partner. Female agency, and any restriction on male privilege, including the right to demand sex, are anathema to such people.[4]

Oddly enough, despite portraying themselves as thick-skinned, rugged individualists—as the action heroes of human civilisation—many white men behave like whingers, furious that their massive socio-economic advantage has been reduced by 10 per cent. They present as sore losers when they've barely lost anything. And despite the quest for victimhood, they have no idea what it's like to be a real victim, to be someone on the receiving end of discrimination, injustice, abuse, violence, harassment—mostly because they're the ones dishing it out. Indeed, when it comes to sexual harassment or domestic violence or racist abuse, white males often *create* victims.

The revolt of the white men is the appropriate context for the debate over the *Racial Discrimination Act* in Australia, and the campaign to repeal its section 18C, which prohibits offending, insulting, humiliating or intimidating someone based on their

---

4   Thus the effort by Trump's Education Secretary, billionaire Betsy DeVos, to roll back guidelines relating to sexual assault and harassment on US campuses, based on the fiction that the majority of sexual-assault complaints on US college and university campuses were fake.

race (under the legislation, that includes religion), with the caveat that it doesn't apply to artistic works, serious research or debate in the public interest.

Section 18C is a clumsily worded limitation on free speech, but heavily restricted to limit its impact. It could readily be updated to lift the threshold test to ensure that certain kinds of harmful speech are prohibited while removing the ridiculous idea that mere offence is grounds for complaint. But fixing section 18C would have negligible impact on free speech in Australia. The big threats to free speech in Australia are defamation laws, the enthusiasm of the court system (or what should more accurately be described as the legal industry) for suppression orders and other forms of court censorship that infantilise the community, the lack of media diversity, the growing surveillance powers of security agencies, the dearth of independent, well-resourced civil-society bodies that act to protect freedoms, and the lack of a rights-based legal framework that would enable them to do so (more on that later). Improving the parlous state of free speech in Australia starts with addressing those problems, not with an arcane section of an Act that almost never winds up in court.

Tellingly, advocates of the repeal of section 18C—lifelong free-speech defender Derryn Hinch excepted—hardly ever show interest in addressing real threats to free speech. As someone who has campaigned on surveillance issues a bit in his time, I can vouch for how many of the section 18C crowd—especially at News Corp—suddenly go missing when the time comes to get into the trenches on national security laws. For fair-weather free-speech fans, it's all about *their* free speech, no one else's. Many of them actually want to worsen the state of free speech through media ownership deregulation,

opposition to any form of a bill of rights and even expanding the powers of corporations to litigate against critics. That's
because, as powerful participants in public debate—as employees of media companies and corporate-funded think tanks, as
politicians (especially senators, who don't have the odious task
of dealing with actual constituents, like their House of Reps
colleagues have to)—they already have all the free speech
they need. What motivates them, instead, is the idea that there
is any impediment to using their power against those they
wish to attack: people who criticise them, and particularly
people who are different to them and who have the gall to
challenge them.

There's a reason why nearly all the advocates of changes to
section 18C are powerful white conservatives, and why the
targets of their 'free speech' are so often Indigenous Australians, LGBTI Australians and Muslim Australians. Those who
lined up to vilify Yassmin Abdel-Magied for a deleted tweet
were almost, to a person, the same crowd who persistently
complain about threats to their own free speech, who argue
that people have a right to offend, that they have 'a right
to be bigots'. What they mean is, white men have the right to
offend and be bigots, and any infringement of that right, any
restriction on their ability to kick downwards at those less
privileged than themselves, is an outrage. They are the real
victims, unfairly constrained in what should be a natural right
to wield the power gifted them by wealth, politics and our
lingering socio-economic favouritism to white men, as they
see fit. Hypocrisy and inconsistency are at the very core of the
revolt of the white men.

Diagnosis

Some of the symptoms outlined in this chapter may prove to be transient. Donald Trump might resign or be impeached, to be replaced by Mike Pence, a deeply strange religious fundamentalist who nevertheless at least has some experience in governing. Pauline Hanson's One Nation may slide back into the sewage pond from which it emerged. Terror attacks may abate.

Some symptoms will definitely not disappear. Climate change is worsening; there are gloomy predictions that the rate is far quicker than expected, which bodes poorly for economic growth in coming decades. Large corporations continue to inflict social and economic damage on wider society. And to see actual Nazis marching through, and murdering people in, the streets of American towns; to hear the constant stream of hate peddled even in mainstream media in Australia, is to realise the march of history is by no means inexorably forwards, that we can repeat the mistakes of earlier generations.

So what can we conclude from the symptoms besetting us? What commonalities emerge from these themes?

First, there is some deep-seated malaise in democratic governments, sufficient to turn some people off the idea of democracy itself, and to massively decrease trust in democratic governments. Governments appear incompetent, not up to the task of performing the basics of democratic politics effectively, especially when it requires acting at odds with the interests of powerful corporations. And yet they demand ever-greater powers over their own citizenry.

Second, there is also deep concern in many Western countries about the overall direction of economic policy, and in particular, the perception that Western economies are controlled for the benefit of the few—corporations and the rich—rather than the many, leading large numbers of voters to turn to those who at least purport to be ready to disrupt the existing economic order and restore control to ordinary voters. Economic business as usual is no more appealing to many voters than political business as usual.

And third, the way that we communicate and exchange information has been, somehow, corrupted. It's not merely the rise of fake news, it's the whole tenor of public discourse that has materially degraded, to the point where the capacity for societies to conduct meaningful debate on any controversial issue now seems questionable.

Focusing on these three areas gets us a long way to understanding what has been going on in recent years, and leads us to a diagnosis of what's afflicting Australia and much of the Western world. In three different, crucial spheres of public life—democratic government, our broad economic direction and communication—we're facing disruption on a massive, indeed historic, scale that has driven apparently disconnected but dramatic events across Western societies. Disruption merely in one of these areas would cause significant impacts in society; disruptions in three areas at once has produced a dislocation of extraordinary magnitude across the West that has culminated in the events of the last few years.

What are these disruptions?

First, the dominant economic orthodoxy of the last 30 to 40 years, neoliberalism, has engendered a dramatic backlash and shown itself to be incapable of providing a political–economic equilibrium. Voters have rebelled against it, forcing an abandonment of the economic dogma at the centre of Western policymaking since the late 1970s, driving a new era of populist reaction against open borders and demanding an end to ever-growing corporate power.

Second, the hollowing-out of Western democratic politics has created governments seen as disconnected and untrustworthy by voters, that have too much power over their own citizens and too little power over corporations, struggling with the electorates' demands for more economically interventionist policies and more effective representation.

And finally, the internet has caused a massive psychological, social and economic disruption that has both inflicted damage itself and helped maximise the upheaval generated by the other forces.

Indeed, none of these forces exist independently of the others. They interact in different ways; sometimes two, sometimes all three. They've played out differently in different countries. The Australian experience has been different from that of the United States or European countries, and some countries have proved more resilient in the face of their impacts than others. But above all they have combined to inflict far more damage and disruption than any one of them could by itself. The remainder of this book is an exploration of how that has happened.

PART 2

NEOLIBERALISM AND ITS DISCONTENTS

Much maligned, often misunderstood, neoliberalism is frequently in the eye of the beholder. And that beholder is usually a hostile one. 'Neoliberal' has become a term of abuse for the Left, denoting virtually any economic or fiscal policy disliked by progressives, regardless of its actual connection to the philosophy espoused by the founders of postwar economic liberalism. But that reflexive hostility doesn't really give us an insight into the impact of neoliberalism. Bland assertions that it's terrible and anti-worker and more or less everything that's wrong with the world deprives us of an understanding of how it has ended up causing disruptions ostensibly a long way from the field of economics, and of how it has had differing impacts in Western countries and developing countries. It's also unhelpful for understanding how it has intersected with the other major historical forces that we're exploring in this book.

As a result, progressives who don't bother doing some hard, informed thinking about what they call neoliberalism are ignoring Sun Tzu's wise injunction to know your enemy if you are to defeat it. And conservatives unwilling to examine the flaws of neoliberalism likewise won't even start to work out how it went so badly wrong and what lessons can be learnt about managing a politically sustainable economic policy.

The story of neoliberalism is of a policy that initially delivered the kinds of benefits that its advocates claimed for it, but which contained within itself the seeds of its own destruction, a tendency to disequilibrium because of the power that it handed a small segment of society at the expense of the rest of the community, and the abuse of that power by those who enjoyed it. In Australia—the country where neoliberalism was most successfully implemented—the years 2016 to 2018 were partly the story of how it fell apart under electoral pressure. In the United States and the United Kingdom, the failings of neoliberalism wreaked political havoc that drove both countries deep into a democratic *terra incognita* of extremism, populism and political chaos.

What is it?

There were significant changes in economic policy in the Anglophone world, and in many developing countries, in the 1970s and 1980s. Following World War II, Western economies had run reasonably successful, high-employment economies as part of a broad political consensus about how to manage the business cycle using the kind of counter-cyclical fiscal and monetary policies advocated by John Maynard Keynes. 'I am now a Keynesian in economics,' Richard Nixon famously said in 1971.[5] By the 1970s, in many countries Keynesianism as an economic philosophy had expanded far beyond the original 1936 arguments of *The General Theory of Employment, Interest and Money*, to include policies of government interventionism little related to Keynes' work, such as import tariffs. But soon after Nixon uttered those words, the economic crises of the 1970s, which varied in different countries—high inflation, loose monetary policy and the oil shock in the United States were very different to the near-collapse of British governing institutions and disastrous industrial relations policies in 1974— brought the Keynesian consensus to an end.

The economic models that replaced it in different countries, in different timeframes and via different institutions, varied considerably. The United States, the United Kingdom, Australia and New Zealand and others adopted different policies, but all with some common ideas: the role of governments in the economy needed to be reduced, markets (especially labour and financial markets) should be empowered through deregulation, protectionism should be ended in favour of freer trade, closed sectors of the economy—especially those where government businesses played an important role—should be opened up to competition, taxation should be reduced to provide an incentive to work and invest, and monetary policy should primarily target inflation.

The explicit foundation of these reforms was as much *moral* as it was economic: an emphasis on individual freedom. Freedom

---

5 Nixon's declaration in retrospect isn't surprising. Despite Watergate and Vietnam, he was probably the third most progressive president after LBJ and FDR. He would be too economically interventionist to fit into the modern Democratic Party, let alone the GOP.

was the guiding light of the first generation of neoliberal econ-omists such as Friedrich Hayek, Milton Friedman and George Stigler, who founded the Mont Pelerin Society with other economists and philosophers in 1947. The individual, in their view, should be free to pursue economic opportunity with as little limitation as possible from governments or communal institutions. The communitarian or interventionist economic policies that were dominant in the postwar world—such as Marxism or Keynesianism, which Hayek regarded as nearly interchangeable—were an irrational and deadening restraint of individual freedom that should be replaced by policies that support individual economic opportunity and competition, such as the rule of law, the protection of property rights, the removal of burdensome regulation and low taxation. Beyond those, the role of government should be limited. Governments were intrinsically, reflexively inefficient and anti-freedom, and must be kept curtailed. In the wake of World War II and a shattered Europe, at the start of a Cold War with a communist superpower, this emphasis on individualism was dramatically at odds with contemporary economic thinking. As we'll see later, their warnings about over-powerful governments were applicable in more areas than merely the economic.

But as even this cursory description suggests, there are inconsistencies within neoliberalism (as there are within any economic system of any complexity). Markets often fail, or produce socially or morally unacceptable outcomes, necessi-tating government regulation to protect consumers, workers and even corporations. Even the United States retains a minimum wage, albeit a low one, in the face of neoliberal arguments that unemployment is only ever 'voluntary' because workers won't accept lower wages. In a medium-sized, small population economy like Australia's, the risk of oligopolistic or monopolistic behaviour by firms is an ever-present threat, necessitating strong competition laws and regulators to enforce them. And even in giant economies some industries tend to oligopoly—infrastructure provision, for example, is particularly problematic given it is frequently a natural monopoly. (We'll get to neoliberalism's struggle with monopolies a little later.)

Moreover, there are tensions between the moral basis of neoliberalism and its economic implementation. The primacy of individual freedom should mean that enabling individuals to participate as fully and effectively as possible in the economy is a key goal of governments, along with protecting private property and the rule of law. But this means, *contra* many neoliberals, ensuring the provision of an effective health, infrastructure and education system that even those without high incomes can access. Without a quality education system, workers are less productive for businesses, and individuals have less opportunity to fulfil their economic potential. Similarly, without a quality health system, workers produce less and have less personal opportunity. Without basic levels of infrastructure, accessing such services, or economic opportunity, is problematic. But markets won't operate effectively in these sectors because the individuals who benefit most from these sectors can't afford to pay for access, and require high levels of cross-subsidy—education involves transfers of resources to the young and families; healthcare requires transfers of resources to older people; infrastructure use in low-population areas like regional communities needs to be subsidised if it's to be affordable.

The individualist ethos of neoliberalism, therefore, necessitates a strong state role in areas such as education and health, as well as a capacity to regulate markets to prevent failure. And some of the early neoliberals explicitly accepted this—indeed, the two most famous neoliberals, Friedman and Hayek, both wrote about the importance of reducing inequality of opportunity via education. Friedman even proposed a universal income, and Hayek supported welfare.

As any number of critics have noted, however, neoliberalism is also inconsistent—and extraordinarily varied—in practice, as well as in theory. And this is where it gets complicated, not merely for supporters of neoliberalism, but its critics as well. The biggest area of confusion relates to fiscal policy. Despite the insistence of neoliberal dogma that the state be curbed, under the iconic neoliberal figure of Ronald Reagan, the US government dramatically *increased* spending and the US budget deficit. (Contrary to common belief, it is always Democrat presidents who oversee falls in US government spending, partly because after LBJ they tended to invade fewer foreign countries.) In the United Kingdom, Margaret Thatcher only reduced spending after it surged in the early 1980s. And the neoliberal government of John Howard in Australia became the highest taxing government in Australian history, and one of the biggest spending.

As a result, government spending as a proportion of GDP is about the same now in the United Kingdom and the United States as it was in 1973. In Australia, it's actually substantially higher—18.2 per cent of GDP under 'free-spending socialist' Gough Whitlam in the 1970s, 25 per cent under 'thoroughly Liberal' Malcolm Turnbull in 2018. It turns out the small government stuff from neoliberals has long been more honoured in the breach than the observance by politicians who profess to champion it.

It's not merely hypocrisy and political calculation that have meant that governments have remained resolutely unshrunk in even the most neoliberal economies. As one of the still-living doyens of the pro-free-market, anti-Keynesian Chicago school of economics, Bob Lucas, put it as the global recession erupted in 2008, 'Everyone is a Keynesian in a foxhole'. When economic crises come along, policymakers of all stripes abandon the hands-off approach dictated by neoliberalism and turn to government spending to offset collapsing demand. Ideological purity gives way to the need to respond to electoral demands to do something.

But the tendency of critics to conflate neoliberalism with fiscal austerity is also flawed. Austerity budgeting—dramatic cuts in government spending to reduce budget deficits—in fact has nothing to do with neoliberalism *per se*. A government that spends 33 per cent of gross domestic product but has to cut spending because of its budget deficit is engaging in austerity; a government that spends 20 per cent of GDP but increases social services spending because it has a budget surplus is much closer to neoliberal theory.

Thus, confusingly, governments seen as neoliberal by critics and criticised for engaging in austerity have actually been big spenders. The Cameron government in the United Kingdom engaged in colossal deficit spending which saw the UK deficit top 8 per cent of GDP in 2012, while the Tories were savaged for their 'austerity' cuts to health and education. Similarly in Australia, the Abbott government's notorious 2014 budget inflicted massive political damage on that government for its perceived unfairness and stringent cuts to spending— but in fact, it maintained a high level of stimulatory deficit spending crucial for preventing the Australian economy from tipping into recession. Indeed, Tony Abbott and his Treasurer Joe Hockey proceeded to inflate government spending to levels far above those of their Labor Party predecessors—and taxation levels as well. The persistent overlooking of the Abbott government's aggressive deficit spending is because the Liberal Party itself was conflicted about its big-taxing, big-spending ways. Even Abbott himself, once his party kicked him out of the prime ministership, reverted to insisting the government should slash spending. Neoliberalism—again, like every other economic philosophy—is implemented in the real world of political compromise, calculation and cowardice that means it has no monolithic character, but different forms in different countries and different political circumstances.

However, there's no confusion about how neoliberalism elevates the individual over the collective. 'There is no society,' Thatcher famously said, 'only individuals, and families.' Perhaps unconsciously, Thatcher was summing up the central tenet of neoliberalism, that communitarian economic thinking had to give way to policies that facilitated the opportunity of the individual above all. And that individual was an *economic being*. Under neoliberalism, your value as a human being—your *only* value—was as a producer and consumer. It was up to you to maximise that value, to get on your bike and seek out opportunity.

Under neoliberalism, you could no longer expect to be protected from market forces. You would not be guaranteed economic security, or at least nowhere near to the extent that people in Western economies had been until the 1970s. It was up to you. People were now free—in both the positive and negative senses; unconstrained by the dead hand of government, but also unprotected by government. You were on your own.

At least, that was the theory.

The success of neoliberalism

And in the beginning, it worked.

After the agony of the early 1990s recession, during which the Hawke–Keating government continued to press on with removing manufacturing tariffs and other forms of protectionism, Australia entered a sustained period of economic growth that continues today. Real GDP per capita is more than 80 per cent higher than in 1992. Trend unemployment in Australia hasn't been above 7 per cent since the 1990s, even though the participation rate is a full two percentage points higher now (the participation rate for women is a full *five* percentage points higher). In the economy that Hawke and Keating created, a significantly higher proportion of our population is seeking work than twenty years ago, and we have the jobs for them.

This isn't a modest or symbolic achievement: those of us old enough to remember the early 1990s understand how massively damaging a recession and persistently high unemployment can be, not merely economically but socially. The recession of the early 1990s was an immensely dislocative event, with hundreds of thousands of workers effectively consigned to the scrapheap and families wrecked by lost incomes, defaulted mortgages and missed opportunities. And unemployment hits the most marginal, those with least resources, and least opportunities, the hardest.

This extended period of economic growth has also delivered strong income growth—Australians are considerably wealthier than they used to be. A Productivity Commission report in 2013 estimated individual incomes were nearly 40 per cent higher in real terms (that is, adjusted for inflation) than in the 1980s, and household total incomes were up over 60 per cent in real terms. Nor was that growth all at the top end of the income scale—all income deciles enjoyed substantial real growth, albeit at varying rates. Australia also has far lower inflation than we used to have. We're now accustomed to sub 3 per cent, even sub 2 per cent, annual inflation, but in the 1980s we had 2 per cent CPI growth *per quarter*, which drove a debilitating and endless cycle of worker pay rises in an effort to keep up with prices. Politicians who now pander to electoral concerns about 'the high cost of living' weren't around in the early 1980s, when we had both high unemployment *and* 10 per cent inflation.

That curbed inflation is due to effective inflation targeting by an independent central bank—one of the tenets of neoliberalism—and has provided more flexibility for the Reserve Bank of Australia to use monetary policy to stimulate the economy when needed through lower interest rates for business and household borrowers. The RBA's cash rate rarely fell below 5 per cent between the early 1990s recession and the global financial crisis, but it's now been below 4 per cent since 2012, and below 3 per cent since May 2013. And whereas most people in the 1980s had only the pension to look forward to in retirement, Australians now have over two trillion dollars in retirement savings in the superannuation system, invested in the share market, property and infrastructure, which also provided key ballast for the economy during the financial crisis. Australians increasingly have the capacity to ensure they have a comfortable retirement rather than relying on welfare—people on the aged pension have traditionally been among the poorest in Australia.

None of this meant that Australians embraced neoliberalism with enthusiasm. Large segments of the electorate still disagree with the major economic reforms of the neoliberal era. Privatisation, in particular, irks most voters—there is surprising unanimity across supporters of different political parties in Australia about how much they hate privatisation, and understandably, given privatisation has been used to fill government- and private-sector coffers rather than produce better-quality services. Indeed, many Australians would still happily re-nationalise icons like Qantas and the Commonwealth Bank. Nonetheless, they seemed happy enough with the material outcomes of neoliberalism to have continually re-elected the Hawke, Keating and Howard governments.

Meanwhile, non-Indigenous Australians have never been healthier: men live 7.7 years longer than they did in the mid 1980s and women live 5.3 years longer. Non-Indigenous Australians are the seventh longest-lived people in the world, and continue to extend their longevity and improve their health. In the 1980s, less than half of Australian school students completed Year 12, now that's nearly 85 per cent, while access to tertiary education has expanded dramatically. We're also safer: rates of both violent crimes and property crimes have been falling for years.

There's a similar economic pattern in the United Kingdom: there was strong real wages growth in that country from the 1980s: in the 30 years to 2010, real wages grew more than 60 per cent. Unemployment was consistently above 10 per cent throughout the 1980s and even for a time in the 1990s, but is now below 5 per cent in that country, off a participation rate well above the average level of the 1980s.

Neoliberalism hasn't been as successful in the United States: real median weekly earnings are only 8 per cent higher there than in the mid 1980s—although they've risen much more quickly for women, by over 20 per cent. But unemployment is below 5 per cent, a point it never reached between the 1960s and the Clinton boom years of the late 1990s.

In Canada, unemployment is above 6 per cent, but still well below the level it was at throughout the 1980s and 1990s. Incomes grew more slowly than in the United Kingdom or Australia, with much of the growth coming in the 2000s, to leave Canadian real wages around 15 per cent above 1980 levels.

So while Australia's embrace of neoliberalism has been one of the most successful in terms of wealth and health, other Western countries have also seen substantial rises in the wealth of ordinary citizens.

But the economic benefits of market-based policies haven't been confined to Anglophone countries. The move to a market-based economy in China lifted around 600 million people out of dire poverty. That's helped reduce the proportion of the world's population living in absolute poverty from 44 per cent in the mid 1980s to under 10 per cent in 2015. Health in the developing world has also improved: in 1980, global life expectancy was 62.8 years, now it's 71.7 years. Infant mortality has more than halved, from 65 deaths per 1000 live births in 1990 to 31.7 in 2015. Since 1990, the global literacy rate has also improved ten percentage points to over 85 per cent. For women, it's improved twelve points. The number of girls not in school has more than halved.

The story of neoliberalism was thus, until recently, one of economic success, growing wealth and improved education and health, for people in both developed and developing countries. But more problematic aspects of neoliberalism also began to emerge—aspects that its adherents, with their relentless focus on individual freedom, never saw or did not consider important in a world where the economy was the only thing that counted. As we grew wealthy under neoliberalism, a wealth of problems was being stored up, because eventually the benefits of neoliberalism stopped flowing to workers and consumers, and began flowing primarily to corporations.

All things being unequal: neoliberalism and inequality

Neoliberalism fundamentally changed the longstanding pattern of inequality around the world. Until the 1980s, Western economies had grown more rapidly than developing economies, meaning inequality between nations increased. But under neoliberal policies, developing countries began growing more quickly—especially China, which in recent decades has racked up double-digit and high single-digit growth. The economic gap between developing countries and developed countries began to close. But *within* developed countries, inequality, which had shrunk until the 1980s, began to widen—and widen significantly. That's because while neoliberalism normally delivered real-income growth across all income groups—as we saw in the case of Australia—that growth hasn't been equal across all incomes. In fact, it hasn't even been close to equal, and never has: people in lower-income deciles have had slower income growth than those in the highest income groups. That is, low-income earners are wealthier in real terms than their counterparts in the 1980s, but their wealth hasn't grown as much as that of wealthier people—and by only a fraction of that of the highest-income earners.

This was the subject of political controversy in Australia in mid 2017 as Labor and the Coalition argued over rising inequality, but no amount of cherry-picking of data and selective use of Gini coefficients[6] by advocates of neoliberalism can disguise the simple truth found in the Productivity Commission's 2013 report *Trends in the Distribution of Income in Australia*. For both labour income and gross household income, every income decile got richer between the end of the 1980s and the end of the 2000s, but the top decile got richer by more. The top 10 per cent of workers enjoyed real-income growth of over 60 per cent compared to the average of around 38 per cent. The top 10 per cent of households also saw income grow by over 60 per cent compared to the overall average of around 42 per cent. And that shift has come despite the increased economic empowerment of women, which has acted to reduce inequality between genders.

It's a similar story across the OECD: since 1980, inequality has worsened, both in countries with traditionally high levels of inequality, like the United States, and European countries with lower levels. In both the United States and the United Kingdom, inequality as measured by the Gini coefficient

---

6   One of the most commonly used statistics to determine the distribution of wealth or income in a nation. According to the World Bank, the Gini coefficient in Australia has risen significantly between 1981 and 2010.

increased markedly during the 1980s (and it continues to worsen in the United States). In New Zealand, the Gini coefficient actually fell in the mid 1980s but surged after that, taking New Zealand near the top of OECD countries for income inequality. And the same measure has deteriorated in Australia, despite social policy achievements like Medicare and superannuation and industrial relations protections, but particularly worsened during the 2000s under the Howard government. Like other countries, the share of national income going to the top 1 per cent in Australia has also increased markedly since 1980—albeit not nearly as much as the United Kingdom or the United States.

This is the point at which many advocates of neoliberalism leap in to insist that neoliberalism isn't the guilty party when it comes to rising inequality. Instead, they argue, much of the increase in inequality in Western countries in recent decades is due to *technological change*, rather than an embrace of market-based economics. Technological change, they argue, has reduced the demand for unskilled labour in Western economies, fuelling a growing income division between unskilled and semi-skilled workers and highly skilled workers. They say the growth in inequality would have happened regardless of the economic policies pursued, because our economies have evolved that way, driven by technological change.

But the problem with the technology argument in Australia is that the Productivity Commission's figures show that it was the second to sixth deciles that had the lowest level of income growth for both labour income and gross household income—while the lowest-income decile had growth much closer to the average. That is, technology doesn't explain why the inequality experience, at least in Australia, is more of hollowing out of middle incomes, rather than the lowest-income earners having the lowest growth.[7]

And as economists like John Quiggin have argued, technological change isn't new—significant technological developments affecting key industries have been going on for one hundred and fifty years, without driving the kinds of inequality we have seen in recent decades. Nor does the technology thesis explain why there are such marked changes in inequality in some countries, and smaller changes in others— the United States, the exemplar neoliberal economy, just happens to be the most unequal major economy, and inequality has markedly increased there since the election of Ronald Reagan. If machines are to blame, they're awfully selective about where they inflict inequality.

We also know *how* neoliberalism leads to greater inequality, both in developed and developing economies. A core neoliberal policy, reducing taxes for high-income earners (individual wealth accumulation and risk-taking must not be deterred) reduces the progressivity of the taxation system, thus increasing after-tax inequality by reducing redistribution. Restrictions on trade unions and the rights of workers—in the name of 'workplace flexibility'—also reduce the power of workers to demand higher wages: the rise in the Gini coefficient in the 2000s in Australia coincides with the Howard government's WorkChoices assault on labour rights.

One of the key institutions of global neoliberalism, the International Monetary Fund, has increasingly focused

---

7   The home of 'hollowing out' is the United States, where middle-income earners have shrunk from 58 per cent to 47 per cent of households since 1970, according to the International Monetary Fund, as low and middle incomes have stagnated or fallen and high incomes have surged.

on inequality and its links with the policies the IMF itself
has promoted for decades. A now-famous 2016 IMF paper
examined two mechanisms by which market-based policies
engender inequality. One was the unfettered flow of foreign
investment into and out of economies which another IMF
paper has shown 'are associated with a statistically significant
and persistent increase in inequality' in developing countries
because sudden, large shifts in capital can exacerbate financial
crises, and tend to benefit the well-off more than the poor.
The paper also examined the costs of slashing government
spending to pay off debt and concluded they were greater than
the costs of allowing debt to reduce organically via growth—
entirely contrary to much of the IMF agenda of the previous
four decades.

Okay, neoliberalism causes inequality—so what? If everyone's richer, what's the problem? But that only holds while
everyone is getting richer. And in the years since the financial
crisis of 2008 and the ensuing global recession, even as Western
economies began growing again, people *stopped* getting richer.
Economic growth failed to bounce back with the same energy
as it had after previous slowdowns. Inflation was also unex-
pectedly low. This has led economists to start considering why
developed economies in the 2010s seem to be stagnating, as
Japan has since the 1990s. Theories of secular stagnation, debt
overhangs and liquidity traps have all been advanced by some
of the world's most prominent economists.

Australia fortuitously avoided stagnation after the end of
the financial crisis thanks to fiscal stimulus and being plugged
into Chinese growth. The challenge for the Labor government
in the years after the financial crisis became how to manage
a mining investment boom without an inflation explosion—a

feat never achieved before in Australia, but pulled off by Treasurer Wayne Swan and the Reserve Bank. But since 2013, Australia, too, has begun marking time economically. Our unemployment rate has remained low by the standards of the 1980s to the 2000s but Australian workers are enduring an extended period of wage stagnation that has, at times, seen them getting poorer as their wages grew less than inflation. For most of 2016 till now, the annualised rate of growth for the best measure of earnings, the Wage Price Index, has been below 2 per cent for private-sector workers, and it's been below 3 per cent since 2013.

Throughout this period, policymakers—both political, in government, and independent at the Reserve Bank—have routinely predicted that wage stagnation was about to end, that a pick-up in wages growth was just around the corner. As each quarter of WPI results has arrived, however, that turnaround has been pushed further and further back. For five years in a row, the WPI forecasts in the budget each May have turned out to be wildly optimistic and have had to be downgraded. In early 2018, the government and the central bank were still insisting growth was about to kick in; private wage growth was still stuck at 1.9 per cent.

This absence of wages growth has confused policymakers; their models are saying wages should be rising because of low unemployment. But the same thing has been happening around the world: falling unemployment and falling wages. Indeed, UK workers faced much worse stagnation than Australians: real wages actually *declined* in the United Kingdom in the six years between 2008 and 2014 and have only partially recovered since then—and fell again in 2017. In the United States, real wages grew more strongly than in the United Kingdom or Australia during Barack Obama's second term, declined again in 2017 despite low unemployment, then only began growing again as the economy neared full employment. In Canada, real wages growth in 2016 hit its lowest level since 1998. In France, wages growth began declining in 2011; the decline only stopped in early 2017. In Germany—where wages were held down for two decades by the aftermath of reunification—growth picked up between 2014 and 2016 but then fell below 1 per cent in 2017. In Italy, wages growth hasn't been above 2 per cent since 2011 and is still falling. In different countries, with wildly different economies, in different free-trade areas and with different governments, workers were all experiencing the same thing: their employers were refusing to increase, or often even maintain, their wages.

Wage stagnation hasn't merely ended the long period of growing real incomes that neoliberalism had produced, it contrasted sharply with continued strong growth in incomes for the very wealthiest, and corporate profits: in Australia in 2017, company profits surged and executive salaries soared while workers enjoyed no real wages growth. The economy, it seemed, was no longer working in the interests of everyone, but for the elite. And this imbalance began feeding into lower economic growth, by reducing demand and undermining consumer confidence despite strong employment growth.

The link between growing inequality and lower economic growth has begun to receive attention in recent years. The OECD produced a study in 2014 suggesting inequality had substantially reduced growth rates in Western countries—it was estimated a big rise in the Gini coefficient could knock off a third of a percentage point of GDP growth each year.

A 2015 IMF study suggested increasing the incomes of the bottom quintile of income earners could substantially boost growth. And its 2016 paper, *Neoliberalism: Oversold?*, noted:

> The costs in terms of increased inequality are prominent. Such costs epitomize the trade-off between the growth and equity effects of some aspects of the neoliberal agenda. Increased inequality in turn hurts the level and sustainability of growth. Even if growth is the sole or main purpose of the neoliberal agenda, advocates of that agenda still need to pay attention to the distributional effects.

Apart from wage stagnation, how else does inequality harm growth? As senior economist and Clinton-era Treasury Secretary Larry Summers and others have pointed out, if the wealthy have a greater share of income, they're more likely to save it rather than spend it—high-income people save a lot more of their income than those on low incomes, who are devoting much more of their income to the basics of keeping alive. So as economies become more unequal, a greater share of overall wealth is in savings rather than fuelling consumer demand. There's also evidence that greater inequality is linked to shorter growth cycles, and the OECD thinks it's because inequality '[undermines] education opportunities for children from poor socio-economic backgrounds, lowering social mobility and hampering skills development'. That is, the kids of people on low incomes struggle to accumulate skills, reducing both economic outcomes for themselves and harming overall growth. Another suggestion is that inequality encourages unsustainable borrowing by some households, leading to greater financial instability.

Undermining growth is about as serious a charge as it's possible to level against any economic policy. In Australia, for decades, to be accused of undermining growth was the economic equivalent of a capital offence. The Howard government famously went to extreme lengths to argue climate action would undermine growth—it extrapolated growth rates under different policies out to 2050 and claimed the cumulative difference between them as an immediate impact of climate-action policies. But it's a particularly serious accusation for neoliberalism, because the *only* thing neoliberalism has going for it is that it makes us wealthier. For all that the moral foundations of neoliberalism lie in the concept of individual freedom, as a philosophy it only offers society one thing. Neoliberalism doesn't bring us closer together as a community. It doesn't do the environment any good. It doesn't keep us warm on a cold winter's night. Economic growth is the only KPI.

Inequality doesn't merely have economic impacts. There is considerable evidence that greater inequality is linked to greater mistrust (which also has a flow-on economic impact as well). We're more likely to trust people like ourselves—and someone with a dramatically different income doesn't fit that description. In fact, some critics of inequality argue it is responsible for a huge range of problems: more crime, poorer physical and mental health, higher rates of incarceration. In these analyses, inequality (and, thus, neoliberalism) is the great demon of contemporary policymaking. That overlooks the fact that inequality is an inevitable result of *any* set of policies that encourages economic growth, since growth will never be perfectly distributed and it's hard to start a society from scratch so that everyone has perfectly equal opportunity. But there does appear to be good evidence that more unequal societies have higher crime and poorer health among low-income earners. Moreover, inequality tends to become self-reinforcing, since it leads to less political engagement by low-income earners, while high-income earners have a greater incentive to encourage policymakers to preserve the status quo that serves them so well.

The starkest demonstration of the growing challenge of inequality relates to executive remuneration, which has been turbocharged by neoliberal policies. In 2009, after Labor asked the Productivity Commission to investigate the issue, that body found the CEOs of Australia's top 100 listed companies had seen their pay rise from seventeen times average earnings to 42 times average earnings since 1993. More recent data for the remuneration of the CEOs of Australia's top 100 companies shows them getting around twenty times average earnings until the mid 1990s, when it starts climbing rapidly, reaching over 70 times earnings in the 2000s—and still around 50 times earnings in the 2010s.

In a paper examining the long-run remuneration of Australian mining giant BHP's CEOs and directors, academic Mike Pottenger and former academic and now Labor MP Andrew Leigh found that remuneration had generally fallen, as a multiple of average earnings, across the twentieth century. But after reaching less than ten times average earnings, remuneration dramatically accelerated at the end of the 1980s such that, having never exceeded 90 times average earnings since the late nineteenth century, CEO pay raced up to over 200 times average earnings.

Comparable data from the United States—where the disparity between executive remuneration and the earnings of average workers has received far more attention—shows a similar decline, then rapid acceleration, of remuneration in relation to average earnings in the 1980s and 1990s. In the United Kingdom, where executive pay is currently around 180 times average earnings, former prime minister David Cameron declared there had been a 'market failure' on the issue and—as many countries have done, including Australia—changed corporate governance rules to give shareholders more say on executive pay.

Companies, CEOs and neoliberal commentators shrug and insist that executive pay isn't a problem—it's simply about the market. To attract high-quality CEOs, you need to offer large packages to lure talent from the global pool of corporate leadership. Oddly, though, companies are less enthusiastic about allowing the labour market to operate freely when it comes to recruiting ordinary workers: during the mining investment boom in Australia around 2010, mining companies that had launched a number of large mining construction projects at the same time, and were thus bidding against each other for engineering and other talent, repeatedly complained that Australia was 'a high-cost place to do business'. And you'll never guess what their solution was—they wanted governments to intervene to reduce the capacity of unions to negotiate wage rises for in-demand labour.

Companies also insist that they strongly link pay to performance. But there's little evidence for, and considerable evidence against, the idea that CEO remuneration is linked to corporate share prices. Even pro-business publications such as the *Wall Street Journal* and *Forbes* have pointed out that some of the United States' highest-paid CEOs run some of the country's worst-performing companies. Poor CEOs often walk away from failing companies with mammoth payouts. Peer-reviewed research has even shown a *negative* correlation between CEO pay and stock performance. This is partly a result of flawed incentive structures that reward short-term performance, and executives who work to juice a company's share price, at the expense of long-term performance or even economic stability. Economists, the World Bank, central bankers and senior economic policymakers have all linked 'misaligned' remuneration incentives to the origins of the global financial crisis—a very direct link between inequality and economic damage.

But no matter the rationales advanced for them, eight-figure salaries and massive payouts look obscene to people, even when ordinary incomes are rising. At a time when incomes are stagnant and large companies have a well-earned reputation for dodging taxes and other misconduct, executives earning many multiples of average earnings—let alone up to 200 times, as was the case a decade ago—seems yet more evidence of an economic system that's working against the interests of ordinary people, not in favour of them. To many people, it seems that inequality isn't a by-product of the larger economic success of neoliberalism, but its entire purpose and lasting legacy.

In theory: complexity and concentration

The differences between neoliberal dogma and its practical implementation aren't merely a matter of the political environment in which it is implemented. Theories of efficient markets, informed individuals maximising their welfare and the virtues of competition tend to play out differently in the real world than in economic models.

Two important principles of neoliberalism are rational choice theory and information symmetry. As functions are transferred to the private sector which, theoretically, can perform them more efficiently than government and send an appropriate price signal to consumers, neoliberalism assumes that consumers (and businesses that consume goods and services) are rational, know their own best interests and always act to achieve them, and have a reasonable level of information symmetry with goods and services providers, which will place pressure on the latter to behave competitively.

In practice, not so much. Take compulsory superannuation, the very principle of which defies rational choice theory. The theory suggests rational individuals would wish to save for their retirement to ensure a comfortable income when they are older. In practice, most people below the age of 40 couldn't care less about their retirement and in any event have more urgent uses for their incomes: student debt, buying a home, raising kids. Only those over 50 really focus on preparing for their retirement. Thus, successive governments in Australia have forced people to save for their retirements. And an entire industry—the retail superannuation sector, mostly owned by the major banks—relies on people not being interested enough in their superannuation returns each year to realise that retail superannuation funds underperform funds run by employers and unions, or corporate super funds, and charge higher fees. Retail superannuation and many parts of the financial planning industry have incorporated consumer disengagement and indifference into their business models.

The problem is more acute in what we might call 'hybrid' markets. Australia has a range of markets dominated by private-sector companies that either rely on taxpayer funding or are heavily regulated, or both. The result, often, is markets of immense complexity. And corporations love complexity, because it provides them with opportunities for information asymmetry over consumers, as well as opportunities to game regulations. In markets like mobile-phone plans or health insurance, corporations are particularly clever at preventing consumers from comparing like with like, thus reducing information symmetry. Companies also rely on absurdly elaborate terms and conditions, which no consumer ever reads, to minimise any legal recourse.

Some markets specifically encourage this exploitation of complexity. Australia's national electricity market was intended to bring the discipline of the market to a key utility, reducing costs and providing reliability. Instead, a byzantine regulatory framework was established to accommodate a mix of private and public generators, retailers and transmission network owners, which gave power companies extensive opportunities to game the system to secure big price increases at the expense of consumers and other businesses.

Aged care similarly offers lucrative opportunities for companies to exploit information asymmetry. Much of aged-care policy over the last decade in Australia, and especially after a Productivity Commission report in the Labor years, has been aimed at shifting more of the cost burden of aged care onto consumers themselves (or more correctly, the families of consumers). However 'neoliberal' this might seem, this is a sensible policy goal: Australia's population is ageing, and we are living considerably longer than we used to. The total cost of looking after ourselves in our final years is thus increasing and can't be met entirely by taxpayers, not without a big increase in the tax burden.

This process of shifting costs involves finding new ways to tap into the assets of seniors and their families, often using financial instruments of some kind, or elaborate contracts with retirement home providers. Inevitably, corporations have moved into a sector traditionally dominated by religious organisations and non-profit providers. The complexity of accessing medium-term accommodation, for an undefined period, by people who are asset-rich but cash-poor, and with the added layer of complexity of their being represented by relatives acting on their behalf, and usually with some urgency, provides significant opportunities for corporations to exploit even engaged and well-informed consumers and their families. The fact that the Australian regulatory framework for aged care is a composite of state and federal rules provides still greater opportunities for regulatory arbitrage and evasion of accountability.

The key lesson from this is one that has been repeated across any number of markets. All the predictions about the efficiency of markets won't make much difference if corporations are able to exploit complexity and information asymmetry for their own advantage—and they will *always* do so, to the extent the law allows them, and beyond if they can get away with it.

Corporations, which believe as a matter of high principle that competition is a wonderful thing except in their own industry, will also seek to eliminate competitors wherever they can, nullifying any efficiency gains from markets and shifting income from consumers to themselves in ways that—like inequality—damage growth. Recent decades have seen substantially greater concentration of ownership in the economies of both the United States and Australia as companies have become fewer, larger and more dominant in their markets. A 2017 study by the economist Luigi Zingales noted: 'In the last two decades more than 75 per cent of US industries experienced an increase in concentration levels, with the Herfindahl index[8] increasing by more than 50 percent on average. During this time, the size of the average publicly listed company in the United States tripled in market capitalization: from $1.2 billion to $3.7 billion in 2016 dollars.'

The Economist, which ran a series on growing concentration in the United States in 2016, similarly reported that two-thirds of all sectors in the United States were more concentrated now than in the 1980s. Economists have identified the finance, retailing, media, and high-tech sectors as particularly concentrated, but there are also problems with dominant companies in agriculture, pharmaceuticals, aviation and others. A 2017 paper by Jan De Loecker and Jan Eeckhout showed that mark-ups[9] by US firms had been stable in the postwar period but then began rising considerably after 1980 and had tripled in the 35 years since then—and this rise in mark-ups closely matched the decline in the labour share of national income that had occurred over that period as well.

Australia has also seen a significant increase in concentration—and our economy, with its relatively small domestic markets, was already more prone to concentration and oligopoly than the world's largest. In 2016, the Australian Competition and Consumer Commission chair, Rod Sims, noted: 'The rise of large corporations in the Australian economy has also

---

8   A widely used measure of market concentration, based on market share.
9   The amount companies can add on to the cost of production when setting prices—a useful indicator of market power.

been substantial. Indeed it seems we have slightly outpaced the United States. Analysis prepared by Port Jackson Partners Limited shows the revenue of Australia's largest 100 listed companies increased from 27 per cent of GDP in 1993 to 47 per cent of GDP in 2015. This compares to the US figures of 33 per cent to 46 per cent.'

Much of that growth occurred in the late 1990s and early 2000s. Labor MP and economist Andrew Leigh has noted that 'since 1990 the number of mergers and acquisitions in Australia has more than quadrupled from 346 (with a combined value of $28 billion) to 1595 in 2016 (with a value of $140 billion) . . . this has led to a substantial increase in market concentration in supermarkets, banking, airlines, meat processing, bottled drinks, telecommunications and a range of other important indus-tries'. Concentration isn't confined to reducing the number of competitors; it can extend up and down the product chain. The vertical integration of Australia's major banks with wealth management and financial advice companies commenced in the late 1990s as banks aimed to use their retail networks to funnel unsuspecting customers into bank-owned funds and other wealth products. It took a decade before the consequences of this restructuring began to become apparent (more of that in the next chapter), and almost another decade before serious action was taken to address the trail of wrecked lives and shat-tered finances this had caused, as the banking royal commission revealed industry-wide misconduct and criminality.

Is concentration a particular feature of neoliberalism? Surely an economic philosophy devoted to the rigour of markets and the virtue of competition would be hostile to the idea of corporations becoming large enough to wield anti-competitive power and the ability to use their size to extract economic rents? And, after all, giant anti-competitive companies are hardly a feature peculiar to the late twentieth and twenty-first centuries—the first great era of trust busting in the United States, when the federal government moved against giant corporations and broke them up, was at the end of the nineteenth century. Companies have known about the benefits of monopolies since Henry VIII first handed out a printing monopoly to the Stationers' Company.

But as it turns out, neoliberalism is highly conducive to growing concentration: the emphasis on deregulation and 'market-friendly' policies mean lawmakers are under constant pressure to remove regulatory impediments to mergers and acquisitions, not add to them. And financial deregulation and the encouragement of the free movement of capital have provided fuel for mergers and acquisitions. After all, what offers a better return: risky investment in a new product or innovative start-up, or buying equity in a large firm that could become even larger and be able to dominate its market, ensuring higher revenue? Legendary investor Warren Buffett, whose Berkshire Hathaway is one of the largest companies in the world and holds major and minor stakes in vast numbers of other companies, famously prefers to invest in companies that can dominate their markets, that are invulnerable to competition, protected by a 'moat' that deters competitors. 'We think in terms of that moat and the ability to keep its width and its impossibility of being crossed as the primary criterion of a great business,' he once said. 'And we tell our managers we want the moat widened every year.' As we'll see later, the bigger corporations become, the greater capacity they have to remove regulatory restraints on themselves—the bigger you get, the bigger you *can* get.

This suggests that, for economies like the United States and Australia, Jan De Loecker and Jan Eeckhout were on to something when they examined the fall in workers' share of national income since the 1970s as concentration increased— that lost share of income has not gone from wages to greater investment by companies, but to higher profits. Increasingly dominant firms extract greater margins at the expense of consumers, downstream businesses and workers, and pass on that profit to shareholders and executives rather than investing it back into the business. Indeed, one prominent investor in 2017 blamed rising monopoly power for the 'abnormally high corporate profit margins' since 2011.

But what about disruption? Aren't we living through a period of massive technological change? As we'll see in Part 4 on the impact of the internet, we are indeed witness-ing a period of great economic disruption. But that doesn't necessarily mean markets become less concentrated. Look at the media, an intensely concentrated market in Australia and highly concentrated in the United States. The disruption in that industry has led to the establishment, in less than fifteen years, of two global monster corporations, Facebook and Google, which dominate the industries they operate in to an even greater degree than the media moguls of the analogue age did.

Neoliberal economists understood the threat to their ideology contained in the rise in concentration in the US economy. Explaining it away, or somehow justifying it, became an urgent task for many of the Chicago School. George Stigler, one of the founders of the Mont Pelerin Society, complained that 'the growing socialist critique of capitalism emphasised monopoly; "monopoly capitalism" is almost one word in that literature'. But how could monopolies be a good thing for neoliberal economists? Building on earlier theories about transaction costs, Chicago School economists argued that mergers were justified by their capacity to reduce internal costs for the merged entity, leading to greater efficiency and economies of scale—and certainly not because the merged entity could extract greater margins using its dominant position. This is why, as even a casual reader of the financial press will notice, all mergers these days are justified as being about achieving economies of scale rather than improving the capacity of a merged entity to extract higher mark-ups from its consumers, or to widen Buffett's 'moat'. Neoliberal economists also argued that monopolies would be temporary, and that in any case, *actual* competition didn't matter as long as a market was 'contestable'—that is, a firm could *theoretically* enter it, even if it was highly concentrated. The mere *threat* of a new entrant would be enough to curb monopolistic behaviour.[10]

The assuming away of the negative consequences of growing concentration by neoliberal economists neither stopped the steady expansion of profits by giant firms, nor the negative impacts of concentration. Building on the work of earlier generations of Marxist and radical economists, researchers are identifying more and more evidence of the extent to which growing concentration inhibits economic growth by curbing innovation and investment, increasing prices for other sectors (remember, business customers are as great a victim of monopolies as individual consumers) and undermining wage growth. Prominent investment manager Jeremy Grantham in

---

10 This 'contestable' silliness, by the way, wasn't exclusively the province of neoliberal economists—as a public servant trying to get sign-off from governments for contracts with monopoly providers, I used it myself.

2017 noted, about the high level of corporate profits in the United States:

> The general pattern described so far is entirely compatible with increased monopoly power for US corporations. Put this way, if they had materially more monopoly power, we would expect to see exactly what we do see: higher profit margins; increased reluctance to expand capacity;[11] slight reductions in GDP growth and productivity; pressure on wages, unions, and labor negotiations; and fewer new entrants into the corporate world and a declining number of increasingly large corporations.

And as we saw with inequality, anything that directs a greater proportion of income away from low- and middle-income earners leads to lower spending; high-income earners save more of their income and corporations hoard profits or return them to shareholders by way of share buybacks to boost their share price. The overall result is less demand in the economy and thus lower growth.

And while the lack of sufficiently rigorous competition regulation clearly exacerbates the tendency to greater concentration, there are other areas in which regulation, rather than the lack of it, is the problem. The best example is 'critical infrastructure'—where governments, keen to be seen to be doing something about national security, construct elaborate requirements for companies operating in key sectors. This is aimed at minimising the risks from disruptive events that might affect the core infrastructure of the economy—energy, communications, transport

---

11 This is, again, De Loecker and Eeckhout's point that concentration saw a shift not to *capital i.e.* greater investment, but to *profit*.

and so on. But as a former bureaucrat who once worked on critical infrastructure, I can tell you: it's a scam.

You'd be forgiven for thinking companies would be reluctant to accept the burden of such regulation, given it would add nothing to their capacity to increase revenue, and would increase their operating costs. Yet most 'critical infrastructure' participants are perfectly happy to comply. If you examine the sectors involved, it becomes clear why: sectors like telecommunications, energy supply and fuel distribution are all highly concentrated, meaning companies are usually in a strong position to pass costs straight on to consumers and other businesses. But that's not the key reason why they love it: greater regulation designed to establish resilience in infrastructure provision and critical services increases barriers to entry and places proportionately greater costs on smaller competitors. 'Critical infrastructure' makes it even harder for new entrants and small firms to compete with established, dominant players in such industries because they can't function without having to direct additional resources to complying with the government's regulatory requirements.[12]

And while a highly active and (compared to the pre 1980s) deregulated financial sector is conducive to fewer, larger companies, Australia has a particular policy that exacerbates that tendency as well: our system of compulsory superannuation, which has created two trillion dollars in savings. Industry

---

12 Something similar is underway in the Australian electricity sector, where the additional regulatory burdens placed by governments on companies in 2017 could be easily funded by the big three retailers but were much harder to fund or pass on to customers for their smaller competitors. Every time governments crack down on the behaviour of the Big Three 'gentailers'— AGL, Origin and EnergyAustralia—which are both electricity generators and retailers, they're entrenching their dominant position.

Super Australia, which represents the employer and union-run super sector, published a series of reports between 2013 and 2015 showing how Australia's financial system became less efficient at generating new investment in capital stock as it grew after the Hawke government–led deregulation in the 1980s.

The ISA—and it was exceedingly brave of the super industry to publish an argument that appeared to criticise the entire sector's very existence—found that 'in the early 1990s, for every $1 of economic resources allocated to the financial services sector there was about $3.50 of capital formation. By 2012, that same dollar of resources allocated to finance yielded about $1.50 of capital formation.'

That was partly because Australia's banks had focused on residential property more than business investment (residential property lending, because it comes with an asset that can be forfeited to the lender if the borrower defaults, is more appealing than business loans). But Australia's fund managers were also more focused on the buying and selling of existing assets like equities, rather than new investment. 'In the late 1990s, the ratio of primary capital raised to the turnover of secondary equity markets was, on average, about 1:10 (i.e., for every $1 of public capital raising there was about $10 of trading activity). In 2012, the ratio was 1:28.'

So while Australian institutions controlled a massive pool of superannuation, a lot of it was simply being used for secondary trading of equities and derivatives, rather than new investment in equipment or in new companies that would produce a meaningful increase in growth and employment. The report also noted the British financial system, powered by the City and its £120-billion contribution to the UK economy, was similarly inefficient and focused on equities rather than funding new capital.

Between our massive savings pool, financial deregulation and compliant governments happy to let corporations get ever bigger, we created a dead weight on economic growth that exacerbated inequality.

Swiss cheese or, Towards a competitive index of competitiveness indices

Let's take a break from hard economic data and relax with some neoliberal propaganda. For many years, the International Monetary Fund and the World Bank were synonymous with neoliberalism, as the chief enforcers of what was dubbed the 'Washington consensus', demanding 'structural adjustments' as a condition of loans to developing countries and governments that faced economic crises. While Chile under mass-murderer Pinochet had been the original test bed for the economic reforms of the 'Chicago boys', and the United Kingdom had been forced to impose fiscal restraint to access IMF loans in the 1970s, it was Mexico in 1982 that became the first example of what was to be an ongoing pattern of the IMF and World Bank imposing neoliberal reforms, often to protect the interests of Western banks.

In recent years, however, the IMF has become a mild critic of the orthodoxy it helped impose, with senior figures such as Sanjeev Gupta identifying the inequality generated by neoliberalism and its damaging impacts. Even the World Bank, while still arguing that global inequality has fallen significantly in recent decades, now targets inequality and says 'the increasing share of income going to the top 1 percent of earners is of great concern'.

Corporate-sponsored fora, however, continue to eagerly promote neoliberalism. Chief among these is the World Economic Forum, a Swiss-based advocacy group funded by the world's largest corporations, which seeks the decidedly novel goal of 'improving the state of the world'. Among the companies that fund the WEF are some of the worst corporate actors on the planet: the Adani Group, Deutsche Bank, General Dynamics, Lockheed Martin, Monsanto, Nestlé, Coca Cola, Walmart, and state-owned companies from some of the world's most brutal regimes, such as Saudi Arabia and China.

One of the WEF's most prominent outputs is its annual 'World Competitiveness Index', which has repeatedly been used by politicians, commentators and business-lobby groups to demand more economic reform—in particular, labour-market deregulation to reduce wages, remove workplace protections and erode the power of trade unions. While the title 'World Competitiveness Index' makes it sound authoritative, it mainly relies on the forum's 'executive opinion survey' of 13,000 business executives around the globe—which translates into a few dozen executives per country. Unsurprisingly, business executives turn out to be biased in all sorts of ways. For example, in 2007, under the Howard government, Australian executives rated their customers eighth in the world on their 'sophisticated analysis of performance attributes' when they shopped, with a score of 5.76. But in 2012, under a Labor government, Australian executives rated their customers thirty-third in the world, scoring 4.2. Australians had fallen from urbane sophisticates to slack-jawed yokels in five short years and one change of government.

Similarly, in 2012, the WEF criticised Australia's industrial-relations system, Labor's *Fair Work Act*. Too 'rigid', the gnomes of Davos declared. Happily, things thereafter took a turn for the better: in the 2017 report, 'the efficiency of the labor market, where Australia used to rank in the 50s, improves further (28th, up eight)—a gain of almost 30 places over the past three years'. There's only one problem . . . the industrial relations system in Australia hadn't changed in the intervening period. The only change had been from a Labor to a conservative government.

And when asked 'To what extent do government officials in your country show favouritism to well-connected firms and individuals when deciding upon policies and contracts?', business executives under the Howard government pronounced themselves pleased with the lack of corruption, rating Australia 4.41, or fifteenth in the world. Scroll forward several years, and under a Labor government, and we'd fallen to twenty-fourth with a score of 4.18. That score placed us behind Saudi Arabia and several other oil sheikdoms, where the entire states are based on nepotism and favouritism.

In fact, the WEF loves oil theocracies. Over the years, it has cooed over Saudi Arabia's 'solid institutional framework, efficient markets, and sophisticated businesses' and at how Qatar's 'high levels of security are the cornerstones of the country's very solid institutional framework'. Bahrain was rated ahead of Australia in 'trust in government'. Qatar's judiciary was rated as more independent than Australia's, even though it is hand-picked by the kingdom's ruling family. All are rated above Australia on 'labour flexibility', which is understandable given they use actual slave labour. Indeed, according to the WEF, Qatar is a top performer in a wide range of competitiveness criteria, reflecting that Qatari executives have a very positive view of their government. But the catch is, many Qatari executives *are* the government, being relatives of the ruling Al Thani family.

Indeed, as the years have gone by, the World Competitiveness Index has become sillier and sillier. In 2016, Australia was comprehensively thrashed by Saudi Arabia on measures to do with public-sector efficiency. On 'wastefulness of government spending' the fundamentalist theocrats of Saudi Arabia were ranked twelfth in terms of efficiency, while Australia only managed fifty-second. On overall public-sector performance, the Saudis ranked twenty-first, Australia thirty-second. Alas, just a few days before the WEF published its 2016 index, the Saudi minister responsible for the kingdom's public servants savaged his workers, saying 'the amount worked [among state employees] doesn't even exceed an hour—and that's based on studies'. Two-thirds of all Saudis work for the government, and government workers are virtually impossible to sack, enjoy a 35-hour week, receive frequent bonuses and soak up 45 per cent of the entire Saudi budget—vastly in excess of the total cost of all public servants across three levels of government in Australia.

Full respect to capitalism, however: the World Economic Forum has spawned its own competitiveness index market. There's now an IMD World Competitiveness Centre at a business school based in Switzerland. Every year it produces its 'World Competitiveness Yearbook'. It, too, has an 'Executive Opinion Survey', about half the size of the WEF report. Confusingly, it has startlingly different results to the WEF index: recently, IMD rated Hong Kong the most competitive economy, which only managed a lousy ninth in the most recent WEF index. And IMD only gave the Germans thirteenth spot compared to fifth in the WEF effort. Likewise, the WEF ranked the Irish below Australia at twenty-third but

IMD gives them sixth. And China knocks off the Brits to steal eighteenth spot for IMD while the WEF has the Chinese at the back of the pack at twenty-eighth. The tax dodgers of Luxembourg are eighth for IMD but a lousy twentieth for WEF. What's a neoliberal to do when they can't even work out who's out-competing whom?

Then in 2007, the Brits got in on the action as Cardiff's Centre for International Competitiveness was established, which, for the purposes of product differentiation, assesses *regions* instead of countries (hilariously, it rates the Canberra region in Australia as one of the world's most economically competitive). There's also a manufacturing competitiveness index, proudly brought to you by consultant Deloittes, and the Boao Forum of Asia has its own Asian Competitiveness Annual Report, which might possibly end up competing with the Lee Kuan Yew School of Public Policy Asian Competitiveness Institute.

The solution, of course, is for some bright neoliberal spark to establish a World Competitiveness Index Index, based on executive surveys of which index corporate execs think is best—until we get two competing index indices, when we'll have to start the whole process over again.

The robots are taking our jerbs

As we discussed earlier, one of the standard defences of neoliberalism against the charge that it is responsible for widespread job losses across the West is that it isn't the fault of market economics and free trade but of technology. In particular, the rebuttal to the oft-made argument that five million manufacturing jobs have been lost in the United States since China acceded to the World Trade Organization is that in that time, US manufacturing output has dramatically increased while employing fewer workers. Don't blame globalisation, runs the argument, blame automation, which enables more production with a smaller workforce. It's a handy argument, because it's a lot harder to stop the march of technology than to close a border or slap a tariff on some goods.

The issue has particular piquancy because the widespread expectation is that automation will continue to consume jobs in an ever-growing range of industries, and shift from manufacturing and mining (where, in Australia, virtually the entire production process might become automated and remote-controlled in coming years) to service jobs in sectors like retail, administration, taxis and even legal and medical services. A recent, if wildly implausible, report estimated around a third of UK jobs could be automated in coming decades, and closer to 40 per cent in the United States. An Australian report suggested a similar figure. Even if these scenarios prove grossly over the top, it's hard to avoid seeing a significant loss of employment due to automation. If 15 per cent of all jobs vanished to automation over a decade in Australia, that would mean nearly two million workers looking for a new career—with the concomitant economic insecurity, sense of vulnerability and social dislocation that would lead from that, as well as the impact on the wider economy.

Some tech entrepreneurs—Elon Musk being the most prominent example—argue that automation is going to lead to mass unemployment and we need to embrace ideas like Universal Basic Income, which in recent years has moved from an idea primarily championed by those on the Left as a kind of communist nirvana, to one embraced (or re-embraced, given Friedman's support for a negative income tax) by some neoliberals.

We'll deal with how wretched an idea UBI is later in the book. But there are reasons to be doubtful that this robo-nightmare will come to pass. For a start, there's a lot of hype about automation that looks unlikely to be fulfilled for years, if ever. Take autonomous vehicles, which are portrayed as, well, just around the corner. In fact, there remain huge problems with that technology, not least of which is there don't yet exist sufficiently detailed maps of even the streets of major population centres, let alone the rest of the planet, to enable autonomous vehicles to operate safely. There's the small problem that rain and snow confuse vehicle sensors. Developers can't work out whether or not to skip past semi-autonomous vehicles—where you can kick back and relax but might have to intervene if something goes wrong—and go straight to fully autonomous, because humans might react too slowly to being asked to re-engage with the vehicle. For the next few years, autonomous vehicles are likely to remain confined to where they can work effectively—curtailed, well-mapped spaces like warehouses, or large, unpopulated spaces like open-cut mines. Australian mining companies are currently world leaders in using autonomous trucks in iron ore mining in the Pilbara, but there is little to run into and the operating space is tightly controlled. And all of that is before you get to the problem of the cybersecurity of even existing motor vehicles, let alone fully autonomous ones. Barring an AI revolution that fixes these fundamental problems, if you make a living from driving, the gig economy is the big threat to you, not robots.

Moreover, Western countries currently face a shortage of workers in many industries rather than a dearth of jobs.

97

With ageing populations and falling participation rates, work-forces are no longer growing except in high immigration countries like Australia. China's working-age population has been in a steady decline for a couple of years and that decline will soon accelerate. Poland, Japan, Italy and Russia—just to name a few—are facing declining populations overall, not just declining workforces. Germany until recently faced a falling population but has managed to stabilise it with higher immigration. Even in Australia, despite high immigration, we import temporary workers in tens of thousands, particularly in service industries, and that will only increase in the long term. Australian policymakers have worked hard to lift work-force participation over the last 30 years, but it is hard to see it increasing further as Australians get older. The first Baby Boomers are entering retirement, and even high immigration isn't going to reverse that demographic trend. Even if automation claims many of the service jobs in health, social care and hospitality for which we currently need to import workers, large-scale unemployment seems some time off.

The robots-will-take-everyone's-jobs thesis is also a thesis of discontinuity. Technological progress has been a constant in Western industrial economies. Machines have taken jobs before. Workers have complained, rioted and destroyed them in response, but the mass unemployment predicted to follow in the machines' wake never happened. Other jobs were created, partly funded by the fact that automation reduced produc-tion costs, thereby freeing up consumer dollars to be directed elsewhere. And it's always been the case that the new jobs weren't identified, or often even conceived of, at the time. In the 1990s, job titles like social media manager, digital market-ing consultant and app builder would have drawn blank stares.

Something, therefore, will have to go fundamentally and ahistorically wrong for the same process not to play out in relation to the current wave of automation. That's not to say that's impossible, merely that history tells us the problem won't be as big as we think it is.

Individualism, identity and the neoliberal economics of self

So far we've dealt with the economically rather mixed story of neoliberalism, most of which is easily verified with recourse to data. Let's plunge into some murkier waters and try to determine what social impacts neoliberalism has had.

Neoliberalism sends a message about individual and group identity; it conveys the extent to which, and *how*, people are valued. We're not talking so much here about how neoliberals exploit racial identity—that's well established and not applicable to neoliberalism any more than other economic orthodoxies. As Lyndon Johnson was apt to note, the issue of race had long been used to divide low-income southerners in the United States, white versus black, to the benefit of elite interests. 'Every election, all they hear is n*****, n*****, n*****,' LBJ loved to say about elections in the South. Powerful elites—whether capitalist or not—have long used race and nationalism as an effective tool to divide workers who had far greater shared interests with one another than with those who shared the same skin colour or nationality but exploited them.

Instead, we're talking about something more subtle here: what do the policies of neoliberalism signal about what is *important* in a society?

First, that there is no such thing as society. Margaret Thatcher's famous statement that 'there is no such thing' as society, 'there are individual men and women and there are families' wasn't merely a powerful message, it was one reinforced by public policy. It encouraged Britons to see themselves as untethered by any social bonds, freed of community ties and responsibilities (had not Norman Tebbitt told Britain's millions of unemployed to 'Get on yer bike' and move to where there were jobs?). Social bonds, after all, could not be valued economically; they couldn't be costed, there was no market, no private sector to which the provision of social bonds could be outsourced. It was up to individuals to seek their own economic opportunities, not to expect that the community—'society'—would look after them.

Neoliberalism in its pure form thus seeks to dissolve community ties and social bonds. There are only individuals—or if there is anything else, it runs a distant second to the primacy of the individual, who is engaged in an eternal competition with others to maximise their economic value.

And while Thatcher relied on the jingoism of the Falkland Islands campaign to secure re-election in 1983, her comment also touched on the problematic issue of nationalism and tribalism under neoliberalism. Except in encouraging a sense of the need to compete internationally to provide the most business-friendly economic environment (the reasoning behind a world competitiveness index), neoliberalism in its pure form has little time for nationalism or racism. Nationalism, national identity, sentiment of any kind, is an incidental aspect of social relations that is meaningless in a market (except to the extent that it can be monetised via flag bikinis, 'Fuck off, we're full' stickers and other patriotic paraphernalia). Under neoliberalism, each of us *only* has an economic identity. Our nationality—like our sexual orientation, or gender, or political views, or skin colour—is irrelevant to our value as a producer and consumer. An Australian worker has no more (or less) innate value than a South American or Southeast Asian or African worker by virtue of her Australianness; only the value she can bring to a business, only her skills, her talent, entrepreneurship and expertise, are relevant. Similarly, the 'nationality' of an investment, the country of origin of capital, is irrelevant—whether an investor is Australian, American or Chinese doesn't matter; what matters is the value they bring measured in dollars.

Accordingly, neoliberals favour open borders both for people and investment. When it comes to borders, neoliberals would find much in common with nineteenth- and early twentieth-century Marxists who decried nationalism as a capitalist distraction: they see borders as meaningless nationalist fictions that can only hamper the free flow of resources—financial, human, intellectual, material—to where the market will make most efficient use of them.

This—confusingly for the Left—often sees staunch neoliberals and prominent business figures vocally supporting the rights of asylum seekers to come to Australia, a position normally seen as progressive. In 2009, the Institute of Public Affairs' John Roskam called for a significant lift in Australia's refugee intake and an end to long-term detention for asylum seekers. During his brief political career, the otherwise right-wing Clive Palmer called for an end to Australia's 'shame' of offshore detention. In 2016, economically hardline former Business Council head Tony Shepherd visited Syrian refugee camps in Lebanon with other senior business representatives and called for Australia's intake of Syrian refugees to be more than doubled. And the Left has its own deep split on borders and globalisation—a naive 'Let them all come' sentimentality toward asylum seekers and illegal immigrants among some progressives, which endorses open borders for anyone who wants to claim asylum, and is often coupled with an instinctive hostility to high levels of immigration or temporary worker schemes, which they see as undermining Australian workers' incomes and harming the environment.

As we've seen in recent years, however, open borders push the buttons of voters, not merely for economic reasons, through perceptions of jobs being taken and wages undermined, but because of the sense of a lack of control over who is coming into the country. Asylum-seeker advocates think this deep-seated fear about border control is a reflection of instinctive racism that could be exorcised from the electorate if only there were politicians willing to explain to voters why they were wrong. But for neoliberals, the sentiment about border control doesn't even make sense—the only issue is the *economic value* of workers, not where they were born or how they arrived; not so much 'Let them all come' as 'Let them all work'. For communities, however, even communities with highly progressive views, open borders are seen as a direct threat, in which the benefits of being Australian, or British, or American, or French, are being taken by those with no claim to them, and in a zero-sum game that means locals missing out.

In Australia, there has been a political shift against foreign workers since 2013, prompted by the Labor Party. Back then, the Liberal Party derided Labor's attempts to exploit community resentment toward the 457 visa category that had become synonymous with foreign, often underpaid, workers—the Liberals, after all, had long supported higher skilled migration and allowing businesses to import temporary labour with as little difficulty as possible. By 2017, the Coalition was trying to catch up, announcing the 'abolition' of the 457 category and slashing the number of occupations for which businesses were allowed to import workers.

Foreign real-estate investors have been similarly targeted in Australia: despite foreign residents being limited to buying new housing in Australia—thereby ensuring they don't compete with locals for the existing housing stock—both federal and state Liberal governments have cracked down on foreign real-estate purchases in response to angst about Chinese investors keeping young Australians out of the housing market. That didn't go far enough for some: in 2018, former prime minister Tony Abbott, ever alert for issues on which to cause trouble for his successor, attacked the government for not massively cutting immigration, which he said was the cause of stagnant wages and congested infrastructure.

But this reaction against the indifference of neoliberalism to nationalist sentiment and social bonds is only the economic aspect of a wider issue around identity. The primacy of *Homo economicus* under neoliberalism has a more concrete effect on identity than just resentment about foreign workers or anomie induced by the dissolution of traditional community ties. As economics scholar Mary Wrenn argued in a 2014 paper, by emphasising the economic value of individuals, above and beyond community or other values, neoliberalism spurs the shift to other forms of identity. If we understand identity as a combination of what we ascribe as our personal identities, the identities society assigns to us and what relationships we choose to form socially, neoliberalism establishes the individual and their economic achievement as both a determining factor in how individuals see themselves, and the determining factor of socially assigned identity. As Wrenn argues, 'If under neoliberalism the market mentality and economic sphere dominate all other spheres of living ... that piece of an individual's identity that is other-assigned should rightly be called neoliberal identity, instead of collective social identity since neoliberal, or more broadly, economic assessments of character will dominate that other-assigned identity of an individual.'

This doesn't merely undermine non-economic social bonds and work to disconnect the individual from the community, it exposes individuals to a greater risk of alienation given the changing nature of modern economies. 'As the division of labor intensifies and the individual becomes more removed from both process and product, the individual is less able to identify herself with any material contribution to society.'

But there's a further problem beyond traditional economic alienation: under neoliberalism, even though 'neoliberal identity is predicated on financial success', as Wrenn explains, not everyone can be financially successful. That's just maths—half the population will be below the average level of income, and even those on above-average incomes will feel as though they are not as economically successful as high-income earners. Debt offers a mechanism to *feel* like an economic winner, even if you aren't one, but that often ends up trapping households in poor decisions. And neoliberalism's intrinsic tendency to inequality means that while even the poorest have become wealthier as a consequence of economic reforms, the wealthy have become a lot wealthier. The public benchmark for the financial success that is the basis for neoliberal identity has thus become harder to meet. As societies, we have told people their value relates only to their economic success, and that they are responsible as individuals for that success, but the rules of the game mean that half of them must be losers and most have to miss out on the ostentatious rewards of the winners.

Neoliberalism thus provides both an economic basis for a nationalist backlash against it due to its emphasis on open borders, *and* a motive to reject an imposed neoliberal economic identity. Wrenn argues, 'As failure of the neoliberal identity intensifies, the individual—whether consciously or not—begins to seek a relational social identity that is non-economic in nature. The individual seeks empowerment via this extraeconomic, social identity.' These other identities are more likely to be achievable for people than the status of economic winner—identity based on nationality, a regional group, a race, or other sexual, religious or political identities. In its dismissal of non-economic forms of identity, such as nationalism, as irrelevant, neoliberalism ends up fuelling them—especially once its primary benefit, that of increasing the wealth of citizens, vanishes.

Sometimes the economic and identity-based drivers of nationalism can seamlessly fuse. The long-running issue of Catalan nationalism flared in Spain in 2017, all the way to a brief declaration of independence, prompting Madrid to reassert full sovereignty over the region. While Catalan nationalism is centuries old, what did Catalan nationalists shout so frequently that the slogan was claimed to be the motto of this renewed push? '*Madrid nos roba*' ('Madrid robs us')—the cry of a wealthy province that believes it is paying too much to a central government and subsidising other, poorer regions. People in the economic powerhouses of Lombardy and Veneto in northern Italy also voted for greater autonomy in October 2017, a continuation of the broader Northern League nationalist movement of the 1990s, that aimed for greater economic control and capacity to halt flows of illegal immigrants from the poorly controlled borders in the south of the country.

This fusion of nationalism or tribal identity and economic concerns can play out in different ways. The link between poorer education, and poorer cognitive and verbal skills, and a greater propensity to hold racist views, is well established among white Western people (and US studies show a similar link among African-American and Hispanic people). But people with poorer education and lower intelligence are also more likely to be economically marginalised and to lack the skills to compete in a market economy. Again, on the Trump-era question of whether economics or racism is driving white voters to support a bigot, it can easily be both.

That link between lower education levels, lower cognitive ability and racism also applies to sexism, though evidently that issue has appealed less to male academics, because far less research has been done on it. The Gamergate 'controversy' in the United States—which involved the targeted harassment and abuse of female journalists by a large group of male gamers—was a foretaste of the extraordinary misogynistic abuse that would be directed at Hillary Clinton by Trump supporters (and some Bernie Sanders supporters). In Australia, a substantial bloc of Pauline Hanson's support comes from older white males aggrieved about the family law system and what they see as the feminist destruction of men's privileged position within families. Former Labor leader Mark Latham—undertaking that time-honoured journey from the Left to the far Right that so many middle-aged *Quadrant* columnists have made before him—has argued domestic violence campaigns are a smear of working-class men by privileged middle-class feminists.

As we've seen, there's a strong element of nostalgia in all this. These are people pining for an earlier era when being a white heterosexual male automatically accorded you status. Women had fewer rights, divorce was more difficult, domestic violence was ignored as long as it wasn't too egregious, and frequently even when it was. LGBTI people and other minorities kept out of sight or were kept out of sight. Society was tailored to meet your white male needs and cover for your inadequacies.

In fact, the revolt of the white men is a tribalist backlash that has been directly generated by neoliberalism. The application of market economics has been particularly bad for the economic opportunities of white males throughout the world. By reducing everyone to an economic identity, the special privilege attached to being a white male is, for most men, diminished. It's not diminished for white males at the top of the socio-economic hierarchy, true—they have been the ones to disproportionately benefit from neoliberalism and the growth of inequality. But the majority of white males aren't in that position; they're lower down on the economic ladder, with poorer education, fewer links to economic networks and less opportunity. And the lower you are, the more your privilege has been diminished and made fragile. Neoliberalism, in theory, is a lot closer to a socio-economic level playing field than many white men—used to being accorded privileged status in Western societies—are comfortable with, because *Homo economicus* is notionally gender-free, race-free, sexual preference-free. It's tougher to be a mediocre white man in a neoliberal world than in the world of the 1970s, and a lot of those mediocre white men don't like it.

But the impact has been more direct, too: the manufacturing jobs that white males used to dominate in the postwar economies of the West have been shifting to developing countries for decades (providing both cheaper products for Western consumers and lifting the income of people in developing countries) and that shift accelerated under the economic reforms of the 1980s and 1990s. As late as the mid 1980s, manufacturing employed nearly 17 per cent of Australian workers (three-quarters of those workers men); now it employs only 7.5 per cent of the workforce (72 per cent of them men).

The disappearance of manufacturing as the biggest employer has been more than offset by the growth of other sectors in the economy, like services. In Australia, the professional services workforce has gone from less than 5 per cent of jobs in the 1980s to around 8.5 per cent of jobs. And health care and social care, which have always been big employers of Australians, became the biggest employers several years ago—more than one in eight Australians now works in health, aged care, social services or childcare. That's where a huge proportion of the strong jobs growth in Australia in 2017 came from, and where wages are rising fastest. If manufacturing was dominated by men, health and social care is dominated by women—77 per cent of that workforce is female. Women also make up over 40 per cent of the professional services workforce. Far more women are now in the workforce than in the good old days when men dominated the job market, and a predominantly female industry has replaced a predominantly male industry as the biggest employer of Australians.

It's a similar story in other countries. In 2017, healthcare became the biggest US employer, and the sector is forecast to deliver 30 per cent of all new jobs in the coming decade. The

US healthcare workforce is 80 per cent female. In the United Kingdom, 12 per cent of all job vacancies in 2017 were in health (a 77-per-cent female workforce) and caring and health and social care is by far the biggest employing sector, as it is in Canada (82 per cent female).[13]

This is, by the way, another area where the progressive critique of neoliberalism fails. The decline of manufacturing has hurt women as well—textiles, clothing and footwear manufacturing, which had a two-thirds female workforce, has fallen from over 120,000 Australian jobs in the 1980s to around 35,000 now. But while factors like the ageing of the population have accelerated the growth of the health sector, neoliberalism has accompanied a significant rise in female workforce participation, which has increased since the late 1970s from 43 per cent to nearly 60 per cent, delivering greater economic power and independence to women. Women were 29 per cent of the full-time workforce in the mid 1980s; now they're 36 per cent of it. That gives women greater economic and financial power and more control over their lives than in the patriarchal Gilded Age of the male sole breadwinner controlling his family.

But for many people on both the Left and the Right, this changing shape of the workforce is something to be regretted. They want manufacturing jobs back. Specifically, they want *male* manufacturing jobs back. The Australian government isn't investing tens of billions in re-establishing a textiles industry in Australia—it's heavy manufacturing, like naval construction, that will enjoy that taxpayer largesse. And the Anti-Dumping Commission—the frontline of old-fashioned protectionism in

13 Unlike Australia, the Brits and Canadians lump wholesale trade (and in the United Kingdom, motor vehicle repair, inexplicably) into retail trade, which makes it technically the largest employing sector.

Australia, established to punish foreign firms for the crime of selling products cheaply to Aussie consumers and business—is almost entirely focused on trying to keep out foreign steel. Even outside manufacturing, protectionism is skewed towards male jobs. Guess what proportion of jobs in coal mining—an industry the Coalition is desperate to keep on life support—are held by women. The answer? Less than 8 per cent.

Driving this decidedly pro-male protectionism is a sexist belief that manufacturing jobs, like any manual labour jobs, are 'real' work, compared to service occupations, which are derided as McJobs. Jobs in which communication skills, emotional intelligence and an understanding of client needs are important—or indeed any skills traditionally seen as 'nurturing'—don't benefit from the dewy-eyed nostalgia for an economic yesteryear that drives protectionists. Manufacturing jobs have a cachet associated with producing a physical object, that apparently well-treated patients, satisfied clients or elderly Australians having some basic quality of life and decent treatment in their last months do not.

W(h)ither the Left

Where was the Left during the triumph of neoliberalism and the ascendancy of free markets? Where was the counter-offensive against an ideology of small government, non-intervention and the removal of protections for industries and workers? In Anglophone economies, notionally social democratic parliamentary parties often *led the way* in introducing neoliberal policies. In Australia, Labor—with the support of the trade-union movement—deregulated financial

markets, corporatised key government businesses and disman-
tled protectionism in the 1980s and 1990s. Under Paul Keating
in the 1990s, it reformed industrial relations, implemented
competition policy and privatised major assets like Qantas and
the Commonwealth Bank. In New Zealand from 1984, the
Lange Labour government began a twenty-year experiment
in radical market-based reforms. In the United Kingdom, Tony
Blair made the Bank of England independent. In the United
States, Bill Clinton reformed welfare. Under both, government spending as a proportion of GDP fell to well below the
levels of Thatcher and Reagan.

Progressives, it turned out, made the best neoliberals.

Significantly, though, in Australia, the implementation of
market-based reforms was accompanied by the (re)introduc-
tion of universal health care. Wage freezes under centralised
wage fixing were accompanied by income tax cuts, and taxes
were reformed both to improve efficiency and end business
rorts. Later, superannuation was made universal. The Howard
government—despite loathing both—retained universal health
care and superannuation for electoral reasons. It concentrated
on attacking trade unions and undermining workers' capacity
to collectively bargain, in an attempt to satisfy the endless
demands of corporate Australia for an ever-greater profit share
of national income.

Blair was heavily influenced by the Hawke–Keating government, but became the global avatar of 'Third Way' politics
(the late twentieth-century Third Way was arguably the third
'Third Way' since the nineteenth century). The Blairite version
sought to combine the communitarian and social engineering goals of socialist economics with the individual freedom
and market economics of neoliberalism. In turn, Blair and his

British intellectual influences like Anthony Giddens inspired, or were aped by, other more derivative figures, such as Mark Latham in Australia.[14]

Like neoliberalism, or any economic policy, there are a variety of Third Ways reflecting different circumstances in different countries, but all attempted to achieve social democratic goals using market forces. Demonised by socialists as simply neoliberalism with a friendly face, what different Third Way varieties had in common was a commitment to economic growth, equality of opportunity, meritocracy, market forces, a social safety net and fiscal discipline. But the central charge of critics—that it was no 'Third Way' but simply another version of neoliberalism—had substance, because 'Third Way' governments like those of Tony Blair accepted neoliberal policies with the in-built contradictions and systemic flaws that were to prove, in time, inherently unstable.[15] Third Way policies inevitably merely delayed, rather than prevented, the consequences of the flaws intrinsic to neoliberalism—the identity backlash, excessive corporate power and the impact of ever-rising inequality still provoked turmoil and ended up creating a new version of populist politics.

With social democratic parliamentary parties either co-opted outright into the neoliberal project or committed to implementing it with a labour-friendly face, opposition

---

14 Those only familiar with Mark Latham *circa* 2018 may be bemused or astonished to learn he once assayed the role of progressive intellectual while among the ranks of the parliamentary Labor Party.

15 Indeed, if anything, the wage falls endured by British workers in the decade after the global financial crisis were worse than those of workers in the US, suggesting the economic legacy of 'Third Way' policies could be just as bad or worse than crude neoliberalism, even if British people had the NHS and a better welfare system than Americans.

to market economics was exiled to the political fringes—often to trade unions, which were in any event suffering a catastrophic loss of membership across most of the West as manufacturing contracted and service industries expanded. This meant that when the internal problems of neoliberalism led to a major crisis, the Left in many countries was poorly prepared intellectually (and institutionally) to respond.

That crisis was the global financial crisis of 2008, a product of widespread misperception of risk, strong information asymmetry between financial institutions and their clients, and, most crucially, the lack of effective regulation of the financial industry and the shadow banking system in key markets. In markets with higher-quality regulation, such as Australia, the impact of the financial crisis was less significant, but still highly damaging.

Despite efforts by right-wing politicians and commentators to blame the crisis on government regulation and progressive efforts to encourage home ownership in the United States, even neoliberal institutions like the IMF argued that the primary cause was the dearth of regulation.[16] And as international sources of bank finance turned off access to capital, confidence vanished and some of the iconic names of global capitalism went under, governments responded to the crisis not with neoliberal solutions—if there are any beyond regarding double-digit unemployment as purely voluntary on the part of the jobless—or Third Way–style market-based incentives, but

---

16 There's been an entire delusional alternative history of the financial crisis and its aftermath written by the Right in Australia, in which nefarious interventionists and heavy-handed government regulators caused the crisis, while plucky mining companies, servicing Chinese demand for Australia's iron ore, saved the economy from recession, not fiscal stimulus.

with Keynesianism. In the words of Bob Lucas, policymakers were in a foxhole, and they turned back to Keynes in a heartbeat, undertaking counter-cyclical stimulus programs intended to support demand and halt the slide into a depression.

This entailed substantial spending that—on top of the cost of bank and industry bailouts where they were needed—sent many governments into deep deficit. In Australia, the Rudd government launched the world's most effective stimulus program in two tranches, aimed at consumers and the construction sector, while supporting the financial system in conjunction with the Reserve Bank. But so pervasive was the neoliberal instinct in Australian politics that the Labor Party struggled to defend the level of deficit spending needed to keep Australians in jobs and keep the economy out of recession. Rather than make a virtue of using the borrowing capacity of the government to stave off the crisis overtaking the rest of the world, in its 2009 budget, the Rudd government failed to make the case to voters that deficit spending was the difference between recession and continuing prosperity.

Ironically, just a few months earlier, Kevin Rudd had penned a typically long op-ed about neoliberalism and how social democrats had to save capitalism from itself, but must not 'throw the baby out with the bathwater'. Within a year, in 2010, Labor was promising a rapid return to surplus that, seven years later, is still as far off as ever despite four changes of prime minister in the intervening years.

In retrospect, the financial crisis was the Left's opportunity to launch an assault on the core tenets of neoliberalism, but it passed with little shift from the managerialist, neoliberalism-with-a-human-face approach of social democratic parliamentary parties in Anglophone countries. Only in subsequent years, as the problems of neoliberalism have become increasingly apparent and the backlash it was creating can no longer be ignored, have mainstream progressive parties begun to turn their firepower against neoliberalism, rather than defending it.[17]

The non-institutional Left moved more quickly and aggressively. The Occupy movement, which included veterans of anti-capitalist protest groups from the 1990s like the 1999 Seattle protests and the 2000 Melbourne protests against the World Economic Forum, gained attention across the globe. In the United Kingdom, where militant trade unionism and radical politics had lurked throughout the New Labour years, there was a virtual takeover of the British Labour Party by the far Left to install Jeremy Corbyn as leader, protect him against a subsequent challenge and produce a platform repudiating much of the Third Way heritage of Blair's New Labour. But the Bernie Sanders' insurgency against the establishment Democratic Party, successfully repelled by Hillary Clinton and the party establishment, demonstrated that institutional representation of anti-neoliberal views in the United States still had a long way to go.

In Australia, the Labor Party, once it had moved on from the toxic destabilisation of Kevin Rudd, more aggressively challenged neoliberal policies, aided by the colossal incompetence of the Abbott government. Labor in opposition retained for support carbon-pricing schemes for climate action (a market mechanism, but in aid of addressing a problem many

---

17 In Australia, the backlash was also delayed by an extended mining investment boom that drove strong employment and wage growth under Julia Gillard and Wayne Swan. Far from having to deal with the stagnation that beset most other Western economies in the wake of the financial crisis, the challenge for Swan from 2010-12 was managing an economy with an historic inflow of foreign investment and a currency that surged above parity with the US dollar.

on the Right refused to acknowledge), committed to dramatically higher spending on education and health, promised to curb taxpayer subsidies for property investment (a policy previously advocated by the Greens), warned it would block foreign workers, rejected company tax cuts and demanded a royal commission into the hated banks. In doing so, Labor ended up dominating the economic debate in Australia, with the conservative government often reduced to apeing Labor's policies (including the ones stolen from the Greens).

But between the triumph of neoliberalism in the 1980s and the financial crisis, the attention of many on the Left was also directed away from economics and into identity politics.

Identity politics—much like neoliberalism—has become an ill-defined punching bag for its critics. Any focus on redressing discrimination, harassment or obstruction of what are inaccurately termed 'minorities' is often dismissed as 'identity politics' rather than accepted for what it actually is—the practical recognition of basic human rights for all citizens. What should be clear to anyone in their forties or older is, regardless of what you call it, this has made a substantial difference to the way most of the population is treated. If you grew up in the 1970s, as this writer did, you'll recall how acceptable it was to mock 'wogs', 'Abos' and 'poofs'. (Homosexuality remained illegal in mainland states into the 1980s, and physical violence against, even the murder of, gay men was a regular occurrence.) You'll remember the casual and universal sexism, the ready acceptance of sexual harassment and workplace discrimination against women. The blindness to domestic violence. The poor treatment of disabled Australians. We're now a much better society than that; we have much further to go but Australia is demonstrably a more inclusive, more tolerant and more comfortable place for people who aren't white hetero-sexual able-bodied men, even if at times now it feels like we're regressing to earlier standards.

The problem is (according to this privileged, white, middle-class, middle-aged male, who never has and never *could* suffer discrimination in his life) when this becomes the *primary* project of progressives, and when campaigning against discrimination because of gender, race, sexual preference, disability or any other form of identity deepens into an ever-more fragmented politics based on a hierarchy of privilege and debate about who can and cannot speak for a particular group. This risks making politics—and broader social debate—all about representation and personal authenticity rather than about evidence, reason and real-world outcomes; one's identity becomes a trump card not merely to win arguments about policy, but to dictate the terms of the debate. Many progressives thereby end up being denounced for failing to be sufficiently intersectional in their thinking. White progressive women, in particular, risk copping criticism from all sides when articulating a feminist position—abused by misogynist males, derided as racists by people of colour, denounced as bourgeois essentialists by the far Left.

Let's take one problematic example. People who utter racist statements in the Australian media are 'called out', usually on social media (where participants stand on 24/7 outrage duty). My friend and occasional co-author Helen Razer is a persistent critic of this 'call-out culture'; for Razer, attack-ing an individual's racism distracts from the fact that racism, sexism and other forms of bigotry have systemic causes, and aren't merely the product of individual malice correctable by a public scolding. She's absolutely correct, and in a much larger sense than about social media spats—'calling out' individuals is only useful if it exposes the systemic nature of what has been identified, rather than treating it as individual malevolence.

But it gets worse when people overlay the process of 'calling out' with a representational matrix such as 'white people don't get to determine what is racist'. At first blush, a progressive probably agrees with this statement. How often have white people got away with saying 'I didn't mean it' or 'it was a joke' as cover for demeaning people of different races? And more importantly, white people often don't understand how racism works, because they don't ever experience it. Whiteness is normalised; white people don't see it, like fish don't see the water they swim in. But a problem arises when you decide that the arbiters of racism can only be non-white people, and that they can decide an utterance is racist regardless of the actual content of it, the intention of the speaker, its context or any other facts. A trivial but telling case: breakfast TV host Samantha Armytage was branded a racist and forced to apologise in 2015 for saying 'good on her' about the red-haired, lighter-skinned member of a pair of non-identical twins, which in fact was a reference to her own problems of having a light, sunburn-sensitive complexion in a country like Australia. But some critics decided Armytage's intention was irrelevant, and that only non-white people could decide what it really was: an expression of her racism. When a person's identity is regarded as overriding evidence, 'white people don't get to determine what is racist' suddenly becomes more problematic than at first glance.

As we've seen, neoliberalism creates the conditions for its own identity-based, tribalist backlash. Identity politics, once it becomes about representation, debate and a hierarchy of privilege, reinforces, rather than mitigates, that tendency to fragmentation, by stressing the overarching importance of whatever social, economic or racial group you have identified with, how you as part of that group have less privilege than other groups, that no one outside your group can understand and represent your identity and the interests specific to that identity, and by undermining the notion that there is a broader community made up of different groups with common, not competing, interests—and particularly shared economic interests. The result: many on the Left weren't merely not combating neoliberalism, they were actively assisting it.

But while identity politics is strongly associated with the Left—and became a term of disparagement from the Right—the tribalist backlash to neoliberalism means identity politics is also potent on the Right. Indeed, the far Right is the home of the most egregious practitioners of identity politics of all: white males railing at women, LGBTI people, non-white people and other 'minorities'. This form of identity politics is based on the myth that white males are under siege, even as they remain the most privileged group across Western societies. The identity politics of right-wing males is an inverted pyramid in which they are, magically, at the bottom of the hierarchy of privilege rather than the top. It's one thing to embrace identity politics; it's quite another to do so based entirely on a delusion that you are a victim when you still dominate Western society.

Biographical note: accidental death of a neoliberal

When I go to work to do my day job as a political writer, I tend to write as a neoliberal. And I've always been one. I grew up during the Hawke and Keating years, and I've seen first hand, over my adult life, how Australia has changed economically and how much wealthier Australians have become.

The family I grew up in certainly wasn't poor, but I was aware of my mother's occasional battle to make ends meet. It wasn't Struggle Street by any means, but Paucity Parade wasn't too far away. School clothing is a good example. My school uniform for St Aidan's in Maroubra in Sydney required a Midford sky-blue shirt and navy-blue shorts, purchased from Gilchrist's, a local shop that specialised in sewing and knitting products, and school uniforms. The Midford shirt cost a lot to buy from Gilchrist's, as a proportion of family income, because back then Australia protected its textile and footwear industry with a huge tariff wall. Nor was there a massive textiles industry in China then, except the one making Mao suits for the Cultural Revolution. So school shirts were precious. If they were damaged during the rough and tumble of a schoolyard—if, say, you ripped your shirt during a game of Cocky Laura (at my school, played on a concrete sloping playground guaranteed to send most boys back to class limping and wounded) our exasperated mothers repaired them with needle and thread. And when winter arrived, my brother's hand-me-down long-sleeve flannelette shirts would be pulled from storage, along with the school jumper, reeking of the naphthalene that hadn't quite kept the moths at bay.

That's the way it was—clothing was too expensive to discard readily.

Ditto shoes. Kids still go through shoes like crazy, of course, but back then they cost far more as a proportion of family income, so purchases were a major event, held off until feet were poking through holes and the shine and the sole were long gone. Then it was off to the shoe shop for, if you were lucky, some Bata Scouts, the one with the compass in the heel (for what purpose, was never clear). Parents, usually mothers, had to plan these purchases because they hit the family budget hard.

Thirty years later, as a parent myself, I experienced none of this. I might have had a higher income than my mum did, but by the time my kids were going to school, uniforms cost very little as a proportion of most household budgets: a red polo-shirt from Big W might cost $12; a pair of runners $25. They wore through a little quicker than the Bata Scouts, but you just bought another pair. Of course, it helped that my kids went to one of Canberra's many fine public schools and we faced no private-school uniform requirements. But even if they'd gone private, Chinese textiles and footwear have dramatically reduced the cost of clothing the kids.

Moreover, by the mid 2000s, Australia's gouging, rapacious retail oligopoly was starting to face competition from the internet. You wouldn't order your kid's school clothes online, of course, but as Australians began to discover just how much they were charged for clothes compared to people in similar econ-omies elsewhere, retailers had to start cutting prices. That was bad news if your kid was looking for a first job doing the occa-sional shift in a shop at the mall, but it was more good news for parents who might have otherwise struggled to afford the basics.

And yes, there were still plenty of things for parents to worry about financially, especially if they lived in a city where property was ludicrously expensive. I don't envy young couples trying to get into the housing market in Sydney or Melbourne now. But for every young couple priced out of the housing market, there's a Baby Boomer enjoying the extra wealth delivered by soaring house prices. That's a zero-sum game in terms of net wealth. But as consumers, *all* Australians benefited massively from cutting protection in textiles.

Ditto major household purchases. A new colour TV in the 1970s cost five times average weekly earnings; now you can buy a considerably larger, much lighter, internet-connected TV for not much more than the dollar value of the 1970s model—and well below a week's earnings. And for anyone regretting the closure of Australia's car industry, the first of the new Holden Commodores in 1978 (manufactured at Holden's Pagewood plant, right round the corner from where I grew up) cost around 43 weeks' earnings. You can now buy a fully imported family sedan that is dramatically safer, far more comfortable and more fuel efficient for less than 25 weeks' earnings. Much of this is to do with automation and advances in computing power, but it's also because of neoliberalism and the globalisation that has come with it—to the immense benefit of consumers, who are able to easily afford products our parents could barely even dream of.

Opening ourselves up to competition hasn't been all upside, I know. We were stuck with automotive manufacturing protection throughout my adult life, but textiles tariffs in Australia went much earlier. Many workers in that industry would never have found other work when they lost their jobs. Textiles had a particularly high level of non-English–speaking female workers, who would have been doubly disadvantaged. But there was a welfare system to support them and their families, and the Hawke–Keating government accompanied major changes with structural adjustment packages. That wouldn't have made the transition away from protectionism easy for those women, but the costs they bore have been more than offset by the benefits to most of the population, which continue to this day, of an open economy. Their pain *was* worth it.

I also liked—and this is a statement that some readers simply won't understand—the fairness of neoliberalism, if properly applied. Whatever the problems of reducing everyone to their economic value, it's a great leveller. Plenty of lazy business executives got found out when the Australian economy was opened up to competition. Plenty of companies that had relied on high tariff walls, and demanding handouts from governments, and quietly colluding with their competitors, were exposed to the harsh wind of competition.

Plenty of unions, too, saw their featherbedding exposed and their cosy deals with employers come under attack. As late as the 1980s, when a pimply young Bernard Keane took a retail job at what was then Super K Mart, it was compulsory to join the union. Woolworths enforced it, doubtless to the delight of the reactionary, homophobic SDA (Shop, Distributive and Allied Employees Association), which got my union fees and never did a damn thing for me—an experience uncannily echoed when my son joined the SDA 30 years later. I had told him that young, inexperienced workers should always join a union because they're the ones who need them, but it turned out the Shoppies were still rubbish a generation later.

But neoliberalism, and the mindset it instils, tends to engender scepticism about every claim made in the economic sphere. The Productivity Commission—which remains *the* temple of independent, non-partisan economic rationalism in Australia—routinely produces reports demolishing nonsensical government policies, no matter who is in power. It is the PC that points out that there are actually no benefits to our anti-dumping system—that it isn't even as efficient a form of protectionism as more traditional mechanisms for looking after selected industries. It was the PC that slammed the Abbott and Turnbull governments for refusing to subject the Trans-Pacific Partnership to independent assessment. It's the PC that points out it's hard to know whether regional grants programs ever help anyone because no one ever bothers to check the results. Neoliberalism is good at exposing bullshit and self-interest when it comes to economic policy.

Ultimately, however, there's a more basic reason why I thought neoliberalism was the best, or perhaps the least worst, approach to economic management: because it suits people like me. As a white able-bodied English-speaking male, with a good education and an occasionally functioning brain, I do even better out of a market economy than I would out of a more interventionist economy. Because I have skills for which there's a global market, I am much more likely to end up in the top tax bracket than most people, and therefore benefit from a less redistributive tax system, and I'm less likely to work in the kinds of industries that are being restructured away from Western countries or replaced altogether by automation. In short, I'm exactly the kind of person who is well placed to capitalise on not merely the embrace of market economics, but the cult of individualism that it celebrates, because I've been born with advantages most other individuals will never have.

And that goes for 90 per cent of the economic commentators you'll read in the mainstream media, too. Most of them are white males and the rest are white women and none of us have known what it's like to be out of work since we were uni students looking for a part-time job in the 1960s or 1970s or

1980s, because back then you didn't need to work six jobs and borrow from Mum and Dad just to get through uni.

Neoliberalism is an economic philosophy invented by white guys like me in academia and think tanks, implemented (mostly) by white guys like me in bureaucracies and parliaments, and which benefits white guys like me. That doesn't mean others don't benefit as well, or that it doesn't harm less privileged white men, nor that you can just wish neoliberalism away as a white-male fantasy. That doesn't excuse its critics from the burden of making the case as to its flaws. But it does mean that white guys like me ought to be constantly double-checking our arguments and our assumptions about it, because we're profoundly biased about it.

Conclusion

Neoliberalism has begun harming workers and consumers even in countries like Australia where it had been implemented successfully with social policy protections and industrial relations safeguards. In particular, economic power has shifted to corporations from workers and consumers. Corporations grew much bigger, and dominated markets more, giving them greater power over both workers and consumers. Union power was curbed, removing a key mechanism for workers to protect their wages. The whole point of neoliberalism was greater economic vulnerability for individuals, unless they had the skills and networks to prosper in the new economy—in which case they were rewarded far more generously than in previous generations. An economic philosophy based on individual freedom thus became about freedom for corporations and the wealthy, with all the consequences of disempowerment for everyone else that that entailed.

But the most profound flaw was that neoliberalism, as we've seen in this chapter, contains features that render it unstable, because it will inevitably produce a backlash. Without strong intervention, neoliberalism will always increase inequality, which will in turn undermine economic growth. It will always drive market concentration, which will also undermine economic growth and shift income and power to corporations. And it will always produce a tribalist backlash, both because of the economic effects of the free flow of goods, capital and workers, and because of the impacts on social identity of its emphasis on economic worth as the only meaningful social value.

Eventually, in any democratic society, neoliberalism must topple over. Equilibrium is impossible over the long term. Worse, neoliberalism isn't merely economically and socially unstable, it's politically unstable as well. That's what we're now going to examine.

PART 3

(UN)GOVERNMENT

Trust is a key aspect of a successful democracy. Voters must believe their government is legitimate, even if it's not of their own ideological orientation. They must believe it's committed to the national interest, even if they disagree with how to achieve that national interest. And they must believe it is committed to delivering outcomes for the electorate as a whole, not just one section of it. A government perceived to be in power due to a flawed process, or committed only to serving a segment of the electorate, will quickly lose support.

The problem is, democratic governments have been losing trust for decades. Indeed, what seemed an absurd question in the 1990s, after the collapse of the Soviet Union—Is democracy the best form of government?—is now openly debated, particularly with some evidence (albeit not compelling) that democracy is not seen as quite as essential among younger voters as it is among older voters.

What drove this fall in trust? How did governments let their electorates down? The answer seems to reflect both long-term forces in politics, and some of the malign consequences of neoliberalism.

The party's over

Party politics in most Western countries is very different now to what it was in the middle of the twentieth century, and seen by voters very differently as well.

A 2005 paper by US sociologist Russell Dalton examined long-term data on trust in politicians or political systems across sixteen developed countries—Australia, most of western Europe and North America. Dalton found a long-term, significant decline in trust in political systems in almost every country from the 1960s or 1970s (the US data went back to the 1950s). Moreover, he demonstrated a correlation with both generational change and educational levels—as education levels improved in each country, willingness to trust governments diminished. And Baby Boomers proved far less trusting of governments than their parents; as the latter died out, mistrust in government grew significantly.

This decline in trust that occurred in the last third of the twentieth century might be regarded as the development of an appropriately healthy scepticism of governments and politicians. Mid twentieth-century people across the West had been through the ordeal of World War II, from which democracies and the Soviet Union emerged victorious. Trust in governments might understandably have been high, given they had managed to defeat the Axis powers. The descent into the Cold War and, in countries like the United States and Australia, the disaster of Vietnam, gave the next generation less reason to believe their governments were innately forces for good. Higher education standards also gave citizens greater civic skills and capacity for critical thinking, reducing governments' capacity to evade scrutiny and critique; television ramped up that scrutiny significantly.

It was during that postwar period that political parties ceased to be mass movements. In Australia, in 1967 over 5 per cent of the population were political party members; now around 1 per cent are, if that. In the United Kingdom, the Conservative and Labour parties once had memberships numbering in the millions; now they can't muster one million between them, despite the big rise in Labour membership under Jeremy Corbyn. In the United States, party registrations have declined and levels of party affiliation, particularly for the Democrats, are at an historic low, and well below the levels of the mid twentieth century. Political party memberships across Europe have declined, except in democratic newcomers like Spain, which was a fascist dictatorship until the 1970s.

In Australia, the major parties also draw a significantly lower proportion of the overall vote than they used to—at 22.7 per cent, the non-major party vote in the House of Representatives at the 2016 election was the highest ever, compared to less than 10 per cent in the 1970s. Informal voting—not casting a proper ballot—has also nearly tripled since the 1970s. According to data compiled by the Australia Institute, the level of voter registration began declining in the 2000s, at around the same time the level of informal voting began to rise (except for a drop in the Kevin '07 election).

Not merely has political activity and major party voting declined, the overall level of interest in politics is low. In 2016, polling showed 45 per cent of voters had little or no interest in that year's election. Over one-third said they would either actively avoid or not make an effort to look at media coverage of the election. Only 28 per cent of respondents said they had a lot of interest in national political news, much lower than local news, weather or international news. In the election itself, despite compulsory voting, the turnout was one of the lowest in decades.

That's in contrast to the United States, where polling showed very high levels of interest in the 2016 presidential election compared to previous years, although that failed to translate into turnout, which was above 2012 but below 2008. In the United Kingdom, voter turnout has been increasing in recent elections, but is still well below the levels of the 1990s and earlier, when turnout regularly exceeded 75 per cent. This is a recurring pattern: in Canada, the 2015 election that brought Justin Trudeau to the premiership was the highest turnout in recent elections but remained well below twentieth-century levels. Like the Brits, Canadian turnout slumped in the 2000s. In New Zealand, the last six elections—since 2002—have all seen the lowest turnout in recent decades—although the 2017 election saw a slight increase on the 2014 election. In Ireland, recent elections have seen higher turnout than the low levels recorded in the 2000s, but it still remains below that of the 1980s.

Clearly some form of political disengagement—across different countries and different voting systems—occurred in the 2000s, on top of the long-term decline in participation and engagement in the postwar decades. It may be mere co-incidence—it's hard to spot the commonalities between New Zealand, where Labour leader Helen Clark was in power, and Ireland, where long-serving conservative Bertie Ahern was taoiseach, although arch neoliberals Tony Blair, Stephen Harper and John Howard were prime ministers in the United Kingdom, Canada and Australia respectively.

Much of this disengagement in the 2000s may derive from the Iraq war and the presidency of George W Bush—then seen as a frightening historical aberration, now positively benign compared to Trump's. The Iraq war was particularly damaging to trust in governments in the United Kingdom, the United States and Australia, and to trust in intelligence agencies—even though it was primarily the Blair, Bush and Howard governments that lied about Saddam Hussein's weapons of mass destruction, rather than the agencies themselves.[18] Indeed, we now know from the Chilcot Inquiry that UK intelligence agencies specifically warned Tony Blair that not only did Saddam not have the capacity to launch WMD attacks, and would not cooperate with Al Qaeda, but that attacking Iraq would increase the risk to the United Kingdom from terror attacks—which, tragically, is exactly what has transpired.

Worse, Iraq became the single greatest policy debacle since Vietnam. The United States, the United Kingdom and Australia are still engaged in combat in the region. The current cost of the Iraq war and its consequences is well over $2 trillion;

---

18 Witness one response to the attempted murder of former Russian intelligence official Sergei Skripal and his daughter Yulia in March 2018, which followed a long history of murders in the West of enemies of the Putin regime: Western intelligence agencies were lying about Russia's involvement just like they'd lied about Saddam's weapons of mass destruction.

it has cost Australia alone over $2 billion just since 2014. The long-term cost of the war to the US government has been estimated at $4 trillion in healthcare costs for veterans and casualties. Far greater was the toll in human life, with hundreds of thousands of Iraqis dying in the ensuing civil war and occupation, and the geopolitical result—the creation of Islamic State and the consolidation of the influence of Iran's brutal theocratic regime. It's almost as if, in the name of winning the War on Terror, Anglophone leaders took exactly the action guaranteed to extend and expand said war into a decades-long conflict.

Nor has there been any accountability that is so important for trust in the political process. Blair, at least, had to front the Chilcot Inquiry; neither Bush nor Howard have ever had to account for an illegal invasion that produced horrific outcomes, or justify themselves to the families of the servicemen and women who died, or the families of Western terror victims killed afterwards. While time has allowed these men to move out of public consciousness, the toxic results of their decisions grow ever worse. Australia, in particular, has no mechanisms to hold politicians to account unless politicians themselves agree to permit one (Labor promised an inquiry into Iraq in 2007, but didn't have the courage to follow through with it once elected). The result is a lingering sense that the system is rigged, that even egregious violations of the law can be overlooked. It also remains the case that the federal government can commit Australia to war without even a *pro forma* consultation with parliament.

Other factors may have also contributed to electoral disillusionment. For example, politicians do little to encourage trust when they make a habit of abusing the rules around public money. Australian federal politicians are all paid handsomely. A backbencher gets over $200,000 a year. The president of the Senate, the speaker of the House of Representatives, parliamentary committee chairs, whips and shadow ministers are all paid extra, as are ministers, up to the prime minister, who is paid $527,000. Every MP and senator also receives a $32,000 per annum electoral allowance, and they also have access to a generous superannuation scheme. And all work-related travel is paid for—only a perfunctory link to their duties as MPs or senators is required to justify taxpayer-funded travel. Inevitably, though, it is travel expenses that generate the greatest angst on the part of voters, who normally don't receive an allowance or tax break to get to and from work. And while few politicians outright rort their travel allowance in the manner of certain high-profile cases, the frequency with which politicians find functions requiring their attendance that just happen to coincide with major sporting events or political fundraisers generates understandable cynicism. Even prime ministers are not beyond this. In 2014, then-prime minister Tony Abbott explained that he had arrived late for a party room meeting in Canberra because he had needed to attend a hospital clinic that morning in Melbourne, to justify billing taxpayers for attending a party fundraiser there the night before.

The United Kingdom, Canada, France, Germany and Italy have also all had major political expenses scandals in recent years. The exposé of rorting in Westminster in 2009 revealed some truly spectacular rorts, eliciting collective apologies from party leaders and leading to over thirty MPs and Lords being sacked, resigning or being otherwise damaged. All these disgraces have derived from the same problem as in Australia: vague expenses guidelines that allow both systemic abuse and a less-than-rigorous approach even from conscientious MPs. Politicians crafted the rules to ensure it would be unlikely anyone on any side would be caught transgressing.

But these episodes in recent decades don't address what drove the postwar decline in direct political participation that saw political parties empty out across the world in the second half of the twentieth century. A longstanding argument is that there's been a broader loss of 'social capital' since the mid twentieth century and that people simply don't *join* things anymore—after all, trade-union membership and church participation have also declined (except in the United States). But people do still join other things in large numbers—football clubs, for example, and even activist organisations like GetUp in Australia, as well as traditional NGOs and environmental groups. People are still willing to get involved, just not with traditional political parties.

Another theory is that the mass media has created an atomised society, in which people's primary social connections have become those mediated by television, for example, rather than traditional, real-world, communitarian bonds. Again, the fact that people are willing to join all kinds of organis-ations, just not political parties, suggests social bonds remain reasonably intact. Moreover, there's also evidence from older sociological studies that the decline of social bonds has been repeatedly observed in societies, even prior to World War II and the arrival of mass media; like the poor manners of young people, perhaps atomisation has always been complained about.

We're on stronger ground, though, if we note that the decline in postwar mass political participation coincided with a signif-icant improvement in living standards in the West throughout the 1950s and 1960s (and, perhaps, the resumption of that improvement in the latter part of the 1980s and the 1990s). As their living standards lifted and a larger middle class was created, citizens had less need to be specifically represented by a party devoted to their interests, reducing the potential for overt class conflict. If in the mid twentieth century in Australia, politics was a parliamentary contest between the representatives of the working class and those of the middle class, by the 1980s politics was more about growing the economy to benefit everyone. (Similarly, the case for belonging to trade unions—currently around 10 per cent of the private-sector workforce—diminished as living standards rose.) This process saw major political parties move from being representatives of sectional interests to bidding for power based on a broad agenda designed to attract enough voters to secure office. (The Australian Labor Party, for example, moved beyond being a purely working-class party to one committed both to the helping working people and the agenda of progressive middle-class people on environmental and discrimination issues—and not without some tension along the way.)

The mass media played a role in this: even if it did atomise the electorate and undermine people's willingness to join political and social movements, it also allowed political parties with sufficient funding to reach the bulk of the electorate—rather than relying on mass membership and large-scale volunteer efforts at elections—and to do so via increasingly carefully crafted audio-visual content that emphasised political personalities. With mass media, a well-funded political party could reach as many, if not more, people than a mass-membership party, making expert campaigners, polling and marketing as important as how many people a party could put on the ground during an election campaign and on election day.

In Australia, political parties also benefit from a factor their overseas counterparts don't enjoy: compulsory voting. Australia's major parties don't need to try to maximise voter turnout, because the law does it for them, further reducing the need for volunteers and an on-the-ground presence.

The continued ability for hollowed-out political parties to function successfully even without mass memberships may appear to be a problem for democracy. A democracy is better, the argument goes, if more people participate directly. But it's hard to see the problem for democracy, and good government, if major parties stop representing sectional interests and instead compete for the votes of a majority of citizens with a broad-based program.

But since the 1980s, another factor has shaped levels of political engagement: the narrowing of differences between the major parties. With progressive parties unwilling to resist, or even leading, the introduction of neoliberal policies— and with the fall of the Soviet Union—the great ideological battles of the postwar era seemed over. This process occasionally worked in the other direction: in Australia, the Liberal Party abandoned its long-cherished desire to end Medicare. But the broad trend was of a progressive surrender to conservative policy. Political disputes thereafter became more about management than ideology. Who was the best economic steward within the framework of market economics? Who was the best fiscal manager? Who could run health and education services best? We swapped contests over the entire philosophical direction of our economies and societies for debates about managerialist expertise—just about the last thing that would inspire mass movements or get people marching in the street, let alone racing to the barricades.

Those who did join political parties increasingly did so as the entry to a career within the governing class. That is, not merely being in government, or in parliament, but as one of a range of occupations linked to public life: political staffer, party executive, MP, statutory board appointee, lobbyist, consultant—and, increasingly, media commentator. Over the last 30 years, politics has become highly professionalised, with its own career ladder from student politics to retirement.

For many careerists, a hollowed-out party is preferable because it is easier to exercise a degree of control within it compared to a party with a thriving branch membership. But such parties need access to large amounts of money to run mass-media campaigns, necessitating a reliance on public funding and donations from large donors such as unions or businesses. The money isn't for the political parties themselves—they don't grow rich on taxpayer subsidies or donations—but instead for ammunition for political battle: the money is transferred to media companies and marketing firms for political advertising, which turns elections into a huge payday for free-to-air television broadcasters and newspapers.

The result is that we have outsourced policymaking to a professional class, which bills us for the cost of tendering for our support every few years, with little and diminishing engagement by voters. This is a self-contained class that often appears uninterested in re-engaging the electorate, that appears focused on its own concerns rather than representing the concerns of voters. In Australia, this is also a highly homogenised class—much whiter, more male (particularly on the conservative side) and older.

This hollowed-out, less ideological, more careerist politics, reliant on external funding sources, is much more amenable to encouragement and direction from powerful donors and lobby groups: the corporate-friendly policies of neoliberalism were being presented to politicians at a time when they were becoming more susceptible than ever before to such influence.

Of the corporation, by the corporation, for the corporation

A crucial element of neoliberal policies is that governments mustn't merely keep out of the way of markets, but must adopt policies that encourage business activity: governments should focus on reducing regulation, cutting company taxes, creating business-friendly environments, being 'internationally competitive' as determined by bodies like the World Economic Forum, and selling off government assets to the private sector. The elevation of corporate benefit to the centre of policy-making—the adoption of the principle famously expressed as 'What is good for US Steel is good for America'—has delivered massive wins for corporations and given business a permanent seat at the policymaking table. Business lobby groups expect to be consulted on significant policy changes—it would be 'sovereign risk' if anything went ahead without consultation. And 'consultation' isn't merely being given the opportunity to present one's case—which is an eminently sensible way to conduct policymaking—but to *get one's way*. Any policy considered unconducive to business interests leads to threats that investors will take their money elsewhere.

To this end, two industries have sprung up in Canberra since the 1980s, devoted to influencing policy on behalf of business: lobbying and economic modelling. There are around six hundred officially registered lobbyists at the federal level, but that's only a fraction of the people dedicated to influencing policy, since most lobbyists in Australia aren't required to register as lobbyists. This is either because they're employed directly by a corporation (some large companies have dozens of 'government affairs' personnel), or because they operate under another guise—legal and accounting firms often offer lobbying services in addition to their core functions.

Economic modelling is nowhere near as large as the lobbying and pseudo-lobbying industry, but it is an important adjunct for business seeking to influence policy—economic consulting firms, often employing former Treasury bureaucrats, can be hired to provide economic modelling to support the policy your company wants advanced, no matter what it is, for a suitable fee.

Lobbying and government relations are so entrenched in Canberra that they have become part of the career ladder for politicians and political staff. If you no longer work in Parliament House—because you lost your seat, or your minister lost government—you can still spend plenty of time there acting on behalf of client companies. Occasionally, some senior political figures end up working for the very corporations they bitterly fought when they were in politics. The lobbyist register illustrates this: it is about one-third former ministers, MPs or staffers, including some of the biggest names of former political eras. Many lobbyists also represent NGOs, charities or community groups. Trade unions also have their representatives, and their lobbyists; naturally they exert greater influence when Labor is in power. But their influence isn't necessarily hostile to business: while notionally at loggerheads and having few goals in common, unions and business have a shared interest in encouraging governments to protect their industries with regulations or taxpayer funding. To this day, manufacturing unions and employers that otherwise fight like cat and dog have a joint interest in protectionist mechanisms such as anti-dumping rules.

And because many formers ministers, political staffers and senior bureaucrats develop expertise and contacts in one particular area, they gravitate towards that area after leaving political or bureaucratic life. This is a particular problem in Australia given the relatively small size of our economy. In the defence industry, there's a very clear revolving door: former military brass and Department of Defence officials turn into defence contractors, where they are welcomed for their understanding of the procurement system and their links with those still inside government. This isn't corruption *per se*, but it's what would allow the corrupt to flourish if they were so inclined.

A 2017 paper by US economist Luigi Zingales, 'Towards a Political Theory of the Firm', argued that the neoclassical theory that corporations were unable to influence the rules of the markets in which they operated was manifestly false and that large corporations were able to create what he termed 'a "Medici vicious circle," in which money is used to gain political power and political power is then used to make more money'. Zingales particularly noted the capacity of firms to offer employment to policymakers *after they leave public life*. He suggests,

a company's ability to obtain what it wants from the political system is highly dependent upon: 1) its ability to make credible long-term promises (for example, future employment opportunities for politicians and regulators), which is highly dependent upon a company's long-term survival probability; 2) the grip a company has on the market for specific human capital (for example, how many potential employers of nuclear engineers there are); 3) a company's ability to wrap its self-interest in a bigger, noble, idea (for example, Fannie Mae and the goal that every American should be able to borrow to purchase a house); 4) the control that a company has through its image in society through employment, data ownership, media ownership, advertising, research funding, and other methods.

In Australia, we have very weak laws constraining former ministers from working with companies or in industries they have previously regulated or otherwise dealt with in the course of their duties. Ostensibly, they are prevented from doing so for two years, but the restriction is laughably easy to evade and it's unclear what action could be taken if they were found to have acted inappropriately, given they have already left politics. The problem was made painfully clear by former prime minister Tony Abbott in 2016, when he lauded the retiring Coalition MP and one-time industry minister Ian Macfarlane for his efforts to destroy Labor's mining tax, saying 'it was a magnificent achievement . . . and I hope the sector will acknowledge and demonstrate their gratitude to him in his years of retirement from this place'. And indeed they did—within a few months Macfarlane had taken a job as head of the Queensland Resources Council. And there have been Labor ex-ministers who have been no better.

And when it comes to transparency and potential for corruption via political donations, things are even worse: Australia has the least effective rules governing political donations in the developed world. Unlike virtually any other developed country, Australia allows donations by foreign individuals and companies. Unlike Canada and the United States, there are no donation limits. Unlike the United Kingdom, there are no campaign spending limits. And because Australia is a federation, a wide variety of different reporting regimes, with different standards, are in place. For example, at the Commonwealth level, if you pretend to 'buy' something from a political party—like a seat at a dinner with a minister—you don't have to declare that as a political donation even though you have both contributed to the party's coffers *and* purchased access—indeed, you don't have to declare it *because* you have purchased access.

Moreover, because of the high reporting thresholds put in place by the Howard government, clever donors can give over $13,000 to each branch of a political party, for nine different donations totalling over $100,000—and neither the donor nor the political party is required to report them (Labor and the Greens, however, voluntarily report all donations over $1000).

Most absurd is the lag between donating to a party and having to report it. Donations only have to be declared once a year, well after the end of the financial year, and those declarations aren't made public until the February of the following year. If you donate to a political party on 1 July, you and they don't have to report it until October the following year—and it's not made public until the February after that, nineteen months later. Malcolm Turnbull's $1.75 million donation to the Liberal Party—crucial to his narrow victory in the 2016 election—only legally had to be revealed in February 2018. Only political pressure forced him to confirm it in 2017.

Moreover, there are no consequences if you don't bother

reporting, or a political party doesn't report donations. Indeed, you can wait until after the release of public donations data in February of each year to issue a *mea culpa* to the Australian Electoral Commission admitting a donation—and only the most eagle-eyed will spot it once it is put online.

So useless are the donation laws that the Victorian branch of the ALP reported a $60,000 donation to Bill Shorten's 2007 campaign in 2015, nearly eight years late—just days before he was due to appear before the Coalition's trade union royal commission, where he would be asked about it. Not that the Coalition was in a strong position to criticise him—then-prime minister Tony Abbott's fundraising arm, the Warringah Club, had revealed a $25,000 donation to the NSW Liberals four years after it was made in 2010. Neither Shorten nor Abbott, nor the respective party branches or associated entities involved, faced any consequences for their years-long negligence.

Political donation disclosure in Australia may as well be voluntary—even your own political opponents won't go after you when you're shown to have egregiously breached disclosure laws. It's mutually assured obstruction.

Worse is when a major foreign donor takes a liking to a particular party or politician. For years, the Labor Party was adept at sourcing donations from Chinese business tycoons; the sums involved were usually in the six-figure range. And while Labor's Sam Dastyari became infamous for sending unpaid bills to a Chinese company linked to a Chinese–Australian millionaire, future prime minister Kevin Rudd, in opposition, had accepted extensive international travel paid for by a Chinese firm, Beijing Aust-China. Nor are the do-nations of foreign companies limited to Labor—both sides have received massive donations from Chinese firms and business figures over the last decade.

We also have no clue as to whom ministers and shadow ministers, or key crossbenchers who can make or break legislation in parliament, are meeting; there is no federal requirement for public availability of diaries, as there is in some states, and in Canada and New Zealand, where diaries are either publicly released or available under Freedom of Information laws.

Nor is there a federal anti-corruption and misconduct body, as most states have, to investigate possible corruption by both politicians and public servants, although in 2018 Labor adopted a policy to establish one. It's true that, given federal ministers rarely deal with planning and property development issues, which are the wellspring of corruption at the state and local level, there's less blatant corruption in Canberra. But political donations, post political and public-service employment and connections between business and union leaders and politicians, and their impacts on policymaking, are all areas worthy of greater oversight than that provided by senate committees. The argument that a federal anti-corruption body is 'unnecessary', as some Commonwealth figures claim, is in effect an assertion that federal politicians and public servants are perfect.

Australia's polity at the federal level, then, is one that is systemically prone to accord influence to powerful bodies. It is only by good luck and, perhaps, the relatively small size of the Australian economy, that we are not completely down the path of the United States, which is as close to an open plutocracy as has been seen in modern times. In that country, one needs to be extraordinarily wealthy to be a serious presidential candidate, powerful establishments run both major parties, and the conservative side of politics is controlled by super-wealthy

businessmen such as the Koch brothers, who have worked assid-
uously for decades to turn the Republican Party into a vehicle
for a pseudo-libertarian, radically deregulatory agenda that
would deliver all economic power to corporations. This has been
done in the name of individual freedom, but in fact it is about
corporate freedom, with individuals' rights a distant second to
ensuring large corporations and the wealthy can operate with
relative impunity from any social or community obligations.

If corporations can't influence, or successfully campaign
against, government policy, increasingly they can litigate it via
Investor State Dispute Settlement. ISDS is a mechanism that
has proliferated in trade and investment agreements around
the world, allowing multinational corporations to leapfrog
domestic courts and sue governments in international arbi-
tration fora for any policy change that they can argue has
cost them money. It was originally conceived as a device for
ensuring companies from developed countries could invest in
developing countries without worrying that a new government could suddenly nationalise their investments. However,
it has become a powerful tool for infringing the sovereignty
of all countries that agree to ISDS clauses in trade agreements,
enabling multinational corporations to obtain compensation
for policy changes no matter how rational or sound such
changes might be—and despite domestic companies having no
such similar rights. Philip Morris, for example, sued Australia
for its tobacco plain packaging laws under an Australia–Hong
Kong investment agreement, after the cigarette manufacturer
had shifted its headquarters to Hong Kong purely to take
advantage of the ISDS provisions in the agreement.

ISDS, which features in the new, America-free version of
the Trans-Pacific Partnership to which Australia agreed in

2017, is a one-way street for governments—they can never initiate litigation against transnationals, they can only ever be sued. And even if they 'win', governments can face significant litigation costs running into the tens of millions—although international fora are increasingly prepared to award costs against companies pursuing frivolous suits, which happened in the Philip Morris case.

Polling in 2015, during the Trans-Pacific Partnership controversy, showed over 60 per cent of Australians opposed ISDS provisions. In the United States, senior Democrat senator Elizabeth Warren campaigned against the TPP based on what she called the 'rigged pseudo-courts' of ISDS. 'This is a case of basic democracy,' another senator, Bernie Sanders, said about Philip Morris' litigation against Australia. 'Do the people of any country have a right to be very vigorous in protecting the health of their kids and their citizens without worrying about being sued by a cigarette manufacturer?' When Trump's administration began renegotiating the NAFTA trade deal with Canada and Mexico, there were widespread calls from across the ideological spectrum for the ISDS provisions in that treaty to be removed as well.

What benefits does ISDS actually provide? The Productivity Commission, which has repeatedly expressed great scepticism about the benefits of the TPP, demonstrated in a report that in a number of trade agreements the presence or absence of ISDS mechanisms had no impact on investment levels. It had no demonstrated benefit to the community, merely benefit to corporations.

That's unsurprising, given the way the TPP was negotiated: in secret by trade ministers. Secret that is, except for senior business figures, who were given special access to the text, while the rest of us only got access when WikiLeaks obtained a copy. Not merely were corporations given privileged access to the draft agreement, they helped draft it themselves—emails obtained under US Freedom of Information laws exposed how the US Trade Representative office had not merely shared details of the draft text with corporate interests but requested their assistance in drafting sections of it. 'These are our rules ... This is a very pleasant surprise,' one chuffed executive emailed when shown what the United States had put forward.

Trade deals occupy a peculiar niche in neoliberalism. Since the Doha round of global trade liberalisation talks ended in failure in the 2000s, countries around the world have pursued bilateral and limited multilateral trade deals. Many of these deals lead to more open borders and curbs on sovereignty—thereby encouraging the identity-based backlash against neoliberalism we've previously explored. But the true neoliberal looks askance at what are called, entirely misleadingly, 'free-trade agreements'. As the Productivity Commission, which one would expect to be supportive of free trade, has pointed out, such deals have virtually nothing to do with free trade—they are merely agreements to adjust trade barriers on a bilateral or multilateral basis between individual countries. Such agreements have minimal economic benefit, since for exporters, they simply amount to shifting trade from one market to another. In fact, given that such trade agreements usually represent an *additional* layer of rules on issues such as country of origin (for example, whether a particular product, made up of imported parts or ingredients but manufactured in Australia, counts as an Australian product for the purposes of its free-trade deal with Japan, and *vice versa*), they can actually *add* to the bureaucratic costs faced by firms.

And when the Productivity Commission examined Australia's oldest bilateral trade deal other than with New Zealand, the Australia–United States Free Trade Agreement, it found that the copyright provisions in it had actually damaged the Australian economy. The AUSFTA was spruiked by the Howard government and Australian business as being little short of an economic miracle and a massive win for Australian exporters when it was negotiated in 2004. Fourteen years later, our exports to the United States, adjusted for inflation, have actually *fallen*, while US exports into Australia have increased.

In the last three decades, the power of corporations to influence policy, even to write it themselves, reached its zenith as governments bent over backwards to please them. But would there ever come a point when corporations would discover they had gone too far? As it turned out, they'd already reached it.

Things fall apart: the corporations cannot hold

In Australia in 2016, the penny began to drop with some of the country's biggest businesses that they were passionately hated by the community.

Australians have always disliked banks. But a regular succession of scandals has given banks a particularly bad odour in recent years. The Labor Party worked this out early on, and began demanding a banking royal commission. These calls were fiercely opposed by the Coalition, which assumed it could merely accuse Labor of seeking to undermine the financial system, and capitalism generally, in order to defeat any push for a major inquiry. But a single moment during the

2016 election campaign put paid to that. 'Mr Shorten wants to put the banks in the dock,' Malcolm Turnbull said during an election debate with his opponent, doubtless expecting the Western Sydney audience to be shocked at this recklessness. Instead, the audience cheered at the prospect, visibly dismaying the prime minister. A former banker himself, Turnbull was unaware of how viscerally Australians disliked them. Within twelve months, Turnbull had himself slapped a special tax on banks and by the end of 2017 had been forced by some of his own MPs to establish a royal commission.

Some business leaders, like David Gonski, had worked out just how unpopular big companies were, and tried to discuss ways to address it. 'Business has taken for granted that business is good for you. And that just doesn't work anymore,' another senior businessman, BHP chair Jacques Nasser, said—as his company was undergoing a major rebranding exercise to try to escape the stigma of multiple controversies and a reputation for tax avoidance. By early 2018, entire business summits were being devoted to trying to work out how to get the community onside again.

That was all before the banking royal commission began uncovering extraordinary examples of misconduct, breaches of corporate law and plain bastardry in the financial services sector that astonished even the most jaded industry observers. At that point, even erstwhile cheerleaders for corporate Australia began angrily demanding tougher regulation, and the ousting of the boards of some of Australia's biggest companies. But many business executives and lobby groups remained oblivious to the growing anger toward corporations. Throughout 2017 and 2018, the Business Council of Australia continued to demand company tax cuts and industrial relations changes to curb workers' rights, while insisting workers would only receive pay rises once companies deemed that profits had risen sufficiently.

Indeed, industrial relations represents a particular blind spot for Australian business. Australia had a centralised wage-fixing system until 1993, when the then-Labor government introduced enterprise-level bargaining with a safety net system of award conditions. In 1996, the Coalition government established individual contracts and stripped back industry awards, then introduced WorkChoices, which removed most protections for workers and restricted union activity, sparking a backlash that partly accounted for the end of the Howard years. The subsequent Labor government established a new framework abolishing individual contracts but leaving the enterprise bargaining system in place. Since then, the Fair Work system has provided ample flexibility for industrial relations in Australia—at least according to the Reserve Bank, and the Productivity Commission, which was tasked by a conservative government with examining it.

In the view of Australian business, however, the *Fair Work Act* is a disaster almost singlehandedly responsible for everything wrong in the Australian economy, and it remains urgently in need of a fundamental overhaul even as households endure their fifth year of low or non-existent wages growth.

So let's do a comparison of how business in Australia fared in 1986, at the dawn of neoliberalism in Australia, compared to 2016.

In 1986, the Australian corporate sector made, on average, $2.6 billion in total profits each quarter of that year—that's about $7.4 billion a quarter in 2016 dollars. Thirty years later, they averaged $42 billion a quarter. Company profits are around 500 per cent higher in real terms, give or take; as a proportion of GDP, they're over 600 per cent higher. In the same period, the incomes of Australian families only grew by around 60 per cent. And companies were paying 46 per cent tax on their profits back then; in 2016, they were paying 30 per cent, and had been promised a fall to 25 per cent.

In 1986, the centralised wage-fixing system meant Aussie workers got a whopping wage rise of around 8 per cent that year—and an inflation rate of nearly 10 per cent. In 2016, workers made do with a lousy 2.2 per cent wage rise while the country's industrial relations body made ready to cut penalty rates for many of the country's lowest-paid workers. Industrial disputes in 2016 were one-twentieth of what they had been in 1986, while the wage share of nominal GDP has fallen significantly, from above 50 per cent to around 46 per cent.

So, can we all agree Australian business has done just fine over the last 30 years?

You're kidding, right? Australia's business leaders are always wanting to know what you've done for them lately. There are always more taxes that must be cut, more workers whose wages must be reduced and more regulations that must be stripped back—and always urgently, lest economic doom overtake us. Australia's corporate sector insists unions are 'out of control', Australia is a 'high cost economy', real wages 'have to fall', company taxes must be slashed, while ever more deregulation is needed to save capitalism from being strangled by red tape. There's always another country that has lower taxes, lower wages, less regulation than us. 'Time to give business a break,' the country's chief business lobby group demanded before the 2016 election, as if they had been the victims of 30 years of reform, not the beneficiaries.

It's a similar story across the West: business has done extraordinarily well over the last three decades. OECD data shows that in Western economies, including the United States, the United Kingdom, France, Canada, Germany, Japan and Australia, the labour share of national income, which peaked at over 65 per cent in the 1970s, began falling significantly in the 1980s and stood at 57 per cent in 2011, although falls were more pronounced in the United Kingdom and the United States. The International Labour Organization has calculated that between 2000 and 2013 labour productivity growth in those countries dramatically outstripped real-wages growth. The share of national wealth going to workers has shrunk, and shrunk significantly, under neoliberal policies; workers are more productive than ever, but business is keeping the benefit of that productivity to itself.

This is never acknowledged by business, which instead has a deeply ingrained sense of victimhood. And when facts don't bear out their complaints, they quietly change the subject. One of the major issues of economic debate in Australia around 2010 was the great productivity crisis—a collective lament by economists, business leaders and politicians that productivity growth, after performing strongly in the 1990s, had collapsed in Australia. For anyone who remembered the economic debates of the 1980s and 1990s, this was very familiar—back then Australians were constantly harangued by business and right-wing commentators that they were too lazy and took too many holidays, especially compared to Asian workers. As long-time Singaporean prime minister and autocrat Lee Kuan Yew declared then, we would become the white trash of Asia.

According to business and the Coalition, this 'productivity crisis' was caused by Labor's *Fair Work Act*. Unfortunately for this argument, in 2011, labour productivity in the private sector surged nearly 3 per cent in one quarter. A few months later, it surged another 1.4 per cent in a single quarter. Business lobbyists dismissed the rise as misleading. But inconveniently, labour productivity in the private sector kept rising, every quarter thereafter, in an unbroken run that stretched through the 2013 economic slowdown and into mid 2014. It was still growing, albeit at a lower rate, in 2017. In 2012, Tony Abbott had declared, 'We have some serious workplace relations issues in this country. There is a flexibility problem. There is a militancy problem. Above all else, there is a productivity problem.' But there was no flexibility problem; according to the Productivity Commission report Abbott himself had requested, industrial disputes had dropped to historic lows— and the productivity problem had already vanished.

By 2017, a Treasury paper—from the conservative government itself—was waving away the productivity crisis as having never existed: 'Despite concerns, Australia's labour productivity growth over recent years is in line with its longer-term performance. In the five years to 2015–16, labour productivity in the whole economy has grown at an average annual rate of 1.8 per cent. This compares to an average annual rate of 1.4 per cent over the past 15 years and 1.6 per cent over the past 30 years.'

But did Australian business ever acknowledge the improvement in workplace productivity—especially given that workers were no longer being rewarded with higher wages for higher productivity? To the contrary. In 2017, the Business Council was still calling for reforms to increase productivity and the Minerals Council was calling for dramatic changes in industrial-relations laws, despite a labour-productivity boom and falling real wages in mining.

Taxation is another area where business—especially big business—has overplayed its hand. The extraordinary extent of tax avoidance and evasion by the world's biggest companies has elicited such anger in both Anglophone and European countries that even conservative, business-friendly governments have cracked down on rorts such as parent–subsidiary loans at inflated interest rates, intellectual property agreements that remit vast amounts of revenue as IP costs to tax havens, and the use of foreign sales hubs to engage in transfer pricing. Multilateral efforts to address base erosion and profit shifting by the OECD and the G20 have been stymied by US efforts to prevent any international agreement that would compel US multinationals to pay tax in other countries—leading to frustrated governments like those of the United Kingdom, Australia and Germany taking unilateral action.

In Australia, the sheer level of electoral anger about tax dodging forced the Coalition government to undertake its own actions, such as a diverted profits tax. In an elegant demonstration of the obliviousness of big business to the reputational damage it was inflicting on itself, business lobby groups such as the Business Council of Australia repeatedly warned against rushing into anti-avoidance laws—even when some of its members, such as Qantas, Energy Australia and Rupert Murdoch's News Corporation, were shown to be paying no tax at all. 'Any debate must be sensible, well informed and rely on facts and evidence. Not doing so undermines the community's confidence in the integrity of our tax system and distorts the debate,' the BCA warned in 2014.

In other words, don't talk about corporate tax avoidance, because people might start to work out that the tax system is unfair.

But the business community in Australia went further and demanded a cut in the company tax rate. The story of that tax cut proposal is a classic example of neoliberal policymaking. Back in 2010, Labor had suggested a company tax cut as part of its rather unambitious, but as it turned out, politically problematic tax-reform package. It was to have been funded by a superprofits tax on the mining sector, then making billions from record-high commodity prices—which had driven the Australian dollar over parity with the US dollar and crunched export- and import-competing sectors like manufacturing. In effect, it would have transferred some of the benefits of the commodities boom to the sectors suffering through the downside.

Six years and four prime ministers later, the Coalition, which had opposed Labor's company tax cut, now proposed its own, more than twice as large as Labor's, having already cut the tax rate for small business. However, this cut was not to be funded by any new source; the anticipated cost to taxpayers over a decade exceeded $60 billion, which would simply come out of existing deficits and future surpluses. The government's reasoning was that a tax cut would spur greater investment, higher economic growth, higher employment, higher wages and higher productivity—in fact, there seemed to be no economic benefit a company tax cut *wouldn't* deliver.

No evidence was ever produced for this 'company tax cut equals economic panacea' claim, beyond economic modelling that relied on a range of heroic assumptions such as full employment and no government debt. Even then, the modelling showed trivial benefits to growth over a decade. Indeed, there remains a major evidentiary problem about the tax cut: countries like the United Kingdom and Canada (which has a very similar, though larger, economy compared to Australia) *had* cut company taxes and underperformed Australia, which had left its rate unchanged, in many of the areas company tax-cut advocates said would benefit. In particular, it was clear from those two countries that the oft-repeated claim that company tax cuts would drive higher wages growth was simply nonsense—despite big cuts in company taxes in Canada and the United Kingdom, wages growth was even lower than in Australia in the decade to 2017; as we've seen, British workers went backwards in terms of real wages.[19]

It was also argued—especially after Donald Trump was elected—that in order to remain 'internationally competitive', Australia had to cut its 'punitive' company tax rate to the levels of other countries, despite no evidence the Australian company tax rate was deterring investment; Australia managed a mining investment boom despite our apparently uncompetitive tax rate. Indeed, between 2008 and 2016, foreign direct investment in Australia set a new record every year, and grew in total by nearly 80 per cent. Judging by our attitude to investment from Chinese sources, we are in fact getting so much investment we're able to pick and choose.

There weren't even any particular benefits to Australian shareholders of companies that would receive the tax cut: due to Australia's system of dividend imputation, a company tax cut would mean lower franking credits for shareholders, thereby increasing their tax obligation. It was primarily foreign shareholders who'd win from a company tax cut.

---

19 When ABC journalist Emma Alberici made these and other points in a February 2018 article, it prompted fury from the government (and personal smears of Alberici by business journalists), leading to the ABC buckling to pressure to censor the article.

And evidence from the United States after Donald Trump handed US business a trillion dollar tax handout showed that, rather than being invested in new economic activity, the windfall ended up being used for a new all-time record level of share buybacks, pushing the share prices of companies up and rewarding corporate executives whose remuneration was linked to them. After months of massive share buybacks, including a staggering $100 billion buyback announced by Apple, no signs of investment growth and no wages boost, even senior Republicans like former presidential candidate Marco Rubio were criticising Trump's tax cuts.

The almost complete lack of evidence advanced for company tax cuts—which Australian business had been claiming were 'urgent' since the mid-2000s—was an example of how the 'rules and conventions' referred to by Keynes, which, 'skilfully put across and guilefully preserved' are so important to a civilised society, have gone missing. In this case, the idea that major policy favouring one sector of the community should be built on a testable rationale; that evidence-based policy should be the default position of any polity, that claims could and should be tested against reality—something company tax advocates and the government simply refused to do, preferring to assert without foundation the wealth of benefits that would flow from handing tens of billions of dollars to corporations. Rather than evidence-based policy, the tax cuts would be the biggest tax avoidance scam in Australian history, with corporations set to reap a $60 billion windfall, all delivered through the political process (Business Council members donated nearly $3 million to the Coalition in 2015-16 and 2016-17 alone), rather than via complicated and potentially risky tax avoidance schemes.

But corporations were so used to getting what they wanted from governments that they had lost any understanding that at some point, they might push their luck too far.

Learned helplessness and its lessons

One of the long-term consequences of the application of the neoliberal suite of policies over decades was that, even if many governments were spending as great a proportion of GDP as ever, the range of things governments actually *did* was substantially reduced. With unrestricted capital flows, monitoring by credit-ratings agencies and the mantra of needing to keep the 'confidence' of business and markets, the policy space within which governments could act without incurring some form of economic penalty or rebuke was perceived by politicians to have narrowed considerably. Moreover, neoliberalism curtailed the *tools* by which governments could intervene in the economy: government businesses were privatised or, at the very least, corporatised, so that they were required to produce a profit. Taxation policy became about how best to incentivise business and risk-taking, rather than about providing the wherewithal for community needs. Trade policy became subject to international rules overseen by the World Trade Organization. The potential for stimulus in the event of an economic downturn was—at least in neoliberal dreams— curtailed to 'automatic stabilisers' (income tax and welfare payments) and monetary policy. Any Keynesian efforts at stimulating demand were forbidden as borrowings would 'crowd out' the private sector and have no net stimulatory effect. Infrastructure investment was limited out of concern for public debt; instead, complex financing mechanisms were found to engage the private sector in infrastructure provision in byzantine deals that often left either investors or taxpayers out of pocket. Even temporary stimulus measures like one-off tax refunds would, neoliberals insisted as the world plunged into recession in 2009, have no effect as consumers would save them, knowing they're temporary. (Fortunately, Australians spent them with glee, apparently unaware they were defying neoliberal dogma, helping to keep the economy afloat.)

The result is that Western governments now do far fewer things than they used to—and thus know *how* to do fewer things. In some areas, this is a definite good: governments used to build roads, but as it turns out, the private sector really *can* build roads cheaper, and quicker than governments, and to the same quality or better. And if people complain about the service from their telcos and ISPs, it's nothing compared to the widespread loathing of Telecom in the 1970s, or its government predecessor the PMG, which were hopelessly engineering-driven, unresponsive and Stalinist in their attitude to the people notionally known as their owners or customers. Forget this at your peril.

In other areas, however, the result is a learned helplessness by governments in functions that can't be outsourced. This weakness tends to emerge at times of crisis: the catastrophic failure of the US government to help victims of Hurricane Katrina in New Orleans in 2005 or Hurricane Maria in Puerto Rico in 2017—in which the richest country in the world sat and watched as their own countrymen and women were left without basic aid—and the failure of the UK government to provide basic help to the victims of the Grenfell tower fire in

2017, are examples of governments that have forgotten how to perform the core task of the state, to protect their citizens. Fortunately most Australian governments remain skilled at providing emergency relief, partly because they get so much practice at it every summer and autumn as bushfires and cyclones sweep the country. The Australian Defence Force has considerable experience in responding to cyclones, and floods; rural fire services, often composed of volunteers, are the frontline against bushfires. The ABC is the trusted emergency broadcaster for regional communities.

But learned helplessness pervades other policy areas in Australia. The greatest example is the National Broadband Network, a policy debacle of the first order in which a major nation-building project was hobbled first by the then-Labor government's requirement that it generate a rate of return for taxpayers—in order to keep the project on the 'capital' side of the Commonwealth budget and out of the budget deficit[20]—and then by the decision of the Coalition to switch to second- and third-rate delivery options involving Australia's ancient copper telephone network that, while promised to be 'faster and cheaper', turned out to be every bit as slow to roll out, more expensive, and with terrible service to boot.

The key problem for the NBN was that the government body best-placed to roll out communications infrastructure—Telstra—had been privatised by the Howard government. This was an entirely sensible decision, childishly opposed by the Labor opposition at the time. But it was privatised as a vertically integrated market giant—to maximise sale proceeds and

---

20 Although, in Labor's defence, the budget was still in surplus when the NBN was announced, and the project was regarded as a likely successful privatisation when completed in the 2020s.

appeal to 'mum and dad' shareholders—in violation of neoliberal orthodoxy, which suggests it should have been privatised in a way that maximised competition in the relevant market, not revenue for government. This meant Telstra both owned the telecommunications network and provided retail services *on* that network, giving it an incentive to prevent competitors from accessing its infrastructure, or to charge them exorbitant access fees, meaning they'd have to roll out their own infrastructure. Telstra could therefore not be relied on to provide a basic broadband infrastructure in a competitive market for other telcos. Indeed, what prompted the Rudd government to pursue an NBN in the first place was Telstra's refusal to participate in Labor's original idea of a fibre-to-the-node broadband network, and other telcos' unwillingness to do so unless they could be guaranteed they wouldn't have to compete with Telstra (or anyone else).

So having sold off its capacity to deliver communications infrastructure, the government had to rebuild a communications infrastructure company from the ground up to do it all again—while insisting it deliver a return on the capital the government was putting into it (something the PMG/Telecom had never been required to do). Unsurprisingly, the NBN had enormous teething problems, and nearly a decade after the beginning of the project, it's a byword for failure and disappointment in the community.

Rolling out a national fibre network in a country so large and so sparsely populated as Australia is admittedly a major logistical undertaking that would challenge any government or private company. But learned helplessness pervades other, simpler, areas, such as regulation. For example, financial sector regulation—quite apart from the global disaster of the financial crisis—has been a nightmare for tens of thousands of Australians who have suffered major financial loss, even the complete loss of their savings, due to the depredations of Australia's major banks and their staff. The Australian Securities and Investments Commission—supposedly the corporate regulator—time and again proved inept at reining in the banks, acquiring a well-founded reputation for going easy on powerful business figures while pursuing minor figures relentlessly. As one of the architects of ASIC admitted, as the banking royal commission revealed scandal after scandal, 'We placed too much faith in the efficient market hypothesis and in light touch regulation . . . with the benefit of hindsight and what's been coming out at the royal commission, the weaknesses of the specialist approach we took to regulation are also evident.'

One example of this learned helplessness in financial regulation will suffice. It relates to the impacts of the 'vertical integration' of Australia's big banks with the wealth management and financial planning industries (which we noted in the previous chapter) on customers who'd sought financial advice and chosen wealth products sold to them by big bank agents. In the 2000s and early 2010s, a number of staff of the financial planning arm of the Commonwealth Bank engaged in unethical and illegal behaviour that inflicted massive losses on their clients, such as forging clients' signatures and switching them, without their knowledge, into high-risk, but (for planners) more remunerative products. By 2017, the CBA had spent nearly $70 million in compensation in two separate remedial programs, but faced tens of millions more in compensation as new victims emerged in other areas.

As it turned out, ASIC had known since the early 2000s that the entire financial-planning industry in Australia was riddled with misconduct and used a remuneration model that encouraged planners to serve themselves first and clients second. And since at least 2007 ASIC had specifically known about the dodgy dealings within the Commonwealth Bank's Commonwealth Financial Planning arm, because whistleblower Jeff Morris had told them. ASIC even wrote to the Commonwealth Bank in early 2008, raising its concerns. By that stage, the Commonwealth Bank itself was aware of at least one planner who had forged clients' signatures to move their funds to different accounts. But ASIC wasn't interested in enforcement action against the bank—instead, the CBA was allowed to establish and run its own 'continuous improvement compliance program'. This wasn't even an enforceable undertaking to do better—simply the bank hiring an independent monitor and reporting to ASIC.

And throughout all this, ASIC didn't bother to tell anyone there were issues with the bank's financial planning services. People continued to use Commonwealth Financial Planning, unaware criminals were working there and that the regulator knew about it.

In 2008 and 2009, ASIC got more tip-offs from whistleblowers. By this stage, there were also former CBA clients complaining to ASIC about the huge losses they had incurred as a result of bad advice from the bank's planners. Internal Commonwealth Bank investigations revealed that not merely had signatures been forged but that files had been tampered with or were missing key documents. In 2009, ASIC received yet another alert about misconduct by planners—this time from the bank itself, as part of the compliance program established earlier. But ASIC did nothing because it *lost the report*. There were *more* complaints from whistleblowers about files being doctored after this but it wasn't until 2010 that ASIC decided to 'get tough' with the bank and impose an enforceable undertaking.

ASIC's problem was that it had been captured by the industry it was supposed to regulate. It prided itself on having an industry-exchange program, in which employees of financial-sector companies would work at ASIC for a period, enabling the regulator to 'better understand' the sector. But the result was a regulator that was far too close to the people it was supposed to regulate. As a 'light-touch' regulator all it ever wanted to do was work *with* big businesses, not actually inconvenience them by requiring them to obey the law— even when the companies themselves alerted them about breaches. ASIC even decided it wouldn't ask the bank to try to fix the files doctored by dodgy planners because, it later said, it might have cost the bank money, and that was apparently unacceptable.

Only after the humiliating exposure of ASIC's colossal ineptitude, and the cost borne by Commonwealth Bank's clients, did the regulator decide to finally start regulating—just in time for a major scandal to erupt in the Commonwealth Bank's insurance division. And within two years of that, the CBA had been sued by another regulator for allowing massive money laundering by drug syndicates.

Energy policy was another example of government helplessness finally giving way to regulatory action. The energy crisis that erupted in Australia in 2016 and 2017 was decades in the making, and a rare example of achieving literally the worst possible outcome of any policy scenario: Australia, a country blessed with an abundance of both fossil fuel and renewable energy resources, found itself struggling to keep the lights on while consumers and businesses faced regular, massive hikes in their power bills, and our carbon emissions continued to rise. The causes were threefold—an attempt to establish a market for infrastructure services that ended up incentivising gaming by participants; a gas 'market' characterised by monopoly, gouging, over-investment and an almost complete lack of transparency; and an investment strike caused by the Coalition's climate denialism and refusal to establish clear rules around long-term energy infrastructure investment.

It is the first of those causes that is the most important for our purposes. The national electricity market—in reality, it was an east coast electricity market—was established as the product of a suite of micro-economic reforms implemented by the Hawke government, though the bulk of the development of the structure of the market took place under Paul Keating, and was finalised under John Howard. Unlike the privatisation of Telstra, the goal was to separate the monopoly aspects of the power industry—transmission and distribution—from the retail and generation aspects of the industry, and to connect consumers together in different states. Victoria and South Australia were privatising their electricity assets at the same time, whereas in New South Wales and Queensland they remained in government hands for another two decades. In this case, privatisation wasn't the problem—it was the corporatised government-owned power companies in New South Wales and Queensland that ended up being the worst offenders in gouging customers, by gaming the complex regulatory framework that applied to electricity infrastructure investment.

The other problem was the ageing fleet of east coast coal-fired power plants, which were coming to the end of their lives without anyone being too keen to invest in new plants which would belch out carbon emissions for the next 50 years. The working assumption on the part of governments had been that gas would be an appropriate intermediate source of power generation to complement the growth of renewables, given gas-fired generators can quickly ramp up and down unlike coal-fired power, and produce lower carbon emissions. But three gas companies had simultaneously built gas liquefaction processors in Queensland for LNG exports, in some cases without even having enough of their own gas supplies to meet their export contracts, and the price of gas on the east coast of Australia increased dramatically—with pipeline owners the particular winners given their capacity to use monopoly pricing power.

Energy policy thus became a perfect demonstration of neoliberalism in practice: poorly regulated, highly complex markets that gave oligopolistic and monopolistic companies (including government-owned companies) endless opportunities to maximise profits at the expense of consumers and other business.

The eruption of the energy crisis in 2016 and 2017 saw the Turnbull government adopt radically interventionist policies: gas exporters were threatened with a domestic reservation scheme (Labor's flirtation with a milder 'national interest' regulation on gas exports had been denounced as raving socialism barely twelve months earlier). Electricity companies had their appeal rights in relation to infrastructure pricing drastically curtailed. Business and sector experts began talking about the *de facto* nationalisation of coal-fired power stations.

Curiously, however, this wholesale abandonment of neoliberal dogma and embrace of large-scale interventionism seemed to have little effect on the Australian economy. Companies kept on hiring people. Investors kept on investing. Business kept on operating. A few diehard neoliberals tut-tutted and the business community expressed its concerns. Somewhere in a boardroom, the phrase 'sovereign risk' was doubtless invoked. Beyond that, the sun kept rising in the east and setting in the west. Perhaps it was because a conservative government had done it, rather than a progressive government. Perhaps, just as Labor had been the better party to implement neoliberalism in Australia, the conservatives might have been the better party to start dismantling it. But after generations of hearing that the markets would punish any government that deviated from what was once termed the 'Washington consensus' of neoliberal orthodoxy, the threats turned out to be more than a little hollow when, in one industry at least, a government threw that consensus right out the window.

The bureaucrats

The Australian public service was once regarded as one of the best civil services in the world. And despite the disaster of the early 1990s recession—for which senior economic public servants were partly to blame—in the 1980s and 1990s, it helped political leaders put in place the basis for decades of economic growth and rising wealth.

But a rot set in during the Howard years—albeit drawing on developments under previous Labor governments—and Australia's federal public service has steadily declined under recent governments. While the criticism of increasing politicisation has often been made (by both progressives and conservatives) the bigger issue has been a growing problem of sheer incompetence—so much so that it is difficult to know where to start on the long list of major bungles of recent years. The worst offender has been the Department of Immigration (or 'Home Affairs', as it now calls itself), which under both sides of politics has offered staggering displays of incompetence, often involving offshore detention of asylum seekers.

The handling of maritime asylum seekers, and the need to deter them from attempting to reach Australia via the highly dangerous mechanism of sailing from Indonesia or points further afield, is a complex policy challenge. Simply accepting tens of thousands of maritime arrivals who would have supplanted refugees from other parts of the world in Australia's limited (though, by international standards, very large) humanitarian program was not acceptable, especially when many died in the effort to reach Australia. And bureaucrats were also tasked with undertaking large-scale solutions to this challenge in extremely short periods of time, to suit the needs of politicians.

But from the re-establishment of offshore processing by the Gillard government onwards, there has been one constant: the Department of Immigration's incompetent letting of, and mismanagement of, the billion-dollar contracts for offshore prison camps on Nauru and Manus Island, as well as the use of a range of practices within those camps injurious to the health of detainees. The department also permitted brutalisation at its facility on Nauru—it was made aware of the sexual and physical abuse of female and child detainees but did nothing except to attempt to prevent evidence from being made public. The result has been dozens of mentally and physically injured asylum seekers needing care in Australia. In some cases, medical treatment has been withheld by the department for too long and asylum seekers have died from treatable illnesses, or taken their own lives.

Other cases of extraordinary incompetence abound; the challenge is which to leave off this lowlights reel.[21] The Attorney-General's Department received correspondence from convicted extremist Man Haron Monis, then on trial in relation to a violent crime, containing advice from Monis that he wanted to contact Islamic State, mere weeks before he entered the Lindt Café in Sydney to begin his siege. The Department did nothing about it, then failed to tell the government's in-house inquiry about Monis' letter, then misled ministers about having done so, a kind of bungle trifecta for which no one has ever been held accountable. Or we can look to the Social Services department, which deliberately breached privacy laws in handing out personal information to a blogger about a client who had criticised its scandalous robo-debt maladministration. The last was a separate fiasco that saw tens of thousands of Australians sent threatening letters for debts that either didn't exist, or which were far below the amounts calculated by inept bureaucrats.

Then there's the Treasury: it poorly served three treasurers in a row by serially overestimating tax revenue, leaving the Gillard, Abbott and Turnbull governments all well adrift of their goal of returning to surplus. For the better part of a decade after the financial crisis, embarrassed Treasurers would be forced to reveal revenue write-downs of tens of billions of dollars at two fiscal set pieces each year—the budget and the Mid-Year Economic and Fiscal Outlook—pushing the

---

21 Immigration has been the subject of a long string of negative audit reports by the independent Australian National Audit Office, covering an impressively broad range of other bungles as well.

return to surplus back further and further. It became a bipartisan ritual that Wayne Swan, Joe Hockey and Scott Morrison all had to endure, despite Swan initiating a review into the problem and Hockey claiming that he'd put an end to it by establishing a new era of conservative accounting within Treasury. Prime Minister and Cabinet, supposedly the very best of the Australian Public Service, were found to have badly bungled the Abbott government's handling of funding for Indigenous programs; that was also the department that sent a filing cabinet full of confidential material off to a furniture shop for sale to the public—fortunately a cowed ABC, which obtained the material, handed it back to the government without publishing any of the documents.

Then there are persistent IT problems right across the public service: the 2016 census debacle, repeated major IT outages at the Australian Tax Office, releases of personal information by departments (more of that later)—not to mention major defence procurement bungles, such as the acquisition of the disastrous, and grotesquely expensive, F-35 fighter that will damage the defence budget, though probably not too many enemy aircraft, for decades to come.

A likely factor in the long list of major and minor bungles in recent years is a clear decline in the overall quality and experience of senior public servants. Less experienced public servants, or those whose only experience of government has been since 1996, are more likely to be 'responsive' to ministers—the code word for compliant with the government's agenda, regardless of whether it is supported by evidence or not, or is legal or not. The Hawke government ended the era of permanent heads of department and moved Secretaries onto contracts, opening the way to the real politicisation of the public service that began with John Howard in 1996 and his sacking of half a dozen Secretaries, including—the stories persist to this day—one who was sacked by mistake.[22]

And inexperienced public service leaders aren't helped by the huge downsizing of the public service under both Labor and the Coalition. Since 2013, the APS has shrunk by nearly 10 per cent, according to official numbers, with some departments losing over 13 per cent of staff. For many years, the best and the brightest of the public service—that ones that are most likely to prosper in the private sector—have taken redundancy and moved on, leaving behind an increasingly mediocre bureaucracy.

Most voters have little knowledge of, or interest in, public service bungles until they affect large numbers of people—incidents like the census fiasco and Centrelink's robodebts that attracted major media attention. Public servants are not warmly regarded by private-sector workers at the best of times, but the sense that the public service struggles for competence further undermines trust in government when voters are increasingly looking to government to be more active and interventionist than in recent decades.

Biographical note: Canberra, so white

I moved to Canberra from Sydney in 1993. At that stage I was doing a PhD and still held vague and, as it turned out,

---

22 Even as the incoming Rudd Labor government restored a small measure of independence by abolishing performance pay in the public service in 2008, NSW Labor was degrading and politicising the NSW public service during its disastrously overlong tenure in government.

absurdly ill-founded hopes of becoming an academic. My public service job was just a temporary thing, I told myself. When I finally escaped to Crikey, I'd been in it fifteen years, and barely made it out alive.

Canberra's not a real city, and doesn't feel like one. Even Wellington, New Zealand's capital, stuck at the wind-blasted bottom of the world (um, so to speak), feels a lot more like an actual city. But I like Canberra anyway: it's a brilliant place to raise kids, far better than somewhere like Sydney, and the schools and hospitals and roads are excellent, even if Canberrans, generally, are the worst, most annoyingly risk-averse drivers on the planet.

But Canberra is frequently criticised as being out of touch. People, I think, tend to be referring to the politicians who spend twenty weeks a year here, but it's actually true of the whole town and its population of 300,000-plus. Canberra isn't immune from the social problems of other places, of course, but it's very different to Australia's major cities and other centres of comparable size in that, by and large, it's wealthy, educated and white. Very white.

Coming from a melting pot like Sydney in the early 1990s, I found Canberra a shock. Sure, there were plenty of Vietnamese and Thai and Turkish and Indian restaurants. But in the corridors of the public service, there was barely a non-white face to be seen. Even non-Anglo faces and names were hard to find. This must be what the 1950s looked like, only without hats, I thought as I entered my new workplace and sat down at my 386 computer.

By that time, the male dominance of the Australian Public Service was ending. Until the 1960s, women had been sacked from the APS once they married. In the 1980s, a generation of female leaders had begun rising through the upper ranks. Helen

Williams—for whom I had the pleasure of working later on—became the first female Secretary in 1985. Others followed, and the gender imbalance at each end of the hierarchy—the top, heavy with men, the bottom ranks, female-dominated—began to shift. It wasn't all smooth sailing—not until then-Treasury Secretary Martin Parkinson in the 2010s committed to a program of increasing the number of senior women in Treasury did that key agency join the rest of the APS in looking a little more like the Australia it worked to serve.

There was poor progress in other areas, though. Throughout my time in the public service, the recruitment and retention of people with disabilities was a top priority, and yet the APS as a whole went backwards on that score. Ditto with the recruitment of Aboriginal and Torres Strait Islander public servants, which continues to be a problem even now. And, ethnically, the public service remained overwhelmingly Anglo. It still is today: the names on desks and office doors could have been there when Menzies was prime minister.

There are other ways in which Canberra is different. Canberrans are highly educated: over 40 per cent of its population has a degree of some kind, compared to less than 20 per cent of all Australians. It also houses a strong diplomatic presence. Because of the make-up of the city, the conversation at kids' sports on weekend mornings tends to be wide-ranging, as doctors, senior public servants, high-profile lawyers, economists, journalists, diplomats and the occasional politician cluster to watch their kids play cricket or kick a ball around.

This, coupled with the city's very low unemployment rate—usually at least a point below the national average, and not once in double figures since the Australian Bureau of Statistics began collecting data in the 1960s—skews perceptions. As a city dominated by the governing class—either public servants, or lobbyists, or journalists, or consultants and economists and other people who make their living from engaging in public policy—Canberra has nothing to fear from economic reform. We're never at risk of being unemployed, because most of us have highly transferable skills. The negative consequences on employment of economic policies are mostly of academic interest to us. We live the neoliberal dream of seamless mobility of employment—if we lost our job, we could get another one nearby, or if we had to, move to Sydney or Melbourne. Or, hey, what about Europe? London? San Francisco? What are the schools like there?

For most Australians, of course, life isn't like that. Economic policies come with real consequences for your job, your mortgage repayments, your kids' standard of living. Life is more economically fragile, there's less room for error. Notionally, politicians are supposed to act as a check on this, representing as they do Australians outside the Canberra bubble. And many of them do exactly that. But politicians are almost as bad as the public service when it comes to diversity: they are far whiter, and older, and wealthier, than the population at large and tend to be drawn from a narrower range of backgrounds.[23] And it's been the politicians who have led the most aggressively neoliberal policies of recent decades, rather than the feral abacuses of the public service.

After the 2013 election ushered in a peculiar coterie of minor party and independent senators—far-right eccentrics

---

23 Especially the Liberals, who currently have significantly fewer female MPs than in the Howard years—his massive 1996 election victory delivered a record number of women into the ranks of the parliamentary Liberal Party.

like David Leyonhjelm and Bob Day, former footballer Glenn Lazarus, car enthusiast Ricky Muir, Tasmania's, um, rough diamond Jacqui Lambie—there was a certain patronising tone to the news coverage and debate about the influence of famous 'preference whisperer' Glenn Druery. As one who patronised with the best of them, I now regret doing so. For all their faults and foibles—and Jacqui Lambie is little short of Pauline Hanson in many of her bigoted utterances—they were far more representative of Australian voters than many of the people elected under major party banners, and certainly far more representative than people like me who populate Canberra. And their lack of political professionalism, thought to be a minus, was in many ways a positive. Some of them, like Ricky Muir, visibly grew under the responsibility of being a key swing vote in the Senate. But with the changes to Senate voting processes agreed by Malcolm Turnbull and the Greens in 2016, the possibility that such people will enter the Senate has now been curtailed significantly. Would-be senators now need not merely complex preference-swapping deals but also high 'brand recognition' to have a chance of being elected. That's why Jacqui Lambie was re-elected (albeit, like many a politician, ending up falling victim to the great section 44 slaughter of 2017), while Ricky Muir and Glenn Lazarus were not. And, of course, the wretched Pauline Hanson, who spent her years out of politics being feted by the media, returned to politics.

Occasionally, I think, it might not be a bad idea to have some Ricky Muirs and Glenn Lazaruses and even, god help us, a Jacqui Lambie in the public service. They wouldn't fix Canberra's ethnicity problem, but they might convey just a little of what the world is like for most Australians to people like me, who sit and opine from atop a pyramid of privilege, safe in the knowledge our lives will never be affected by the economic policies we advocate for.

Neoliberal tragedy: how Reform was ignored to death

When Labor returned to power after eleven years in opposition in 2007, what would be its agenda, the commentariat collectively wondered. In particular, would it continue the process of economic reform begun in the 1980s?

The idea of 'reform' is crucial to neoliberalism. The sclerotic, Keynesian, protected economies of the postwar era had to be 'reformed' to make way for markets. But this wasn't a finite process. Liberating the economy is never-ending—there are always ways in which the economy can be tweaked to make life easier for business. Regulations can be removed, budgets can be cut, assets can be sold, workers' rights reduced. The ideal neoliberal politician is engaged in a Sisyphean task, the endless pushing of a huge boulder of Reform—at least until they retire and take several company directorships.

By 2007, Reformists were becoming concerned. The Howard government had lost its way on fiscal policy—despite racking up huge surpluses thanks to the mining boom, it was spending wildly and taking an historically high proportion of GDP in tax. It had implemented the kind of industrial-relations reforms that business had wanted, but companies had so egregiously exploited the new laws that an electoral backlash had swept Howard from power, and now Labor was poised to re-establish basic protections for workers. Fortunately for business, Labor leader Kevin Rudd had promised to 'take a meat axe' to government spending, and established a ministry for deregulation.

But politics aside, there was another problem: it was unclear exactly what Reform was now required. For several years, economists had been urging governments to address the 'human-capital agenda'—maximising productivity by improving the health and skills of Australians—as the next major Reform challenge. Given the proportion of the economy devoted to health and education, increasing the efficiency and effectiveness of those sectors was at the very least an important fiscal opportunity, especially given the ageing population. There was also a lack of a broadband network, not to mention the challenge of climate change, which both sides of politics had promised to address through a carbon-pricing scheme.

For many commentators, however, these weren't Reform. Proper Reform must always involve pain—preferably on the part of ordinary Australians. Around this time, the first mutterings of what proved to be the fictional 'productivity crisis' were heard. When Labor eventually established its new industrial relations system, commentators and the Coalition were appalled and warned it would lead to job losses, wages blow-outs, productivity falls and industrial disputes. When Telstra refused to cooperate with the government's broadband plans and the government decided to build its own network, the commentariat was aghast at the interventionism and the cost. And Labor's proposed carbon-pricing scheme, already absurdly generous to Australia's biggest polluters, was savaged by business for threatening the economy.

Labor did pursue some traditional Reforms—regulatory harmonisation between the states, establishing a national water market. After the need for stimulus in response to the financial crisis had passed, it committed to return to budget surplus quickly and began cutting spending. And it set up a major tax review which, like the tax review later initiated by Malcolm Turnbull when he was prime minister, was to cause all sorts of problems. But when Tony Abbott replaced Turnbull, the cause of Reform was doomed. As opposition leader, Abbott—notorious among his colleagues for having no grasp of policy or basic economics—aped the US Republicans in opposing everything his opponents did, regardless of merit, unless it was in his demonstrable political advantage not to. He appointed another economic illiterate, Barnaby Joyce, as shadow finance minister. Joyce promptly declared that Australia was about to default on its debt, before he was sacked. Later, as our New Zealander deputy prime minister, Joyce had no problem presiding over net debt four times greater than the one he had warned was about to usher in the Fiscal Apocalypse.

For Abbott and Joyce, using a pricing mechanism to reduce carbon emissions was 'a great big tax on everything'. Small reductions in middle-class welfare proposed by Labor as part of its spending restraint were 'class warfare' and 'the politics of envy'. Labor's cuts to the company tax rate to offset the impact of the mining investment boom were blocked. Efforts to end particularly egregious tax rorts by the car leasing industry and wealthy superannuation account holders were opposed. And Abbott, to the dismay of his party, developed his own paid parental leave scheme that disproportionately benefited the wealthy.

But despite Abbott's hostility to Reform, his election success in 2013 seemed to pave the way for its return. After all, his treasurer, Joe Hockey, had declared an end to 'the age of entitlement' and Abbott had promised that he was the 'fiscal fire brigade' that would fix Labor's budget mess. Months before the 2013 election, Hockey promised that the Coalition would produce a surplus in its first budget and in every subsequent budget. A National Commission of Audit was established to go through the Commonwealth's accounts, line by line, to identify areas for savings. Abbott had declared WorkChoices 'dead, buried and cremated' but also warned that Australia had a productivity problem that needed to be addressed through the industrial-relations system. Cuts to welfare payments that dwarfed the 'class warfare' reductions of Labor were unveiled.

But—who'd have thought it?—governing proved much, much harder than sloganeering. Even as a range of unpopular cuts to government programs were imposed and the subsidised car industry was forced to close, spending under Abbott and Hockey actually went up, and by a lot. By 2015, when Abbott was dumped by his own party, government spending had reached a higher level as a proportion of GDP than when Kevin Rudd had responded to the financial crisis—but without a global meltdown in sight. This meant that despite the overall tax take rising, the budget deficit had gotten worse, rather than being extinguished by the 'fiscal fire brigade'.

Advocates of Reform were now sick with worry. Where were the 'swingeing'[24] cuts? Where was the industrial-relations reform? Abbott had made a big deal of deregulation, but the much-hyped Deregulation Day amounted to the repeal of ancient acts dealing with lighthouses and distillation and regulations for how long a senior cadet drilled for. It was closer to

---

24 One of those words, like 'beleaguered' and 'rebuked' and 'slapped down', that only political journalists use.

a tour of the Museum of Quaint Regulation than an all-out assault on red tape.

What had gone wrong for Reform? Many neoliberal commentators—myself included—put it down to a failure of communication. No one in the current generation of politicians, we lamented, had the vision, courage and communication skills of Paul Keating and Bob Hawke, who had steered Australia through its initial period of major economic reform. First, we said Wayne Swan (whom nearly all of us grossly underestimated as Treasurer) couldn't communicate well enough. Then we complained Hockey and Abbott couldn't communicate either. Without effective communication and brave leadership—leadership that recognised, in Keating's phrase, that 'good policy is good politics'—the case of Reform was lost.

As it turned out, we were talking rubbish (in my case, even more rubbish than usual).

What was becoming clear was that Reform *itself* was the problem, not the communication of it. The packaging was irrelevant, it was the contents that sucked. Voters were, at best, deeply ambivalent about decades of Reform. They passionately hated privatisation, in particular. When Queensland Labor proposed privatising major state infrastructure assets, it was reduced to single-figure representation in that state's parliament. Campbell Newman, Anna Bligh's conqueror, then lost office at the very next election courtesy of a voter backlash against *his* neoliberal agenda. Tony Abbott's prime ministership was permanently damaged by his 2014 budget, seen as a draconian imposition of neoliberal dogma, and he was replaced by his own party barely two years into government. Malcolm Turnbull, forced by his party to retain much of Abbott's agenda, only narrowly avoided defeat in the 2016 election.

None other than Keating himself—the man whom we have wanted current politicians to channel—joined those calling time on neoliberalism. 'We have a comatose world economy held together by debt and central bank money. Liberal economics has run into a dead end and has had no answer to the contemporary malaise,' he said in 2017. Jim Bolger, the former conservative New Zealand prime minister who pursued New Zealand's experiment with free markets even more aggressively in the 1990s, similarly declared neoliberal policies 'have failed to produce economic growth and what growth there has been has gone to the few at the top'. By late 2017, beleaguered Theresa May had pronounced 'as Conservatives, the arguments that we thought we'd had and won during the 1980s about the importance of free market economies—I think we thought there was a general consensus on that. And we now see that there wasn't.'

It had been a long, slow awakening for policymakers and commentators, one that required the jolts of Brexit, Trump and the 2016 Australian election to make us realise our Reform-centric world view was the problem. We once thought we were leading nations to a brighter economic future. Now we look hopelessly out of date.

Abbott, Trump and the role of conventions in government

One of the lessons from Tony Abbott's time as leader of his party is similar to an issue at the forefront of the Trump presidency: how Keynes' 'rules and conventions' can be easily wrecked by self-interested politicians. As polities, we are dependent on political conventions—unwritten, sometimes even unspoken, rules that identify what is acceptable conduct and what is not—which play an important role in enabling governments to deliver effectively for voters.

The core convention of any democratic politics is a strict division between self-interest and the public interest. While Donald Trump has trashed any number of conventions, the most flagrant has been his enthusiastic annihilation of the convention that the presidency should not be about enriching oneself and one's family. Instead, Trump and his family have set about using the presidency as a commercial advantage to be exploited as aggressively as possible. The rank nepotism and naked self-interest often seen in corrupt Third World dictatorships is firmly in place in Trump's White House, with the Trump family's commercial enterprises continuing to be run by his sons and son-in-law, half a billion dollars in loans being made to Jared Kushner after White House meetings with lenders, Trump profiting from using his own properties as presidential palaces and his relatives playing key roles in his administration and even sitting in for him in meetings. And Trump has set the standard for his Cabinet, with multiple scandals involving Cabinet members attesting to the fact that, in the words of one historian, Trump leads the most corrupt administration in US history, worse than those of Grant and Harding.

While some of the behaviour of Trump and his family may be unconstitutional—under the emoluments clause of the US constitution, receiving any benefit from a foreign government is illegal—by and large it is a breach of conventions around ethics. Instead of acting to curtail the behaviour of the president and his family, the Republican-dominated Congress has studiously ignored it. There are immediate benefits to this for the GOP, but in the long run it will be enormously damaging to the US government. Damaged conventions don't miraculously repair. A precedent has now been established that ethical conventions can be ignored with impunity, that presidents can brazenly continue to enrich themselves while in the White House as long as their party prefers to ignore it.

Other conventions are about policy. In Australia, under Tony Abbott, the Coalition's stance on climate action broke a number of conventions. Abbott and his opposition persistently and egregiously lied about the impact of a carbon-pricing scheme. They called it a tax when it was no such thing (later admitting they had lied about that). Abbott himself had publicly supported both a carbon price and a carbon tax at various points, and lied about the benefits of removing it, claiming, *inter alia*, its removal would see electricity prices fall. In fact, prices have dramatically increased since 2014.

But while Abbott's lies about both climate change and carbon pricing were extraordinary, it's accepted that politicians routinely lie for political advantage. Abbott's stance was more problematic because it represented a position directly contrary to the approach to policy of both Labor and (particularly) the Coalition since the 1980s—that markets were the most efficient way of allocating resources and achieving economic outcomes. Instead of a pricing mechanism that would have allowed markets to efficiently identify the best ways to reduce carbon emissions, Abbott wanted a big-government, big-spending solution involving government bureaucrats handing out money to companies to undertake emissions abatement activities that had no accountability (and were often merely energy-efficiency projects they would have undertaken anyway). That this was always a farcical policy was demonstrated by the fact that the Coalition itself abandoned it after three years in government.

Abbott's cynical attacks on carbon pricing didn't merely contradict his party's entire approach to economic policy, they were directly contradictory to the commitment the Coalition had taken to the previous election. Then-prime minister John Howard—for whom Abbott was a senior minister—had committed the Coalition in 2007 to 'an emissions trading scheme that will be the most comprehensive in the world'. This in effect matched Labor's 2007 election policy—Australia had a bipartisan commitment to emissions trading as the primary form of climate action. Under the leadership of Malcolm Turnbull, the Coalition had reached a deal with the Labor government on an emissions-trading scheme—albeit a poor one, which would have delivered little in the way of genuine emissions abatement until the 2020s at the earliest—and agreed to support an amended bill to implement that. Abbott broke that commitment as well as his own party's election commitment, to advocate a policy squarely at odds with the principles that informed his party's economic policies.

It's true that Labor, in opposition, had at times campaigned hard against sensible reform by the Coalition. Its campaign against the GST in the 1998 election was embarrassing and its opposition delivered us a consumption tax riddled with flaws once the Australian Democrats—a party now, deservedly, gone into the dustbin of history—got their paws on it. But Labor had been opposed to a GST since the 1980s, and John Howard had explicitly and forever ruled out a GST—'never ever'—in 1995 before changing his mind. And while the GST campaign was essentially a debate about economic efficiency and equity, Abbott's opposition to a carbon price was both ideological—Abbott was and remains a fervent climate denialist and wanted to sabotage effective climate action—and driven by political self-interest.

Conventions, even political conventions, aren't to be observed merely out of some sense of altruism and commitment to a broader public interest, but out of self-interest too. They are really an understanding that what you do to the other side, they can do back to you, even if they have to wait a while. The Coalition discovered the cost of relentless negativity once it was elected, and found Labor blocking everything it could, including policies that Labor had advocated while in government. By that stage, some understanding had penetrated conservative heads that they were merely being repaid in kind. Even Tony Abbott admitted in 2016 that one of his most notorious moments of negativity—blocking Labor's attempt to establish a deal with Malaysia to exchange asylum seekers—had been unjustified.

And, however inconsistent, Labor was entirely correct in repaying the Coalition in kind. The only way to repair broken conventions is to illustrate the high price of breaking them, such that in the future your opponent will revert to adhering to them out of a sense of self-interest. This is what game theory tells us: if the other participant in a game 'defects' from a win–win scenario because they stand to gain more from a win–lose scenario, the smartest strategy is to punish that defection in the next round, providing an incentive to revert to the win–win scenario.

The problem with that is the short-term impact is to render politics dysfunctional because nothing that requires any degree of cooperation can be achieved. For those politicians focused on actually achieving something in public life, this can be immensely frustrating. For politicians like Tony Abbott, whose primary interest is in attacking opponents— no matter in which party—and tearing down any progressive achievement, it's ideal.

The war on scrutiny

While governments have ceded more power to corporations on economic policy, they have simultaneously given themselves more and more power over their citizens. The hostility of the original neoliberals—Hayek, Friedman *et al.*—to government power in the economic sphere has turned out to be well justified in the sphere of civil liberties and personal freedom, with the irony that many of the most devoted, deregulatory-minded political neoliberals have been the ones eager to extend the powers of the state at the expense of individual rights. In recent years, governments across the West have dramatically ramped up the monitoring of their own citizens and removed many basic legal protections, under the pretext of protecting them from terrorism, despite the dearth of evidence that it has made citizens safer. And that's in addition to the vast amount of information that digitisation had made readily available to governments about their own citizens, accumulated in the ordinary course of providing services.

We'll look at the issue of surveillance further in Part 4 because it's fundamentally bound up with the internet, but here suffice it to say that in an age when trust in governments is diminishing, governments are further undermining trust by demonstrating that they can't protect our information despite blithe assurances that our privacy is properly guarded. Australian Medicare numbers—a crucial identity document in Australia—have been sold online by data thieves. The Department of Immigration accidentally published the names of over 10,000 asylum seekers, exposing them and their families to reprisals from the regimes they had fled. Health authorities have published medical data that could be easily de-anonymised. In a recurring theme when it comes to poor data security, private contractors providing outsourced services to government departments have been hacked, resulting in private information about tens of thousands of Australians being stolen.

It's the same in other countries. In 2015, the personal data of six million citizens of the US state of Georgia, collated from voting lists, was distributed in error. The tax records of over 700,000 Americans was hacked from the Internal Revenue Service. Chinese hackers stole the data of 21 million Americans from the Office of Personnel Management, including anyone who'd applied for a non-military security clearance in recent years, giving foreign intelligence agencies a vast trove of data on US public servants, including those working in highly sensitive areas such as trade. And United Kingdom authorities at the national and local level have a long history of losing control of valuable information. Undaunted, governments continue to collect as much information as possible on their citizens, primarily because they *can*, not because it's needed.

At the same time, governments have actively sought to *reduce* the amount of information their own citizens are able to access about them, and to curb media scrutiny of them.

An amusing game to play as WikiLeaks released the Chelsea Manning materials in 2010, and as various media outlets in 2013 released Edward Snowden's revelations, was to catch out progressives who lionised Pentagon Papers leaker Daniel Ellsberg but were outraged about Manning and Snowden. One such is former Australian foreign minister, New South Wales premier, and China booster Bob Carr, a big fan of Daniel Ellsberg who found himself having to split hairs when it came to Chelsea Manning, saying Ellsberg hadn't released information just for the sake of it. Daniel Ellsberg himself disagreed, and lauded both Manning and Snowden.

Bob Carr was a mere youth when Daniel Ellsberg leaked the Pentagon Papers, earning the adoration of generations of progressives and liberals. Like Carr, many of those fans have since entered governments, and adopted a very different attitude to whistleblowing and leaking. Pre-eminent among these was Barack Obama, a civil rights lawyer, who promised to make life easier for whistleblowers before being elected president. Once in the White House, Obama launched the greatest assault on whistleblowing in US history, with a particular focus on prosecuting whistleblowers as spies under the United States' World War I espionage laws. Obama declined to prosecute anyone involved in the torture program used by the CIA to interrogate alleged Islamist militants (many of them innocent) during the Bush years; the only person gaoled in relation to the torture program—under which at least one man was tortured to death—was John Kiriakou, the former CIA officer who revealed the program's existence. Chelsea Manning was prosecuted and sent to military prison for releasing details of US war crimes in Iraq and Afghanistan. Intelligence officials who revealed the waste of hundreds of millions of dollars of taxpayer money within their agencies were prosecuted. Whistleblower Edward Snowden was forced to flee to Russia (remarkably, given his circumstances, Snowden is a regular critic of the Putin regime). Obama also prosecuted and subpoenaed journalists in other whistleblower cases.

Obama's war on whistleblowers and journalists opened the way for the Trump administration to go even further. Tormented by a constant flow of leaks, which mostly resulted from internecine wars within a chaotic White House, Trump's Department of Justice massively increased its resources for pursuing leakers and announced it was considering amending laws to force journalists to reveal their sources, a major step that Obama and his Attorney-General Eric Holder had not taken. Trump also mused publicly about stripping broadcasting licences from major television networks that revealed embarrassing details about his administration and harming Amazon commercially because Jeff Bezos owns the *Washington Post*.[25]

This war on whistleblowers isn't confined to the United States. In 2017, Theresa May's government—which already has established draconian powers that allow security agencies to access Britons' communications and internet search histories—sought to increase the penalty for leaking national security information. A 2015 UK review also found that, under May as Home Secretary, police had got warrants to obtain information on journalists' sources over 600 times in three years, or more than once every two days.

Improbable as it seems, however, Australia is even worse—it's just that our media pays little attention to it. The Abbott government gave itself power to prosecute journalists who

---

25 Trump also proposed former CIA torturer Gina Haspel to be the new head of that agency.

reveal intelligence operations. Mass surveillance laws have made it easier to use metadata to find out who has contacted whom. In the notorious Witness K case, a former Australian Secret Intelligence Service officer who, following advice from a former Inspector-General of Intelligence and Security, legally revealed ASIS's illegal bugging of the East Timorese cabinet under the Howard government, was raided by ASIO and had his passport confiscated to prevent him from giving evidence in East Timor's legal action against Australia. Australia's Attorney-General George Brandis then threatened to gaol both the former officer and his lawyer. To this day, the government refuses to return his passport, despite even ASIO acknowledging it is safe to do so.

Under Abbott's successor Malcolm Turnbull, the Australian Federal Police also raided the offices of a Labor senator and the homes of his staff, and then Parliament House itself, in what turned out to be an improper attempt to track down the sources for media stories that had embarrassed the National Broadband Network company. The AFP were also kept busy trying to track down the sources for leaks about Operation Sovereign Borders, which turned back boats containing asylum seekers, and the conditions in which asylum seekers were held in detention camps in Papua New Guinea and Nauru—including at one stage illegally accessing a journalist's phone records to hunt down a source. The government even tried to give itself the power to gaol health professionals who blew the whistle on child abuse in detention camps, but was forced to relent. More recently, the government has tried to criminalise the mere 'handling' of secret information by journalists.

However lazy governments have appeared to be in trying

to regulate corporations, they have displayed plenty of vigour and enthusiasm in going after whistleblowers or those who had embarrassed them. Paranoid about 'sovereign risk' and failing to extensively consult with corporations about new regulations, they're happy to wildly overreach and ignore community concerns when violating individual rights.

Terrorism and why it will never be defeated

Some years ago I caused a minor kerfuffle by pointing out that if you counted every Australian victim of terrorism, at home and abroad, since the 1970s, terrorism accounted for fewer deaths than falling off ladders, workplace electrocution, being crushed by a tractor or accidents involving firearms. This was seen by some as seeking to downplay terrorism and pretend the great scourge of Islamist mass murder was trivial.

In fact, the point was that people who decide how to allocate limited government resources make decisions all the time that result in someone living or dying, or being injured or staying healthy. Extra spending on a road, for example, may prevent fatal car accidents. More money for hospitals, or perhaps on preventive health programs, may save lives and keep people healthier than they would otherwise be. A gun buyback scheme might reduce accidental and self-inflicted shootings. More money in mental-health programs may reduce the rate of suicide. More effective prevention programs designed and managed by Indigenous communities might reduce cardiovascular disease and lung cancer. And, perhaps, more money on national security might prevent terror attacks that kill dozens of people.

That is, lacking unlimited funding, people who determine priorities about where to spend public money are, whether they know it or not, making decisions that affect how many Australians die, of various causes, directly and indirectly.

How do policymakers decide between so many different options? Of course, they don't start from a blank slate—as a society we already invest according to certain patterns that, if you established some new utopia, you probably wouldn't embrace. But policymakers *do* make decisions about where to direct new spending, above and beyond what decades of government policy have already locked into place.

One problem is that we don't have a consistent perspective on the value of life. Some deaths are more invisible than others. The deaths of non-Australians are almost entirely invisible to policymakers, as they are to voters. The deaths of non-white Australians are less visible than those of white Australians. For the last decade, successive governments have committed to 'closing the gap' between Indigenous Australians and non-Indigenous Australians, yet the former still have vastly higher mortality rates than non-Indigenous Australians, and die far younger than the rest of us. And deaths in our regional and rural communities—agriculture is by far the most dangerous occupation, for example—tend to be invisible to most Australians, who reside in cities and think little about where their food and clothing come from. In contrast, terrorism (unless it is perpetrated by a non-Muslim) earns wall-to-wall media coverage, prime ministerial press conferences and much chin stroking from the commentariat, even if no one dies.

There's undoubtedly something about terrorism that prompts such a reaction—that's obviously the point, and why extremists have been using it for two centuries. But if anything, the reaction to terrorism is more febrile now than it was in the 1970s, when Europe, the United Kingdom and even the United States were, at various points in that decade, subjected to far more numerous attacks, including fatal attacks, even than we've seen in the last three years.[26] This may be down to the Other nature of Islamist terrorism. While there was considerable anti-Irish sentiment in the United Kingdom due to the actions of the IRA, ultimately such terrorism was 'home-grown', like that of far-left terrorists in Italy, Germany and France, or the Black Panthers in the United States. Even Palestinian terrorism was understood as political in nature. But terrorism by the likes of Al Qaeda and Islamic State, in being perpetrated by people claiming to be Muslims and being linked to a religious agenda, seems to prompt a very focused sense of hysteria that was never seen when the IRA routinely conducted Christmas bombing campaigns and murdered members of the royal family.

But by allowing our decisions about public policy to be dictated by such visceral feelings, we end up with policies that lead to more deaths than might otherwise be the case. They may be hard to spot—it's difficult to put down an increase in the road toll, say, to a specific failure to spend money; the lack of additional spending in hospitals is hard to link to specific patient outcomes. The victims of such policies are, in effect, invisible, rather than the highly visible victims of a terror attack. But they're just as dead. Their loss is just as keenly felt, the grief their families and friends feel is just as real, despite the lack of media coverage and prime ministerial media conferences.

---

26 Then again, if you count mass shootings in the United States as a form of terrorism (inflicted by the prominent terrorist organisation the National Rifle Association), there's been a significant increase since the 1970s.

To talk about deaths from terrorism compared to deaths from falling off ladders is thus to speak up on behalf of those invisible fatalities, which might not have occurred if we took a more rational approach to policy, one that focused on ensuring that we were attempting to *maximise* the number of lives we saved.

Let's take one recent example, which draws heavily on a methodology developed by John Mueller, professor of political science and chair of national security studies at Ohio State University, and Mark Stewart, an engineering professor at our own University of Newcastle. For the last decade, Mueller and Stewart have been looking at how much the United States spends on counter-terrorism, and whether that spending has been worthwhile. Their methodology is basically to work backwards: establish how much has been spent on counter-terrorism measures and then, with the help of generous (to governments) assumptions, establish how many terror incidents would have needed to have been stopped to determine if the spending was justified.

The short answer for the United States is, it spends so much on counter-terrorism that unless it is stopping a couple of 9/11s a year, it is grossly excessive.

We can go one better in Australia because governments are now in the habit of explaining exactly how many terror attacks they've thwarted. Both the head of ASIO, Duncan Lewis, and the former Attorney-General, George Brandis, have said that security agencies have thwarted a dozen terror attacks since 2014. A media report says police claim to have thwarted not twelve but fifteen terror attacks. One major attack, involving a plot to bomb an aircraft, was also uncovered after the event, but only because a foreign intelligence agency alerted Australian agencies, not through the actions of local agencies.

We also know how much money has been spent since 2014 on national security—the government has told us that too. In the 2015 budget, the government declared that it was 'investing $1.2 billion in new funding for national security in the 2015 budget, building on the $1 billion in funding we announced in the 2014–15 MYEFO [Mid-Year Economic and Fiscal Outlook]'. The allocation included funding for Operation Okra and Operation Accordion, the military operations to bomb Islamic State and train the Iraqi army. In the 2016 budget, the budget papers showed the government allowed for an additional $671.6 million in spending, most of it on Okra and Accordion. In the 2017 budget, Okra and Accordion received funding of $650 million, and there was another $30-odd million in funding for the AFP and other security agencies.

The total in extra national security spending since 2014 is thus, according to the government's own budget papers, $3.55 billion or thereabouts. Was that spending worthwhile?

Let's assume all fifteen thwarted attacks would have gone ahead. Let's also assume a casualty figure for each. Many of them appear to have been unambitious plans to 'kill a random stranger'. None intended to use a vehicle as a weapon, but some involved explosives. Let's assume, for each one, the death toll of the London Bridge attack in 2017: eight casualties.

What's a human life worth? We know that as well: according to the Department of Prime Minister and Cabinet's 'guidance on how officers preparing the cost-benefit analysis in Regulation Impact Statements should treat the benefits of regulations designed to reduce the risk of physical harm', the cost of a human life is $4.2 million in 2014 dollars, or $4.4 million today.

So if all those attacks had proceeded, the monetary value of the lives lost, according to the government's policymaking guidelines, would have been $528 million.

But terrorism doesn't merely have a cost in human lives. There are the people who are injured and who need medical care, there is infrastructure damage, and the cost of the investigatory and, perhaps, judicial processes, even imprisonment—as well as economic effects from the shock to confidence a terror attack causes. It's hard to estimate the impact of relatively low-level attacks; the British share market shrugged off the 2017 London Bridge attacks, but it would surely have had an impact, if only temporary, on tourism. If we assume every one of the fifteen thwarted attacks would have occurred in a place with a potential economic impact on tourism or some other industry, let's assume, say, a $75 million cost for each attack. That's another $1.125 billion in addition to the $528 million.

So if all fifteen attacks had proceeded along the lines assumed, the cost would have been $1.653 billion.

But there's a problem: the Commonwealth is not the only counter-terrorism actor—state and territory police forces are involved as well, sometimes as the lead agencies. But it's difficult to factor in state and territory counter-terrorism funding, so let's assume away the states and territories: all fifteen plots would have been thwarted by federal security agencies alone.

And there's yet another problem. We already spend over $35 billion a year on national security, defence and law enforcement, according to the 2015 budget. The extra spending since 2014 has been only a small addition to the money we were already giving to security agencies—the billion-dollar-plus annual budget of the AFP, for example, and the half-billion annual budget for ASIO. How many of those fifteen attacks would have been thwarted if resourcing had stayed exactly as it had been in 2014? Probably most of them. Perhaps they were thwarted more quickly with the extra resourcing, but it's improbable to say that the ASIO and AFP, at 2014 funding levels, would have been utterly in the dark. So we have to make some sort of estimate of what additional terrorism-thwarting benefit we've got for the additional funding.

Mueller and Stewart dealt with this problem by generously assuming that the new expenditure increased the capacity of US agencies to stop attacks by 45 per cent—that is, in their example the new spending had directly led to a 45 per cent reduction in terror attacks, in addition to the reduction in terror attacks from existing national security resourcing.

Let's be even more generous than Mueller and Stewart and assume that the additional funding since 2014 has led to a 60 per cent increase in these agencies' ability to stop attacks, above and beyond their preventive capacity before their additional funding. This is entirely implausible, but let's assume it out of an abundance of caution for the counter-terrorism case. So the benefit from the extra spending is 60 per cent of $1.65 billion. That's $990 million in additional benefits, from an additional expenditure of $3.55 billion.

So we wasted over $2 billion.

Using the numbers set out above, there would have had to have been 54 thwarted attacks (all involving the Commonwealth agencies) since the end of 2014 to justify the additional spending.

This may seem a deeply cynical calculation. But it's one at the heart of policymaking. That's why there's an actual government guideline about how much to value a life when devising a policy. And it's quite possible that a similar calculation applied to road funding would produce a similar disproportion—although better roads reduce travel time, which has economic benefits as well. But it's also possible that spending on other initiatives would save much *more* in terms of both life and economic outcomes, too. The lives saved by that spending would be invisible—no one talks about 'thwarted road accidents' or 'thwarted heart attacks'—but real nonetheless. As long as we obsess about terrorism, however, we'll make bad decisions about dealing with it.

Sloppy thinking—if that's all it is—pervades our analysis of the causes of terrorism as well, which among politicians and the media is dominated by both racism and a bizarre essentialism.

The racism derives from an apparent inability to call terrorism by white people (almost invariably, white men) terrorism, despite far-right terrorism being regarded by US police agencies as a greater threat than jihadist terrorism, despite the long and lethal history of terrorist attacks by white supremacists and right-wing extremists. Our instinct is to regard terrorism as a purely Muslim phenomenon, and to see white people purely as victims, even if they hate others. 'Islamophobia hasn't killed anyone,' Tony Abbott said, just days after a white American Islamophobe murdered two people in Portland, Oregon, after abusing young Muslim women.

The framing of white people as innocent victims of irrational Islam-derived violence is a key part of the essentialist narrative that politicians and the media promote about terrorism. The essentialist thesis goes back to George W Bush, and consists of some variant of 'They hate us for our freedom', as if the mere existence of a post-Enlightenment West is a motive for mass murder by Muslims, as if white people were politely minding our own business of being free before we became the arbitrary object of Muslim rage.

The problem for the essentialist thesis and its adherents, who are by no means confined to the Right, is that the people specifically charged with fighting, investigating and preventing terrorism disagree with it. There is now a long tradition of current and former intelligence and defence officials acknowledging that Western actions play a key role in motivating terrorism.

John Brennan, then head of the CIA, admitted in 2015, 'We have to recognize that sometimes our engagement and direct involvement will stimulate and spur additional threats to our national security interests.' The former head of MI5 told the Chilcot Inquiry in the United Kingdom that, 'Our involvement in Iraq radicalised, for want of a better word . . . a few among a generation . . . who . . . saw our involvement in Iraq, on top of our involvement in Afghanistan, as being an attack on Islam.' Pentagon officials told then–Secretary of State Donald Rumsfeld in 2004:

> Muslims do not 'hate our freedom,' but rather, they hate our policies. The overwhelming majority voice their objections to what they see as one-sided support in favor of Israel and against Palestinian rights, and the longstanding, even increasing support for what Muslims collectively see as tyrannies, most notably Egypt, Saudi Arabia, Jordan, Pakistan, and the Gulf states . . . Therefore, the dramatic narrative since 9/11 has essentially borne out the entire radical Islamist bill of particulars. American actions and the flow of events have elevated the authority of the Jihadi insurgents and tended to ratify their legitimacy among Muslims.

Former officials now working in the field of counter-terrorism agree. 'At what point are you going to start listening to the perpetrators who tell you why they're doing this?' said one of the world's foremost counter-terrorism experts, Marc Sageman. 'The same applies to the videos of the 7/7 bombers [the 2005 London bombings]. At some point you have to be grounded in reality.'

The essentialist thesis isn't an arbitrarily selected misinterpretation of events or simple misreading of terrorist motivations, but an argument that benefits particular groups—the politicians who use it to justify curbing civil rights, the defence companies that profit from increased military expenditure, the media that attracts readers and viewers by hyping terrorism. But it also benefits the terrorists. As the Pentagon officials writing for Donald Rumsfeld put it so succinctly, the essentialist approach, and the Western reaction to it (invading, bombing and occupying Muslim countries) '[bears] out the entire radical Islamist bill of particulars' confirming the radical Islamist narrative of Western victimisation and producing more alienated, aggrieved people open to radicalisation. There's a reason why we are not demonstrably safer sixteen years into the War on Terror: both terrorists and governments benefit from perpetuating it.

Conclusion: interactions with neoliberalism

Neoliberalism didn't cripple and hollow out governments. Neoliberalism didn't professionalise politics. It doesn't drive governments' hatred of scrutiny or the venality of so many politicians across the West. But it certainly benefits from the consequences: it's far easier for corporations and lobby groups to influence policymaking when we've outsourced policy-making to a professionalised class that relies heavily on money to keep themselves in power. And it's far more likely that the electorate will be disaffected and disengaged if they see policymaking as an insiders' game, one that isn't about the interests of the community but about the interests of corporations, and of influential organisations like trade unions. Another of Keynes' 'rules and conventions' is the belief that a society must balance competing interests; that where one group is systematically favoured, without justification, over another, then that is unfair and must be remedied. In particular, Keynes recognised the importance of a society addressing poverty that resulted from economic conditions rather than treating it as an unfortunate by-product of the natural functioning of the operations of capital. A society that failed to balance the interests of low-income earners against those of the owners of capital was unsustainable and at risk of revolution. The power wielded by corporations over policymakers and the community as a whole in recent decades breached that crucial convention in convincing the community that the economic system no longer worked for them, but in the interests of the powerful. As the cases of the energy and financial industries in Australia demonstrated, however, this corporate dominance carries the risk of backlash. At some point, even the most strongly pro-business politicians must accept electoral reality if powerful corporations have alienated and angered enough voters that supporting and protecting them is no longer viable. The tendency to economic disequilibrium within neoliberalism is paralleled with a tendency to political disequilibrium. Eventually, corporations push their power too far and the ensuing community and political backlash can be highly damaging.

And then there are the second-order effects—the disaffection and cynicism felt by citizens about the tax system when they believe the powerful get to pay what they like. If electorates in democratic countries were already feeling disempowered by the professionalisation and hollowing-out of politics—a process that they themselves were partly responsible for—the shift of power from governments to corporations made this sense of disempowerment worse, at the same time as governments, reluctant to challenge corporations, were giving themselves greater powers over citizens.

In that sense, neoliberalism happened at the worst possible time, when electorates across the West were losing their postwar faith in democratic politics, and growing more disengaged than ever from democratic political systems. The two phenomena, accordingly, reinforced each other, multiplying the social damage they inflicted. When waves are in phase—peaks combine with peaks and troughs combine with troughs—it's called constructive interference, and it means the peaks of the waves are much higher and the troughs much lower. The disaffection generated by the hollowing-out of democratic politics was 'in phase' with that generated by neoliberalism from 2016 to 2018, maximising the peaks and troughs of dislocation as the waves spread across Western societies.

But worse, there was another powerful dislocation occurring at the same time. Its cause arrived much more recently than either of the phenomena we've considered so far, but that didn't mean it was any less damaging or chaotic. The arrival of the internet created a third massive wave of disruption that synced up with those created by neoliberalism and the hollowing-out of politics.

ENTR'ACTE
THE AGES OF UNREASON

'People in this country have had enough of experts.'

That was right-wing British politician Michael Gove during the Brexit campaign, encapsulating not merely his view of the direct focus of his comment—the British economists forecasting (accurately, as it turned out) economic damage from a Brexit vote—but a wider decline in the belief that informed expertise, or factual evidence, should be regarded as an important contribution to policy debate.

A new scepticism was abroad in 2016. Not a healthy, rigorous scepticism, not a scepticism persuadable by sufficient evidence, but a scepticism that was more accurately denialism—the rejection of any facts, no matter how well-founded, if they didn't fit with people's world view.

In a previous book, written with Ms Helen Razer, I devoted a chapter to denialism and the role of what is called 'motivated reasoning' in it—and the long intellectual tradition of emotion versus science in Western thought, particularly in the context of the Enlightenment. I was reminded of that when critics began accusing Donald Trump, and the passionate rejection of facts that he personified, as representing a contradiction of the Enlightenment and the values it gave to the West. Trump was the end of the Enlightenment, many a thinkpiece suggested in 2017. But it is more accurate to see Trump, and the rejection of reason, as a *mutated* form of the Enlightenment, one reflecting the prime role of individualism in European modernity coupled with the identification of reason as a tool of elites.

To explain, we need to go back further than the Enlightenment, to the Reformation. By coincidence, 2017 was the 500th anniversary of Martin Luther publishing his theses against the Catholic practice of indulgences, which launched what remains the most important intellectual moment of Western history, greater even than any of the three Renaissances, the invention of the printing press (which helped cause the Reformation), or Einstein's reshaping of physics.

At the core of the Reformation was an idea that has fundamentally shaped the West ever since and which is also at the very core of neoliberal economics: individualism. The most important difference between Protestantism and Catholicism wasn't doctrinal disputes over obscure matters such as indulgences or transubstantiation—although plenty of lives were lost in the fights over those questions—but Protestantism's focus on the individual's direct relationship with god, in contrast to the Catholic model in which a priest, backed by the 1500-year-old institutional church, was trained to mediate the laity's connection to their god. Or, to put it another way, in the Reformation, people had had enough of experts.

Instead of relying on priests as their source for divine revelation, people would pursue it themselves via the Bible, which was increasingly available in their own language, and reasonably cheap thanks to printing. In his examination of the impact of printing, Marshall McLuhan talked about how it 'split the head and the heart of Europe'. The Reformation was the beginning—but not the end—of that split, starting a chain reaction that embedded individualism into the very fabric of European life and carried it all the way to the Mont Pelerin Society after World War II.

The chain reaction was powered by the inherently destabilising nature of individualism: once ordinary people began to explore their own spirituality, rather than rely on the teachings of authorities, where did that exploration stop? It began a constantly splintering process of institutional transition in religion: Lutheranism and Calvinism, Huguenots, Anglicanism, Presbyterianism, Independency, Shakers, Quakers, Anabaptists, a multiplicity of Protestant churches in the newly settled east coast of North America, evangelicalism, great awakenings— on and on it went, in a process that continues today in drive-in religious services and megachurches across America.

But individualism could never be confined to religion— especially not when church and state in the early modern era were so closely bound together; there was no forcing the individual back into the bottle once she was out. The chain reaction led to a rejection of authority in political spheres, even as monarchs asserted their status as divinely appointed rulers.[27] In England, John Locke established a contractarian basis for kingship centred on individual consent and rights, providing the philosophical underpinnings for England's limited, Protestant monarchy model, and relative toleration of religious dissent, after 1688. In the Dutch Republic, Baruch Spinoza argued systematically for freedom of conscience and speech on religious matters, in works so controversial scholars many decades later were still banned from arguing against them, lest that was enough to spread his ideas.

Spinoza's legacy found strong expression in the work of the *philosophes* of the radical Enlightenment. While the Enlightenment in France was anti-clerical and rationalist, much of it was highly conservative—figures like Voltaire had more in common with eighteenth-century 'enlightened despots' than contemporary liberals. But there was also a strain of *radical* Enlightenment, that followed reason and universal rights to their logical conclusions rather than halting at anti-clericalism and support for limited monarchy. Why have any social orders? radical *philosophes* wondered. Why shouldn't *all* individuals have basic rights, including women, including Africans, including native Americans, including slaves, including homosexuals? That was where Denis Diderot, the editor of the *Encyclopédie*, ended up, along with other key figures of the radical Enlightenment such as Baron d'Holbach and Jean d'Alembert. *These* were the ideas that would prove profoundly influential in the twentieth century, not the hierarchical, conservative Enlightenment of Voltaire.

---

27 That canny Scot, James I, understood the chain reaction. 'No bishops, no king,' he remarked in 1604, in response to Presbyterian proposals to reform the Church of England.

The full bloom of philosophies of individual rights that marked the radical Enlightenment—was thus the culmination of a process that had been in train since Luther nailed his challenge to indulgences to a Wittenberg church door one autumnal day in 1517. True, Luther and every other major Reformation figure would have been deeply mortified by what they had wrought, but the intellectual and political lineage was a direct one, particularly in England, the Dutch Republic and among the slaveholding elites of the new national experiment across the Atlantic, the United States of America.

And this complemented the emerging economic philosophy of capitalism. Max Weber famously sought to connect capitalism to Protestantism in the oft-misunderstood *The Protestant Ethic and the Spirit of Capitalism*, which linked capitalism to the desire to display one's elect status. Being 'elect' was John Calvin's doctrine that not merely, as per Luther, was it impossible to secure salvation through good works you might carry out in your lifetime (like buying indulgences), it could only be done through *faith* alone. You could never 'achieve' salvation, you simply were saved or not through your faith. But there was a catch: because god was thought to be omniscient and eternal, your salvation had been determined aeons before your birth. It thus became a question of *displaying* your elect status as saved, not earning it, because it had been decided before there were any stars and planets.

Even in its understated, rather than caricatured, form Weber's argument that a desire to display one's elect status fuelled capitalism is flawed and probably unverifiable anyway. But at the heart of the capitalist project, and particularly prominent in neoliberalism, is the very same individualism that animated first Protestantism and then the radical Enlightenment. It's probably going too far to say that the Protestant personal link to god, a faith unmediated by communitarian institutions and their sacerdotal experts, was paralleled by a capitalist's personal link to the market, unmediated by governments and other communitarian institutions. But even so, the atomic-level combination of capitalism and contemporary Western society provides a fair analogy for the way in which religion and Western society were fundamentally intertwined in the early modern period—and individualism became key to both.

But there's another eighteenth-century figure who represents a different strand of thinking, one that redirects the rational, anti-authority scepticism of the Enlightenment in a less healthy direction: Jean-Jacques Rousseau. This deeply problematic figure, who has enjoyed unjustifiably positive press for two and a half centuries, occupied the margins of the Enlightenment: he contributed to the *Encyclopédie* but fell out with Diderot, as he fell out with virtually everyone he ever met. Rousseau was also, as is frequently overlooked, quite profoundly misogynistic, even by the wretched standards of the eighteenth century. For Rousseau, women, who 'are the sex that ought to obey', could not be citizens; instead, their place was in the domestic sphere. On the other hand, Rousseau was one of the few major thinkers of the eighteenth century who wasn't virulently anti-Semitic—few *philosophes*, radical or more conservative, extended their liberal-mindedness to European Jews, but Rousseau did, contrarian to the last.

Rousseau's own philosophy was fundamentally anti-Enlightenment: far from celebrating reason, he believed it was the entire problem for humankind and that we'd all been better off in a blissful pre-reason state of nature. In place of reason—the blight that had corrupted humankind—Rousseau championed *feeling*. Patriotism and religion, and one's own emotions, were to be preferred over philosophy; the humble wisdom of the peasantry over the claims of 'physicists, geometricians, chemists, astronomers'. Rousseau, too, had had enough of experts. 'Why should we build our happiness on the opinions of others, when we can find it in our own hearts?' Rousseau said.

> Let us leave to others the task of instructing mankind in their duty, and confine ourselves to the discharge of our own. We have no occasion for greater knowledge than this. Virtue! sublime science of simple minds, are such industry and preparation needed if we are to know you? Are not your principles graven on every heart? Need we do more, to learn your laws, than examine ourselves, and listen to the voice of conscience, when the passions are silent?

Notice how individualistic his celebration of emotion is, even as it lauds the common sense of the peasantry? Not for Rousseau the path to knowledge through the learning and reason of others. Rather, true wisdom is found through examining *one's own feelings*.

But while Rousseau's elevation of feeling inspired an entire movement, Romanticism, his contempt for reason was all the more important given his political philosophy. Rousseau was a democrat, but hated the idea of any sort of *representative* democracy—he believed in a direct, authoritarian democracy in which representatives of the people would be constantly constrained and monitored for any deviation from the popular will, and any disruptive ideas shut down as quickly as possible, not by debate and argument but by censorship. Those who disagreed with the common consensus must be—to use Rousseau's own phrase—'forced to be free', and there must be strong censorship to prevent the common, feeling-based consensus being subjected to criticism. Like the early Reformers who put to death those who deviated from their teachings, Rousseau wanted it both ways—you were to look in your own heart for wisdom, but if the wisdom you found there didn't accord with other people's, you wouldn't be allowed to explain it.

So Rousseau didn't merely propose a dichotomy between the reason of the *philosophes* and the emotional truth of the common people, but argued that the former must be forcibly suppressed by the latter for the common good. Absolutist monarchs had long censored and suppressed philosophers but Rousseau was now doing it in the name of the emotional sovereignty of the ordinary Frenchman. Rousseau's system was an Enlightenment world turned upside down: the rationalists, the *philosophes*, were the domineering and out-of-touch elite, not restless minds whose rigorous thinking undermined fragile *ancien régimes*. The 'physicists, geometricians, chemists, astronomers' were not soldiers in a war of liberation from superstition, clerical tyranny and monarchical and aristocratic rule, but enemies of the people, the exemplars of how it had all gone wrong for mankind once man (Rousseau would never have regarded women as in any way representative of humanity) began to reason.

Unsurprisingly, it was Rousseau who was the dominant philosophical influence on the Jacobins during the French Revolution: they, too, saw reason as a corruption of the simple wisdom of the labouring classes—wisdom as interpreted, of course, by the Jacobins and their supporters, the *sans-culottes* of Paris. Those *philosophes* still alive by the time of the Terror were executed or forced into hiding, demonstrating exactly the kind of censorship Rousseau must have had in mind in *On The Social Contract*.

Rousseau's philosophy of suppressing reason in the name of the emotional truth of the masses places him at the start of an intellectual tradition that leads deep into twentieth-century (and twenty-first-century) fascism, but also continues to echo in every denialist who insists that 'experts' defy common sense and fail to grasp the essential truths known to every ordinary person. Such people are the deformed descendants of the individualism of the Reformation, but the true children of the anti-rationalism of Rousseau.

Rousseau's writings reflect a profound fear of the *philosophes*, a near-hysteric rejection of their entire world view. Due to his congenital incapacity to form lasting friendships and his seething hatred of women, Rousseau lived as both an intellectual and social outsider for most of his life. His philosophy reflects alienation and hostility to what he saw as an intellectual group that rejected him. In an insightful 2016 article in *The New Yorker*, 'How Rousseau Predicted Trump', writer Pankaj Mishra identified the strands in Rousseau's that anticipated Trump and the political climate exploited by him, particularly around the importance of fear, and his resentment of what we now call 'elites'.

> ... because Rousseau derived his ideas from intimate experiences of fear, confusion, loneliness, and loss, he connected easily with people who felt excluded. Periwigged men in Paris salons, Tocqueville once lamented, were 'almost totally removed from practical life' and worked 'by the light of reason alone'. Rousseau, on the other hand, found a responsive

echo among people making the traumatic transition from traditional to modern society—from rural to urban life.

The point is well made, given the attempt by the fake populists to exploit the fears of those feeling disempowered by economic and political change, who feel like outsiders in their own society. Trump, Pauline Hanson and other far-right figures appeal to those making the transition from a traditional industrial economy to a globalised, information-based economy. It's not the end of the Enlightenment that they represent, but an irrational anti-elitism that was provoked by and simultaneous with the Enlightenment. And the individualism it draws upon has roots that reach even deeper into the fertile soil of Western intellectual history, back 500 years to Wittenberg.

PART 4

THE INTERNET—WEAPON OF MASS DISRUPTION

Do people living through times of rapid change—even revolutionary change—know it? If you're in the middle of a violent political revolution, obviously yes. And these days, courtesy of adjective inflation, pretty much everything is 'revolutionary'. But what about living through, say, an economic revolution? Did English people in the late eighteenth or early nineteenth centuries think they were seeing an industrial revolution? Did people in the first third of the sixteenth century realise they were witnessing a religious and political revolution that would reshape Europe?[28] Were people in the middle of the twentieth century aware they were surrounded by and participating in a mass-media revolution?

---

28 And problematically, back then, 'revolution' was used in its literal sense, meaning to turn 360 degrees back to a starting point.

These terms tend to get applied later, after the fact, when we have a clearer idea of the dramatic long-term consequences of what at the time might have seemed to be unconnected events. The pace of change can make assessment difficult—most of us, even journalists, are poor at comparing how things were, say, ten years ago, because we're too busy leading our lives, raising our kids, doing our jobs.

It was clear back in the 1990s that the internet was going to lead to dramatic economic and cultural change. But what that change would be wasn't clear, and a lot of rubbish was written, both by internet evangelists and critics, about the wonderful/frightening things that might happen. As it turned out, the impacts of the internet *were* and *are* revolutionary, but often in ways that no one predicted, and that we're still trying to understand and measure. The mass-media age of the mid twentieth century needed a genuinely innovative and original thinker to shift the focus away from media content to the impacts of media itself, and to redefine media more broadly. Alas, there's been no Marshall McLuhan for the digital age—perhaps there couldn't be one anyway, given how fragmented our mediascape is now compared to the media in which McLuhan was ubiquitous in the 1960s. But the fact that, fifty years on, we're still looking to McLuhan for insights into what the internet is doing to us and our culture shows how we've struggled to comprehend the disruption and dislocation caused by the internet—and how it has interacted with the disruptions of neoliberalism and politics to maximise their impacts.

No biggie, but the internet is changing your brain right now

While neoliberalism was changing our economies and social relations, governments were infantilising themselves, and political parties were increasing the gap between the governors and the governed, the greatest technological change in history was well underway. It was messing with our heads, and with pretty much everything else as well. It's the biggest thing to happen in generations and we're living through it.

The internet has been the subject of much panic over the last decade. If there's a social problem, it will be blamed on the internet. Allegedly, it encourages suicide, makes us dumber, incites incivility, encourages violence toward women (because there was never any of *that* before the internet), enables gambling and other forms of antisocial behaviour, corrupts young people and wrecks relationships.

As anyone with even a nodding acquaintance with social history knows, most of these charges have been levelled not merely at previous generations of media technologies but at all kinds of cultural innovations. Socrates was executed for corrupting the youth of Athens. Reading gave the poor ideas above their station. The waltz was banned in the early nineteenth century because it led to promiscuity. Radio programs caused juvenile delinquency. Television made us all dumber and anti-social. Video games desensitised us to violence. Rap music—remember all the ills rap music was ushering in, just like rock'n'roll before it? As each new phenomenon emerged that could be blamed for social problems, the previous one promptly vanished from the list of concerns. No one complains about the waltz anymore, with the exception of people who buy their mothers André Rieu CDs.

Once we get past the urge to blame the internet for every social ill, we can begin the more fruitful discussion of how the internet, like *all* media, changes us, both in terms of our interactions with each other and, separately, in terms of its direct impact on our brains. To illustrate that distinction, let's take the example of Marshall McLuhan's argument that the printing press led inevitably to nationalism, since it homogenised and disseminated individual national languages while simultaneously 'detribalising' society by removing orality as a key means of transferring information.

The link between the impact of printing and nationalism has been made often enough, and the importance of language in the development of nationalism is also clear, even if it is hardly the sole factor. But in addition to those social and cultural factors, McLuhan also argued that our physical and mental engagement with the printed text altered us *neurologically*. In *Understanding Media* he wrote: 'Psychically the printed book, an extension of the visual faculty, intensified perspective and the fixed point of view. Associated with the visual stress on point of view and the vanishing perspective there comes another illusion that space is visual, uniform and continuous. The linearity precision and uniformity of the arrangement of movable types are inseparable from these great cultural forms and innovations of Renaissance experience.'

Even if you disagree with or struggle to follow McLuhan, that media technologies affect our brains makes intuitive sense: the brain is plastic, and changes depending on how we use it, and our use of media—even using a very limited definition of media, rather than McLuhan's conception of media as anything that extends us—is one of our most regular mental activities. The internet has also developed and spread much more quickly than previous emergent media. The origin of writing is lost in the mists of history but it must have developed across civilisations and centuries; the impact of printing took decades, if not centuries, to manifest. The spread of radio and television was more rapid, and set thinkers like McLuhan in hot pursuit of how they were changing us—but they still spread relatively slowly compared to the internet, which has been widely available for barely twenty years. Luckily, the arrival of the internet has coincided with our ability to detect specific neurological changes, and behavioural studies that can examine how those changes affect us.

The most obvious and uncontroversial impact of the internet relates to memory. We remember differently now than twenty years ago—mainly we remember less, because we don't need to. Instead, we have access to a universal source of electronically stored information. Forgotten where you've seen that actor before? Look her up. Can't remember where you saw that statistic? Google it. Forgotten how to tie your bow tie because you only tie it once a year? Ah, there's that video (ahem, yes, I do that). Evidence for the impact of the internet on memory is backed up by both behavioural evidence and neuroimaging. While 'knowing' less, we are much better at knowing how and where to find information in quantities that far exceed the total of human knowledge of previous generations.

However, we've made similar shifts in our use of memory before as technologies increased our capacity to store information somewhere other than in our heads. We undoubtedly underwent the same loss of memory when writing began supplanting orality, albeit without hysterical articles about how clay tablets were ruining your child's brain and putting poets who could memorise thousands of lines of verse out of work.

Other neurological and psychological impacts of the internet are harder to pin down (and how you'd test for McLuhan's linearity is anyone's guess). A common claim is that the internet has reduced our capacity for concentration, since we're now trained to seek constant stimuli online. Hard evidence that schoolchildren now struggle to concentrate is limited, but teachers report that this is the case (while also believing the overall impact of the internet on education is a positive one). However there is solid evidence, both self-reported via surveys and from more objective sources, that many adults now struggle to pay attention to tasks for an extended period without being distracted (and, indeed, I checked Twitter halfway through writing that sentence). One verifiable piece of data is that we now spend less time on, and read less of, each web page we visit. There's an argument that this is a positive; that even if highly distracted we're now able to multitask more effectively, which potentially make us more productive. However, some psychologists dispute this, saying there's a cognitive cost every time we switch to a different task, and that multitasking and constant exposure to information makes us more stressed.

Apart from changes to our memory process and capacity for extended concentration, what else do we know about what the internet is doing to our brains? Social media, the apps we use online and some of the most commonly used web applications, are purposefully designed to take advantage of an addictive cycle of cue, action and reward: we're constantly fed 'rewards' in the form of social interactions or virtual currencies to keep us engaged—and producing information that can be used to shape how we are advertised to. And the cues are particularly effective when we're lonely or bored or unhappy or angry—especially social media, which is good at provoking

outrage and encouraging users to participate by venting anger/
devising an insult/offering a *bon mot*.

This is much the same cycle as the cue-routine-reward
process that forms habits in us—and understandably, because
the people manufacturing social media platforms, apps and
websites want us to become habituated to using them. This is
why we're glued to our phones so much now, at the expense
of face-to-face interaction: they are literally devices of habit,
or often addiction, that provide us with a stream of tiny hits of
pleasure in the form of ego boosts or some form of pseudo-
asset, in exchange for our time and privacy.

What about the relationship between spending more time
alone and interacting more via a screen, and communication
skills and empathy? Studies show there is evidence of a fall in
empathy in recent years among US college students—with
the caveat that the decline predates the internet, but *accelerates*
after its widespread adoption. If the evidence of psychological
effects is strong, it's less clear exactly *why* it happens. Many
suggest anonymity is key: being able to express ourselves online
without fear of it being linked to our real-world identity is
judged to encourage the worst in humankind.

This isn't something peculiar to the internet; anonymity
has always both encouraged participation in public debate, and
lowered the standard of it. Political discourse in the United
States has been pulled into the gutter by Trump, but he's not
the first to do so by a long stretch. The founding fathers, such
as Thomas Jefferson, Alexander Hamilton and John Adams,
vilified each other via pseudonyms and proxies in the 1790s.
Jefferson paid for a newspaper to attack George Washington
while serving as Washington's Secretary of State (he even leaked
cabinet documents). The same attack-dog newspaper called

Adams an hermaphrodite and Hamilton corrupt and treasonous, and accused both Hamilton and Washington of wanting to establish a monarchy. Hamilton anonymously revealed that Jefferson had sexual relationships with his slaves; Jefferson's proxy revealed Hamilton's own affair. Hamilton wrote of the 'great and intrinsic defects' in the character of Adams, who was head of Hamilton's party. Back then, it was the leaders' comments, not the readers' comments, that were the problem.

Evidence of the neurological and psychological impacts of internet use will grow over time; the first generation that has always had access to the internet is only just now coming to maturity. And our own understanding of internet use has evolved as well—for years, critics of social media complained that it replaced 'authentic' real-world interaction with 'inauthentic' virtual interaction. Given the universality of internet use now, we're more likely to understand that people are engaging in online and offline interactions for the same reasons—friendship, commerce, relationships, finding a partner, entertainment, civic engagement. The internet isn't distinct from real life, but part of it, and vice versa.

The greater access to information afforded by the internet is a positive, except, of course, that it has also given us many more things to worry about, particularly when social media arrived and gave us raw, uncensored access to news events from around the world. Compare the disruptive events of 1980, the election of Ronald Reagan[29], and 2016, the election of Donald

---

29 This is not to suggest a comparison between Reagan and Trump beyond the apparent dislocation to political business as usual that both represented. As it turned out, Reagan, with his massive increase in government spending and aggressive foreign policy, was more like LBJ or Nixon than anything in the current Republican Party.

Trump: Reagan's win received some limited coverage in a country like Australia, but it was impossible to closely follow that campaign from outside the United States. In contrast, anyone with an internet connection can now consume as much coverage of US elections, and especially presidential races, as they can take—they can watch debates live, they can read US media coverage, they can participate in online fora. In short, interested foreigners could, and did, consume more coverage of presidential elections than the majority of Americans themselves.

Much greater exposure to the 2016 election led to much greater emotional investment, particularly for progressives, and many conservatives, mortified by the prospect of a Trump victory. But in the same way, social media is very good at bringing all kinds of conflicts, atrocities and disasters into our lives that we would otherwise hear little or nothing about. This gives us an endless succession of tragedies that distress us, enrage us, worry us, or give us a general sense that the world is going to hell, none of which we would even have heard of twenty years ago. I'm convinced the psychological impact of this is significantly underrated: social media delivers a pervasive sense that *everything is shit*. It also misleads us: it's easy to see the world as a place filled with violence, hate, stupidity and mediocrity because it's served up every minute in your Twitter feed, but that obscures the fact that humanity as a whole is doing better than at any time in its history in terms of living standards, health, education and longevity. We're just much better informed about the awful lives of most of the rest of the planet than we have ever been before.

To come back to McLuhan: if the arrival of printing led to epochal changes in Western history (nationalism, the

Reformation, the development of centralised states) as well as profound changes in how Western people thought about and saw the world—if it so profoundly changed the Western mind and Western history—how much change is the internet now creating around us on a much shorter timescale? How different are our brains becoming when bombarded with a constant supply of things to worry about, and an addictive cycle of engagement and reward, from the black rectangle in our pocket that never leaves us? Only our descendants may be able to fully answer that question.

Joining imagined communities

Until the 1990s, humans' direct social relationships were limited to their homes, to their local communities, to their workplaces. We could travel the world, we could watch news from another country, we could phone foreign relatives and friends, but our social lives were mostly lived in a world defined and limited by physical space in a way little changed since the dawn of humankind. But the online communities that emerged in the 1990s could be regional, national or international in character. They were initially on a limited scale—more like a text version of a telephone party line than what we think of as the internet. These bulletin boards, newsgroups, email discussion lists and, later, blogs, were never mass scale, and accessing them and participating in them often required specialist skills, meaning the communities that were formed—even the biggest—were limited in size.

In the 2000s, however, social media platforms emerged that enabled users to connect on a mass scale, dramatically increasing the size and range of online communities, and providing multiple platforms for different kinds of social tasks and different users. You could now choose the community you wanted to participate in. And no matter how unusual you might believe your identity or interest to be, there's a page, a group and an FAQ for you only a google away.

And after geography had been defeated—the communities you participated in were no longer just a product of where you were physically located—smart phones and internet-enabled tablets meant the community you chose to participate in could go anywhere with you, never further away than a glance at your phone. Participating in online communities no longer required being stationary, or in the home or workplace, or 'dialling up'—they were always available and wherever you were.

That we can now choose with whom we form communities plainly has positive and negative consequences. People once isolated by geography, disability, sexual orientation or other physical or social restrictions can connect with others and form communities around shared interests or lifestyles. As anyone who was in a long-distance relationship before the internet can attest, staying in touch with loved ones is now far cheaper and easier than in the days of expensive phone calls and constant letters. Inevitably, too, people willing to harm others, who before the internet might have struggled to connect with other like-minded criminals, can also now form communities. Paedophiles, terrorists, anti-vaxxers and Nickelback fans can use the internet to seek each other out and link up in ways impossible before the internet, greatly extending their capacity to do harm.

Not merely do online platforms enable connectedness between people, they disable the control formerly exerted by

the mass media, which was once the only means for the dissemi-
nation of disaffection beyond fringe print media. Consider the
shift in the operation of One Nation between the late 1990s
and 2017. To build her movement in 1997, Pauline Hanson had
to travel around regional Australia, organising events for the
marginalised, the disaffected and the racist. Much of the media
demonised Hanson, which may have improved her image for
many people, but nonetheless meant her message was filtered
through a mainstream media view. But now Facebook delivers
hundreds of thousands of people to her for the direct dissemi-
nation of her views; Facebook provides an online community
for her supporters to interact, encouraging and validating each
other, their hatreds, and their enthusiasm for Hanson.

The analogue media world was a hub-and-spoke model,
with media organisations controlling the flow of information
to the rest of us. Whatever its (many) flaws, the advantage of
that model was that it provided a relatively unified space made
up of a limited number of television and radio channels and
newspapers. Communities, cities and nations saw and heard
similar media and read the same newspapers. There was an
agreed set of facts even amid partisan division. Readers and
audiences were exposed to the same—limited—number of
views in the media. We were thus a community that shared the
same facts about the world, however selective or filtered those
facts may have been.

That controlled, hub-and-spoke media has been replaced
with a network of media nodes in which the people formerly
known as the audience—a passive community that absorbed
whatever was fed to it—not merely access any content they
want, but produce their own. The internet fragmented the
unified media space of the analogue era. People no longer

consume the same media; they can pick and choose their sources of information like they pick their own communities—indeed, often those self-selected communities became key channels for news. The very connectedness that brought people together online also guided them into clusters—or to use a more common term, echo chambers—that share little with other clusters online.

Political scientist and historian Benedict Anderson described the nation-states that emerged in early modern Europe as 'imagined communities' created by the unifying media of print. In contrast, the 'imagined communities' of the twenty-first century reflect a fragmenting digital media. They're more selective, and exclusionary, because they reflect cultural, linguistic and social commonalities rather than geographical ones, powered by individual choice and a technology that had fundamentally altered the nature of human connection. At the very moment neoliberalism was generating a backlash across the West, creating a hunger for non-economic forms of identity, nationalism and tribality, the internet was giving people an unprecedented ability to connect with communities of their own choosing.

Dead set on disruption

While the internet is rewiring our heads and fundamentally altering the way we connect with each other—big enough societal changes on their own—it is also inflicting massive economic change, and that process, if anything, is accelerating. Technology such as automation has driven other kinds of economic change for centuries, but the internet's capacity for disintermediation is intensely disruptive even for industries where automation has traditionally played a role. Any industry that is based on acting as an intermediary between customers and services or products is vulnerable to digital disruption.

Retail is the most obvious example: in the United States, Amazon and other online retailers have driven a massive increase in online shopping and corresponding fall in real-world shopping. By one calculation, around 200,000 Americans lost their jobs in retail between 2013 and 2017, with layoffs recently accelerating, not slowing down. The primary victims are traditional, especially mid- and low-market, department stores, as anyone who has been into one in the United States in recent years will know. And the ultimate symbol of US retail, the shopping mall, is also under siege—the number of malls in the United States once topped 5000, now it's down to around 1000 and falling, creating opportunities for zombie apocalypse filmmakers and not much else.

Not all of that has been because of e-commerce: US consumers have shifted part of their spending away from goods to services—particularly eating out, but also holidays and online services. This is a widespread phenomenon not merely in the United States, but in Australia, the United Kingdom, Europe and even in India—it's called 'the experience economy', whereby we're spending more on doing things than owning things. Why have consumers changed in this way? There are various explanations (millennials, inevitably, have been blamed) but one plausible argument is that the rise of social media, and our constant exposure to other peoples' experiences via Facebook, Instagram and the like, encourages people to want to do the same—to travel, to eat out, and put the results into their social media feeds. The cue–reward process of addiction on social media has had real-world consequences for the way we spend our money.

So one way or another, traditional retail is being hammered by the internet—although that's not necessarily a bad thing in terms of employment. E-commerce creates jobs too, and Amazon's warehouses actually pay better than Walmart, one of corporate America's most repugnant major employers. Consumers are still spending, which is the key thing—they're just not spending in traditional retail.

Postal services are another example of how the internet disrupts, but doesn't necessarily destroy. Postal companies, whether government owned or private, have been smashed by the internet: people rarely exchange letters now and companies and governments are now billing online. The once profitable Australia Post descended into loss in 2015, slashing thousands of jobs and reducing mail delivery services. But logistics companies (often owned by the same postal companies, like StarTrack in Australia) have seen significant growth as the task of storing and delivering e-commerce freight has dramatically increased.

The internet disrupts in this way because e-commerce has lower costs than the intermediaries it challenges—including lower entry costs, meaning intermediary industries that have gouged customers suddenly face greater competition. Australian retailers, for example, exploited Australia's distance from world markets for generations to rip off consumers and other businesses, until online retail allowed Australians to shop overseas.[30]

---

30 Typically, the response of Australia's retailers was to demand that the government punish consumers by imposing taxes on internet purchases.

Some of those intermediary costs aren't monopolistic rents, however, but the regulatory requirements of a civilised society—minimum wages and other labour protections, environmental protections, safety standards, insurance. 'Gig economy' companies like Uber base their business model on removing these protections and standards from the cost base of the service they provide by pretending their employees are contractors. That's why they bitterly resist any effort to treat their relationship with their employees as like that of an employer—even in a labour market as hostile to workers as the United States, being an employee is better than being a contractor, especially when it comes to health insurance.

This becomes a classic corporation–union philosophical split: employers claim the gig economy and casualisation is being driven by workers themselves, who want greater freedom and flexibility, whereas unions portray it as a corporate assault on job security, and blame it for wage stagnation and lower consumer spending. Conservative governments in Australia, encouraged by employer groups, have long pandered to the myth of the independent contractor—the idea that all workers really want to be freelance agents, proto-small-businessmen and women selling their skills in a free market unencumbered by labour laws, unions or other 'red tape'. In practice, instead of unleashing the animal spirits of rugged individualists, this *Homo economicus* fantasy has led to a wave of sham contracting, where workers—often foreign workers with poor language skills—are classified as contractors and employed without basic protections or entitlements. As disintermediation spreads, the pressure to turn employees into contractors will grow ever greater.

We earlier looked at the claim that technology—primarily automation—threatens mass unemployment. The internet has long been regarded as a levelling technology—lowering barriers to entry, reducing transaction costs, giving people greater access to services, information and markets, especially in developing countries. And while there's evidence that the internet has been an important tool for economic development, with information and communications technology strongly linked to accelerated economic growth in developing countries in Africa, there are downsides to the economic impacts of the internet.

As we noted in relation to neoliberalism, market concentration, while ostensibly inimical to the precepts of market economics, has become one of its fundamental features, an outcome that has shifted resources away from workers toward corporations, increased inequality and delivered ever more political power to multinationals. The internet has exacerbated this trend to huge corporations. Five of the six largest companies in the world by market capitalisation are US tech firms—Apple, Alphabet (Google), Microsoft, Amazon and Facebook (the fifth largest is Warren Buffett's Berkshire Hathaway). Ten of the top twenty companies are tech or telecommunications companies. Google and Facebook both dominate their industries and, like Apple and Amazon, have leveraged their dominance into other sectors. The internet amplifies network effects so that the more a platform grows, the more reason there is to use it, and the more damage it can inflict on competitors, consumers and even political processes.

The internet also gives greater power to employers in an era when anti-union and pro-corporation policymaking has already shifted the power balance in favour of employers and away from workers. It enables radically greater surveillance of employees both within and outside the workplace and, as mobile phones and email have been doing for over twenty years, lets employers encroach on staff out of hours; even relatively junior employees are now expected to be reachable all the time and respond overnight. Ironically, consistent with the tendency of futurists and tech people to portray everything in a utopian newspeak, much of this is framed as 'empowering employees' rather than the reality, which is tethering them to employers ever more closely.

The growing reliance of both governments and corporations on algorithms for carrying out tasks once performed by humans is another mechanism for increasing, rather than reducing, inequality. The move from humans to AI doesn't remove bias in the activities of a system it merely shifts the source of bias from the human operators to the humans who write the algorithms. It's bad enough that Facebook's algorithms were designed to serve up entirely fictional news as equally authentic as legitimate news sites during Trump's run for the presidency. But algorithms can inflict disproportionate damage on low-income earners in other contexts: algorithms that delete the applications of job seekers because they have an arrest record, even if the arrest was the result of police harassment; algorithms that are based on flawed 'personality tests' conducted by employers; algorithms that lower people's credit scores if their mobile phone shows they're connected to other people with poor credit histories; even healthcare algorithms based on data from white males that lead to poorer outcomes for people who aren't white males.

In 2017, Google went to the extent of releasing a PR video explaining how bias can creep into AI and what it was trying to do to prevent it from happening. But one of the worst forms of bias is the one that's hardest to remove: the tech sector (in both the United States and Australia) is overwhelmingly male, and in some areas has a culture that is deeply toxic to and intolerant of women and ethnic minorities. In Australia, female participation in the tech sector is now less than a quarter and has been falling in recent years, as has the number of girls and women studying science, technology, engineering and mathematics subjects that act as precursors to tech careers. As more and more products and services designed by male tech engineers become crucial to society, so too do the biases of those men become embedded in society.

Disintermediating the media

The business model of the media is—or was—to make money from connecting content creators with paying audiences, and to sell audiences to advertisers by aggregating those audiences using content. Both of these processes proved highly amenable to disruption by the internet.

Unusually, it was the audience itself that initially disrupted the business of connecting content creators to people willing to pay for content, by taking advantage of digitisation and the internet to share content among themselves rather than paying anti-competitive intermediaries. The fact that the intermediary companies like music and movie companies refused to allow access to content with the prices and conditions consumers wanted provided a considerable incentive for this. Indeed, many content companies refused to make content available in some markets at all, and then complained when consumers used the internet to share the content among themselves.

The music and movie industries, however, managed to survive. Despite predictions from the industries that the cost of file sharing would run into the trillions of dollars, both the music and film industries are now enjoying massive profits. Having finally worked out that consumers will readily pay for content if it's provided on reasonable terms, the music industry enjoyed its most profitable year in a decade in 2017 courtesy of streaming, which delivered double-digit revenue growth in both 2016 and 2017. Better still, live-music ticket sales are at all-time highs. Similarly, the movie industry is racking up record profits globally—movie revenue in 2017 was the highest ever. Sometimes disruption does not equal death.

Disruption of the other media business model—aggregating and selling audiences to advertisers—was slower to hit, but has over the longer term proved far more damaging. Mass media operate by drawing large audiences together for entertainment or information so that they can be advertised to. As with movies and music, once audiences could access content more cheaply and effectively elsewhere, they began to leave, making mass platforms less appealing to advertisers. That's been the fate of television broadcasters in Australia, who have lost audiences to content delivered online (whether paid for or for free). Television broadcasters still remain the only means of aggregating Australians in their hundreds of thousands, but viewing audiences are now consuming content via a variety of online platforms, particularly US-based platforms that can deliver the prestige drama that Australian networks no longer make (Australian free-to-air TV now relies more heavily on cheap'n'cheerful reality shows rather than local drama). High-value sports content is also starting to move online as sports realise they can make more money selling their product directly to consumers, rather than allowing media companies to clip the ticket on the way through.

But news media have it much worse: not merely are their consumers obtaining content from elsewhere, thus reducing news media's appeal to advertisers, but advertisers are abandoning them for a better way of reaching audiences. The ad revenue that once funded journalism has shifted to more efficient intermediaries that have massively lower costs and can tailor advertising to individuals in a way no mass medium could possibly hope to. Not merely do Google (via search) and Facebook (via social media) attract mass audiences, but those companies collect vast amounts of information on every single audience member, enabling them to offer targeted advertising aimed at individuals. Compared to traditional media, where you have to spend millions of dollars to advertise to a mass audience in which only a fraction of viewers might be interested in your product, targeting individuals that have already been profiled as likely to be interested in whatever you're selling radically reduces the cost, and increases the chances of a sale, per ad.

And that's separate from the impact of specific online platforms that target bespoke markets—real estate, trading, recruitment, dating—that were traditional revenue sources for newspapers via classified advertising, but have been subject to the same process of disintermediation seen in other industries. In Australia, the major real estate sites are owned or controlled by the remaining major newspaper companies, Fairfax and News Corp, meaning they haven't lost access to this flow of revenue entirely—although they face investor pressure to spin these successful units off from loss-making newspaper assets. But the overall collapse in ad revenue means media companies are left trying to convince people to pay for news and current affairs, despite the fact that many companies offer it for free (as do government-funded broadcasters in the United Kingdom, western European countries, Canada and Australia).

And while journalists and editors and producers may lament the collapse of the traditional funding model for journalism, it's worthwhile to stop and ask why this is a greater concern than any other disruption caused by the internet, or by automation—or by any previous technological advance. Journalists in Australia's mainstream media cheered on the wave of micro-economic reform in Australia that ended protectionism, accelerated the decline of manufacturing and sent hundreds of thousands of Australian workers to the dole queues, especially during the recession of the early 1990s. Now that it is the media's turn to suffer the cold grip of market forces, so what? After all, the end of protectionism was an economic success in Australia. We might have lost manufacturing jobs, but the economy prospered nonetheless. Perhaps we should be as relaxed about the long-term consequences for the media.

One answer, of course, is that the media is 'different' or 'special'. This is the argument used by *every* industry demanding protection and assistance—that there's something unique about an industry because it generates additional benefits beyond the purely economic. Advocates of automotive manufacturing used to maintain it was a 'strategic industry' because, to quote one former industry minister, if you can build a car you can build a fighter jet (in fact, despite the reputation of Australia's defence industry for cost overruns, delays and inferior products, we probably could have done better than Lockheed's F-35). More recently, protection advocates have deployed 'security' as a latter-day version of 'strategic'—we need to protect local industries for food security, or national security, or energy security, or resource security. So claiming media is 'special' requires a demonstration that the media really does have some additional benefit beyond the economic, one so important it can't be provided any other way. Information security, perhaps? News security?

But, as a society, we already treat the media as special and have done so for generations—the ABC is publicly funded (as is SBS Radio; the less said about the pseudo-commercial SBS TV, the better) and to the eternal fury of its far-right critics and News Corp, the ABC is far and away the most trusted media outlet in the country, despite its many problems. Unless you're an ideologue or work for the Institute of Public Affairs, it's universally accepted that Australia needs a genuinely independent public broadcaster because there are things that even a healthy commercial media (which we haven't had for a long time) can't provide. The two best examples are genuinely independent high-quality news and current affairs, and children's programming that isn't primarily a vehicle to sell rubbish to kids.

And broadcasting in Australia, as in most countries, has traditionally been seen as requiring particularly stringent regulatory requirements because of its influence—it has additional regulation beyond simple competition regulation, designed to ensure diversity and certain standards, including local content. So for better or worse, we've been treating the media as 'special' for a long time, for reasons most of us agree with. But in dramatically curbing advertising revenue for the media, the internet has curtailed its viability and thereby undermined the media's capacity to produce one of its 'special' non-economic benefits—public interest journalism, which is expensive to produce and generates little revenue on its own, especially in a market the size of Australia.

Public interest journalism is crucial in a democracy—it's one of the 'rules and conventions' that has allowed us to maintain Keynes' crust of civilisation, because it checks the powerful and prevents their use of the polity for their own purposes at the expense of the public. No amount of institutional regulation and independent oversight can replicate the effect on public life of a free press. And politicians would never allow such rigorous regulation or oversight anyway: witness the longstanding resistance of federal major party politicians to countenance a federal anti-corruption commission. Without the work of Kate McClymont over the last 15 years at Fairfax, serious corruption within the NSW government and within the NSW Labor Party would likely have remained unrevealed. Widespread lawbreaking across corporate Australia and the slack response of the alleged corporate regulator ASIC would probably have remained hidden but for the work of her colleague Adele Ferguson. The consistent pattern of major misconduct in Australia in recent years has been regulatory action and political response—if any—only following on the heels of the exposure of that misconduct by the media.

That kind of journalism, all the more necessary as governments have handed more power to corporations and become ever more distant from voters, is becoming rarer and rarer in Australia. The 'replacement media' of Google and Facebook, which have hoovered up the revenue that once flowed to media outlets, are incapable of producing it. Indeed, they are unable to even tell the difference between journalism as we understand it—something that reflects actual events—and propaganda disguised to resemble news. When your 'editor' is an algorithm rather than a thinking human, it is inevitable that the product will be propaganda of the kind that potentially played a role in the election of Donald Trump.

For all that Facebook and Google plead they are now working hard to more effectively filter out propaganda, these problematic consequences of the decline of traditional news-gathering media will only grow worse. Quality public interest journalism requires not merely the financial resources for a top-flight journalist to work for an extended period on complex issues—only some of which will produce stories—but also the financial wherewithal to fight off legal challenges. Citizen journalists and bloggers don't have the capacity to fight suppression orders, defamation suits, FOI appeals and litigation by powerful interests, all intended to prevent the public from learning what they are doing. And the absence of such journalism isn't noticed by the public—the powerful and the corrupt are simply able to hide more successfully from scrutiny.

It's not merely investigative journalism that we're losing, it's quality public-policy journalism. Major newspapers used to employ more journalists who specialised in one or two 'rounds' and therefore became knowledgeable about, and had relevant contacts for, particular areas of policy. Increasingly, journalists have to cover multiple rounds, as well as provide content for multiple platforms and to multiple deadlines, diminishing the time and effort they can devote to providing an informed analysis of policy issues—a space that political spinners and PR people are happy to fill. Readers now get poorer quality reportage and analysis from hard-pressed journalists—often more junior journalists than in the past, more experienced journalists having taken redundancy packages and headed for greener pastures (like public relations).

Diminished revenue has forced some media companies to alter their editorial stance to pander to their remaining readership. The best example is *The Australian*, which is now primarily read by elderly white people—one of the last groups in the community to actually buy newspapers. Over the last fifteen years, the paper—always conservative—has become ever more shrilly partisan and denialist, to match its readers. While this undermines the quality of public debate, it makes perfect commercial sense for News Corp to try to hang on to the one readership still buying its product. It's also firmly in the tradition of the US media of the nineteenth century, and the United Kingdom today, where partisan newspapers have been a central and accepted feature of the media.

The result, however, is to strengthen the echo chamber effect created by the fragmentation of media in the digital age. In addition to cutting resourcing for the funding of public interest journalism, as we've seen, the internet facilitates consumers selecting their own sources of information and entertainment, meaning we're less likely to see stories that don't fit with our world view, either because they're not covered, or they don't receive the same prominence, or they are reported through a filter.

And while the internet can be blamed for giving consumers the tools to filter the information coming to them, the traditional media isn't blameless. In fact, it is the media that has trained its audiences to regard news as just another product packaged, marketed and sold in a competitive marketplace.

While newspapers are currently in terminal decline, newspaper circulation across Western countries has been steadily contracting since the 1950s. The obvious cause to suspect is television, the arrival of which coincided with the start of the decline (although newspaper-advertising *revenue* continued to grow, riding the postwar surge in prosperity in Western countries). Television had a clear advantage over newspapers and radio in being able to present news with video, an even more powerful advantage once colour television arrived.[31] And while the presentation of news has always been the product of editorial, political and social ideology, television news, far more potently than its competitors, was able to present news as *narrative*. This was partly a result of the nature of the medium—a newspaper is a set of disconnected stories and views, whereas television news is presented as a coherent suite of individual stories, all guided by an authoritative newsreader speaking directly to the viewer. But it also reflected a decision by television news producers to rely more heavily on narrative.

There's nothing innately wrong with using narrative to convey news and current affairs. Which is more effective: a dry recitation of facts, or an emotionally engaging presentation that delivers the same facts in a way that elicits greater attention from the viewer? Narrative is a core element of the journalistic craft.

The story of television news, however, has been one of training audiences to see news and current affairs as packaged emotional stories rather than as an insight into domestic and world events. The bulk of this predates the internet, and began with the transformation of television news from a

---

31 For people under 40, audio-visual content like television and movies used to only be in black and white, and not in the crisp, cool black and white of music videos, but in crappy, low-def.

public service function that, in the 1950s and 1960s, attracted little advertising revenue, to a key source of revenue for television networks in the 1970s. By that time, long gone were the days when the head of CBS would declare he could rely on Jack Benny to subsidise quality news—the newsroom was now expected to contribute to the bottom line of networks. News ratings thus became crucial, encouraging a move away from hard news and reportage to more narrative-based, personality-based, emotion-based current affairs programs and more sensationalist news coverage, that relied heavily on the adage 'If it bleeds it leads'. That line is attributed variously to legendary US journalists or McLuhan, but it appears to have originated in the late 1960s or 1970s. By the mid 1970s, the commercialisation of news programming was sufficiently well-known in the US to be the subject of an award-winning film, *Network*, which would have made no sense at all to audiences ten years prior.

With the sale of television networks to non-media proprietors in the 1980s in both the United States and Australia, cost-cutting and the demand for economies of scale loomed ever larger in news media. Ironically this saw, in many cases, *more* news and current affairs programming, as networks sought to extract as much content as possible out of an expensive area of production. In Australia, reflecting US trends, current affairs programming shifted away from hard news to soft, lifestyle-oriented narratives, brilliantly parodied in *Frontline* in the mid 1990s. In Canada, the shift to emotionally manipulative, ritualistic news production was likewise savaged in Ken Finkleman's hilarious *The Newsroom*. Current affairs programming—even 'hard' current affairs programs like *60 Minutes*—increasingly avoided public policy or political stories; it became rare, for example, for politicians to be interviewed on commercial current affairs programming.[32]

So the internet arrived when television had already educated viewers to understand news as a consumer product—a lifestyle accessory they could select based on personal preferences and interests. Audience were primed to assume that the selection of what facts and events were 'newsworthy', the packaging and editing of the reports, and the news program framework within which they were presented, could and should be a matter of production artifice and personal preference. We didn't abandon the belief that accuracy is important— even today, ABC television and radio remain the most trusted sources of news and current affairs for most Australians, far ahead of newspapers and commercial broadcasters. But the audience had been taught to pick and choose news programming based on its entertainment value, its packaging and its personal appeal to them.

The impact of the internet on news advertising revenue thus exacerbated long-term trends.[33] Television news resources were cut back, and the same process that had been playing out in newspapers arrived in television newsrooms—fewer journalists, fewer editors and fewer producers, all required to produce more content across more platforms. Indeed,

---

32 In recent decades, this has created a vacuum that others moved into: Jon Stewart's *Daily Show*, Stephen Colbert's *The Colbert Report*, and now John Oliver's *Last Week Tonight* all routinely offered or offer more in-depth analysis of public policy, in the guise of comedy, than the bulk of current affairs programs. In Australia, similarly, *The Project* became virtually the only commercial free-to-air television program that treated public policy seriously, again framed as light entertainment.
33 The Ten Network, which went into administration in 2017, had also been in receivership in 1990.

traditional distinctions between journalists, editors and producers began to blur as news employees were expected to prepare and film their own pieces to camera, edit them and upload them, SEO them (*i.e.* make sure they'll appear prominently in search engine results) and push them onto social media.

As with newspaper journalists, the remaining TV journalists have more to do and less time to do it, and bring less knowledge and reflection to bear on their reporting. The departure of older journalists also means a loss of long-term memory. In political coverage, this is a formula for an increased focus on what's dismissively termed 'horse-race journalism', when everything is examined through the lens of who has won and who has lost on an issue, in contrast to its policy substance. Contrary to many media critics, there's an important place for 'horse-race' analysis in political journalism—politicians and policymakers in a democracy are always functioning in a contested space and a politician who can't 'win' doesn't get the chance to implement any policy at all. But policy analysis is also crucial, and it's harder to do for journalists, especially younger, less experienced journalists who don't have the time to get across a particular policy area.

Television journalists face another challenge. Political journalism, with its reliance on talking heads, the lack of visual action, and the often complex nature of stories, can be a tough sell to news producers whose main goal is to keep viewers watching through the next commercial break. Political television journalists thus must compete with what one former head of the ABC once described to me as 'car crashes on Parramatta Road'. As television attracts fewer viewers and generates less revenue, it becomes tougher for political journalists to produce the journalism that a successful democracy needs.

Surveillance

In affording us the means to connect with one another in ways humanity has never before achieved, the internet has also exposed us to surveillance and privacy intrusion never before achieved, by both governments and corporations. People in Western societies, especially in highly intrusive states like the United Kingdom, are under greater observation than at any time in history, in ways that authorities in Stalin's Soviet Union or the East German Stasi could only have fantasised about.

Consider the extent to which others are privy to the details of our lives. With the right access, someone can work out when you wake up, because your ISP records show when you've gone online, even if not which sites you visited. They likely know how much sleep you got, because of how long you've been offline. They know what you had for breakfast because your 'rewards card' (which is actually a surveillance device that trades your information for a small amount of pseudo money) records what groceries you purchase. They know when you drive to work, because our toll roads record you, or road traffic cameras do, or police cars with automated number-plate recognition systems do, and if not that, then they can simply use the location data from your phone. They know what train you caught, if you've linked your credit card to your public transport debit card, or via the surveillance cameras linked to facial-recognition software at the station. They know what time you arrived at your office because maybe you swiped a pass there, then you logged on. Your credit card tells them where you went for lunch. They know if you went to a shopping mall, because your number plate was recorded for a parking fee and your face is recorded on cameras that are designed to track your movements from shop to shop. They can learn what you purchased online. They know where you went for a drink and whom you were with, because you posted a photo on social media, maybe with its geographical data unedited, or you tweeted about what a great place it was. They know when you're ill, because they have the metadata from your phone call to your GP. They can probably work out any health issues you have from the specialists you called. If you're active on social media, they know when you're outraged, or sad, and probably why. And they know when you went to bed, and, based on phone location data, probably who with.

Much of this information is located in different places, controlled by different laws and different people, agencies and corporations. It's also held with different levels of security, though virtually none of it is held securely. But the common theme is the great difficulty of avoiding surveillance if one is to participate in any meaningful way in twenty-first-century life—or even live in a large city. Unless you abandon a mobile phone, stick to cash in your transactions, stay off the internet and wear something that obscures your face, you can be tracked.

Better yet, the 'internet of things'—or, to use its much more apt nickname, the internet of shit—will dramatically increase surveillance. The fridge that records what's inside it. The child's toy that records your kid. The helpful virtual assistant in your phone, TV, or smart speaker, that records you. The internet-connected car that records everywhere you go (and when we finally have autonomous vehicles in the 2030s, it will be impossible not to be tracked in your vehicle). And much of this information is stored insecurely, or accessible to hackers—perhaps because you didn't bother changing the default password on your baby monitor until your toddler told you she was terrified of the strange voices she heard from it at night.[34]

Exacerbating this threat of 24/7 surveillance is the fact that the government agencies charged with protecting us from cybercrime are instead actively undermining our own cybersecurity. For years, information activists and cybersecurity specialists warned that the global spying alliance to which Australia belongs, the Five Eyes, was placing us in danger through one of their primary signals intelligence techniques: exploiting weaknesses in commonly used commercial software. According to former senior National Security Agency official Chris Inglis, that agency—which is supposed to protect US governments, companies and citizens—reports only 90 per cent of the vulnerabilities it discovers in software to the software manufacturers, so that they can fix them. The other 10 per cent it keeps to itself, with the intention of exploiting those vulnerabilities for its *other* role, that of breaking into the IT systems of America's 'enemies'.[35]

To do so, it must either develop its own 'exploit', which will use the identified flaw to gain unauthorised access to IT systems, or purchase one from the world's thriving, multibillion-dollar exploit market. In that global market, criminals, spies, police, hackers and software proprietors themselves offer information on vulnerabilities in the world's most commonly used software, and code that exploits those vulnerabilities, to obtain access to information stored in IT systems.

---

34 Yes, this has actually happened.

35 The Australian counterpart agency, the Australian Signals Directorate, has a similarly confused role, as revealed in its motto: 'Reveal their secrets, protect our own'.

Leaving this 10 per cent of vulnerabilities unreported means other, malign online actors can also exploit them. For years, cybersecurity experts warned of the risk, until 2016 when the entire troves of exploits put together by the National Security Agency and the Central Intelligence Agency to exploit software weaknesses were both stolen, placing dangerous malware in the hands of anyone who cared to use it. The result was a wave of ransomware attacks around the world in 2017, such as WannaCry—attacks that were Made in the NSA. Microsoft—the target of one of the exploits—publicly criticised that agency for failing to warn it of a weakness.

But the risk to our privacy doesn't even necessarily emanate from the spectral world of hackers and spies. In Australia, the quinquennial census has now become an extraordinary exercise in surveillance. The traditional census was problematic in terms of privacy—in effect, the government demands that you hand over highly personal information—but it was intended to be a *momentary* snapshot of your life. For the 2016 census, that changed: henceforth, the Australian Bureau of Statistics would link your name and information to a unique identifier. A permanent file of your personal information would be created that would be added to over the course of your lifetime, creating a rich, living document of personal data on every Australian that would be used by government and whatever companies the ABS sold the data to. The one-off snapshot of each citizen was to become a personal video of everyone.

Prior to 2016, the ABS had already been tracking more than one million Australians since the 2006 census, matching up information subsequently gathered in order to individually profile them. None of these people knew; the ABS did not seek their permission to assemble this life-long profile. It insisted that because the name and addresses of each person had been stripped from the data, there were no privacy implications. In fact, it's been known for decades—long before the rise of Google and the data-mining industry—how simple it is to identify individuals from ostensibly anonymous publicly generated datasets with even relatively limited information, let alone the deep dive into an individual's life that the census represents. That's why Australia's Privacy Commissioner has warned businesses about the need to treat anonymous information with the same care as personally identifiable information—because having it stolen can create the same problems.

Nor, despite the ABS's protestations, was this data safe. It would be straightforward for a future government to take the data from successive censuses and other information accumulated by the ABS, re-identify participants and use the richly detailed picture of every citizen that it provided for political purposes. More likely, the information could be stolen. In an era when not even the CIA and the NSA can keep its data secure from thieves, what hope is there for a poorly funded clutch of bureaucrats in Belconnen, ACT?

Because of digitisation and the internet, and governments' and corporations' desire for information about us, surveillance is now the background radiation of twenty-first-century life, ever-present, inescapable, penetrating into every space, subtly shaping us and our behaviour, the way we communicate and what we communicate. Rather than being a 'surveillance state', this is more accurately described as a surveillance civilisation. This, too, shapes our brains. It exacts a psychological toll, most importantly on trust, because surveillance is a solvent of trust. Detailed studies of Stasi surveillance in East Germany revealed long-lasting social impacts such as loss of trust and less social participation—as well as less innovation and poorer economic outcomes. Because Stasi surveillance was primarily via informants, it may have had particular interpersonal consequences that electronic surveillance doesn't have, but the chilling effect is the same—people are less likely to be forthcoming or open, whether surveillance is interpersonal or electronic. The steady creep of surveillance, and thus the steady shrinkage of the private sphere, that personal space in which neither government nor strangers, but only our loved ones, are welcomed, is another breach of Keynes' 'rules and conventions'. Western societies have long relied on an acceptance that governments, and certainly private companies, have no business monitoring our personal lives, our homes, our relationships, our intimate moments. We even balance some negatives—such as the inability to prevent and detect crime—against the need to protect that private sphere, because that sphere is innately valuable to civilisation, and less valuable the more that others have access to it. A 'surveillance civilisation' is in a crucial sense an oxymoron—our privacy from government monitoring is a feature of our civilisation, not a bug that must be removed by algorithms, data retention and CCTV.

Further, because mass surveillance makes everyone, in effect, a suspect, and because we know those who hold our data are unable to keep data secure, it also undermines trust in government—particularly if you're part of a community that is the target, not the beneficiary, of surveillance. And what's significant about our surveillance civilisation is that it encompasses *everyone*. Well, duh, that's the nature of mass surveillance, surely? But many groups in society are *used* to being under constant surveillance. Women, particularly, are the subject of constant scrutiny for their appearance, their behaviour and their reproductive choices, not merely by men but by other women as well (some of us have even written novels about such things). Women have always lived in a surveillance environment aimed at ensuring their compliance with social codes. The realisation that *all* of us are under constant surveillance represented an extension of this state to men as well. As Canadian writer Madeline Ashby put it so well back in 2012: 'That spirit of performativity you have about your citizenship, now? That sense that someone's peering over your shoulder, watching everything you do and say and think and choose? That feeling of being observed? It's not a new facet of life in the twenty-first century. It's what it feels like for a girl.'

That feeling has now been extended to men as well. Even white men. Even powerful white men, even the men normally doing the surveilling, the ones operating the CCTVs, the ones hacking into information systems, the ones cyberstalking, the ones rating every woman they meet on her attractiveness. That last privilege, that of the Male Gaze, has been taken away, or rather reflected back: now all of us are the object of a gaze that objectifies us, all the time. No wonder white men are angry at their loss of privilege. Now they have to endure, at least to a small degree, what women have endured for millennia—constant scrutiny and inescapable, silent, and often not-so-silent, judgement.

The result is more disempowerment: the balance of power between citizens and governments has become weighted significantly in favour of the latter, as they have accrued greater and greater powers to monitor citizens. This isn't merely thanks to the internet: the proliferation of CCTV cameras in metropolises across the world, and the spread of facial-recognition algorithms, provides governments and corporations with a handy tool for tracking people who aren't even online. None-theless, the internet, in connecting us all together, has enabled governments to connect up to us in ways we can't control, and don't want.

This mass surveillance has not contributed in any way to greater security. No terrorist attacks have been thwarted due to the vast eavesdropping surveillance established by our govern-ments. No would-be terrorists have been stopped because mass surveillance has enabled security agencies to spot their activities. In the words of the American Civil Liberties Union, 'The pesky, rather inconvenient fact is that the government's mass surveil-lance programs operating under Section 215 of the Patriot Act have never stopped an act of terrorism. That is not the opinion of the National Security Agency's most ardent critics, but rather the findings of the president's own review board and the Privacy and Civil Liberties Oversight Board . . . there is no evidence that it has helped identify a terrorism suspect or "made a concrete different in the outcome of a counterterrorism investigation."' Virtually every perpetrator of terror attacks in recent years—and some mass shootings in the United States as well—had already been known to authorities as a potential terrorist or criminal, but had not become the subject of any additional monitoring that prevented their actions. Nonetheless, governments insist ever greater powers of mass surveillance are required.

The digital trails that we leave behind, the routine collec-tion of information about us as we go about our lives, is also used to relentlessly manipulate us. Consider how much infor-mation Facebook provides to advertisers about you: where you live, what you do, what kind of computer and internet connection you use, what kind of friends you have, how fast you type or move your mouse. All of that is obtained before you produce any content on the site—and much of it is available to *any* website you visit. Once you begin interacting on Facebook, you dramatically expand the amount of personal information you are providing—particularly your family circumstances, your politics, how much you travel and where to, what you consume. Nor is this merely an arithmetic effect of adding more data to an existing electronic profile of you: as you provide more personal data, the data you have previously provided also becomes proportionally more useful.

The purpose of that information is to enable these companies—Facebook, the advertisers who generate its profits and the firms who develop marketing strategies—to target advertising at you in ways that—as we saw in relation to the disruption of traditional media—traditional broadcasting and newspapers could never hope to do. Facebook itself boasts of the case of Republican senator Pat Toomey, who in 2016, after spending a couple of million dollars on Facebook ads, was able to lift his polling by double-digit figures among what are deemed 'persuadables'—based on the personal data accumulated about them by Facebook. While controversy erupted in early 2018 over the role of the political marketing firm Cambridge Analytica in the 2016 US election and its use of Facebook data, it was merely doing exactly what Facebook itself does and which is central to Facebook's hugely successful business model: construct personal profiles of people using information they themselves have put online in order to sell things to them. You may think you're not important enough to warrant surveillance but corporations and political parties disagree: the more information they can find out about you, the more they can tailor their marketing to you. Political parties across the world have been compiling databases on individual voters for decades to enable the better targeting of campaigns during elections; in Australia, the major political parties specifically exempted themselves from the Commonwealth privacy framework so that voters can't find out what each party has accumulated on them. Facebook, Google and other online actors merely offer parties another and richer source of information about voters to supplement their already detailed profiles.

Did this kind of granular profiling and highly targeted marketing actually achieve the kind of results that Cambridge Analytica executives—and Facebook itself—boast of? They would certainly like us to think so, since it makes their product more attractive. Moreover, plenty of progressives would prefer to believe that dark political arts and manipulation delivered Donald Trump and the Brexit campaign victory, rather than accept that they won fairly. More likely, as with 'fake news', these techniques probably didn't play a major role in Trump's victory—but will expand in their sophistication and use in coming years, unless we decide to stop putting so much personal information online.

Biographical note: disillusion, delusion and intrusion

I've covered surveillance, national security and online activism for a decade and the scariest thing that I've discovered is how unevil evil actually is.

I've met, spoken with, hung out with, been on panels with, questioned or observed at close quarters many important people in what I call the online security space. I've seen first-hand what long-term, arbitrary detention has done to Julian

Assange. I've done webinars (yeah, I hate that name too) with Barrett Brown, whom I was happy to support a little while he was in gaol for the crime of challenging the US cyber military-industrial complex.

I've also spoken with a thoughtful, intelligent US ambassador about Assange, WikiLeaks and copyright. I know that some politicians genuinely work hard to try to resolve the tension between the constant pressure for action against terrorism and protecting basic rights. I've quizzed the former Director of National Intelligence James Clapper, whom I'm in the habit of referring to as a perjurer. I've spoken to tech people at the coalface and in executive positions in companies. I've spoken to ministers and shadow ministers in the cybersecurity space and some of the world's smartest civil-rights activists.

None of them are the one-dimensional characters that their opponents—some of whom include me and people like me—would have us believe. There are now serious concerns about WikiLeaks' role in the 2016 US election and the Trump campaign, but I still believe WikiLeaks is one of the most important forces for transparency and good government of the twenty-first century. I believe someone like James Clapper was a flawed bureaucrat tasked with the impossible job of ensuring something like 9/11 never happened again while also ensuring no one's rights were ever seen to be violated. I believe executives in the world's most powerful tech corporations do indeed pursue the interests of their shareholders, and if that conflicts with the interests of customers, the latter lose out. But I also think many of them have a genuine grasp of the importance of privacy—even if only because users have shamed them into it—and in the case of Google and Apple, can be successfully pushed to better protect it.

All of these people have made mistakes, and, no, they're not all equal in terms of good will and morality. The mistakes and lies of someone in power are far more important than those of people outside the hierarchies of power, or those who seek to hold the powerful to account. But it's hard to avoid having a more human understanding of the way different people confront different challenges.

In 2011, I'd written an ebook called *War on the Internet* about how the internet was another of history's waves of connectedness—like Protestantism and trade unionism—and authorities should accept they would be powerless to stop it.

In retrospect, it was an almost charmingly naïve work, not because the central thesis wasn't correct, but because I entirely failed to grasp that if individuals could connect up, governments could connect up even better, as could corporations, and that the internet offered unparalleled opportunities for governments and companies to connect up with the rest of us—by monitoring all of us.

Moreover, governments and corporations did this systemically. I don't mean there was a conscious effort to turn the twenty-first-century West into a surveillance civilisation. Rather, that happened as a function of how governments and corporations are designed and operated—as a function of the way they work as *systems*. Unless actively and tightly constrained, governments and corporations will, by their natures, seek more power over the rest of us. The internet has merely enabled this existing tendency to develop in a much scarier direction, because it provides new opportunities for the acquisition of power by accessing and controlling our information.

The people that drive this process are the mid-level functionaries, the government and corporate bureaucrats who keep these systems ticking over. The Assistant Secretary in the Attorney-General's Department who prepares a cabinet submission on mass surveillance. The company executive who negotiates a deal to sell customer data to an ever-wider variety of creepy marketing firms. The politician who chairs an intelligence committee with the aim of promoting himself, rather than taking the responsibility seriously. These people act thoughtlessly, without regard for the impact of their actions. They see themselves as doing perfectly reasonable things, concerned never to do anything that might reflect badly on themselves or harm their prospects.

This, I've come to realise, is the important dividing line. It's not between, say, information activists and intelligence officials, or civil-liberties advocates and security agencies. It's between those who understand that we've created a surveillance civilisation and think seriously about what that means, and those who should understand but don't care, for whom thinking critically about such things is more than their job's worth. You can have serious disagreements with the former, but they speak the same language and understand the same concepts. As former intellectual property lawyer and US Ambassador Jeff Bleich once said to me, they 'get it'. But the latter, the jobsworths, are the ones who drive the system that enmeshes us.

The jobsworths cluster in bureaucracies; Canberra is full of them. They are what makes the whole thing systemic, who keep it ticking over even in the absence of strong direction from people in power. Personable people who go home to their families every night after a day of unreflectively stoking the boilers of the system, thoughtlessly keeping it operating, ensuring its reach extends ever further. And they're very hard to stop, precisely because they don't think critically about the tasks they are engaged in, and because they form a vast apparatus that has extraordinary power and money. It takes strong leadership from senior people to halt them, and reversing their progress is rare and very difficult.

And the fact that I used to be one myself is probably the reason they infuriate me so much.

Conclusion: perfect storm

The internet is the great dislocation of our time, disrupting us psychologically, socially and economically. Previous disruptive new media may have spread as quickly—like television—but did not have the same economic impact. Previous economic disruptions did not have the kind of neurological and social impact of the internet. Disruptive innovations that changed the way humans thought have previously taken decades and centuries to cause change. Rarely, if ever, have such fundamental changes occurred at the same time and over such a short period: our heads are being rewired, the way we relate and communicate with others has fundamentally altered and expanded, one of our key civic institutions is vanishing, we now live under permanent surveillance, and a large-scale process of economic disruption is underway that will not be concluded for decades. And all this from a standing start around 20 years ago, when the internet stopped being a tool for academics and researchers and became widely available.

But the internet doesn't merely inflict disruption and dislocation by itself; it accelerates and enables the dislocations caused by neoliberalism. For those excluded from economic identities, the internet furnishes a perfect mechanism for discovering non-economic and even anti-social and tribal identities, regardless of geography. The internet is the perfect 24/7, go-with-you-anywhere delivery mechanism for the backlash against the economic identity imposed by neoliberalism. The surveillance enabled by the internet gives corporations ever finer-grained information about consumers to target and manipulate them, eroding trust and increasing the sense of disempowerment among ordinary people. And giant internet companies that dominate their markets are among the world's biggest tax avoiders, exploiting their cross-border activities to evade the restrictions of nation states.

The internet has also played an important role in exacerbating the decline in the effectiveness of our political systems. It has splintered what used to be a relatively unified information and media environment, in which people were forced, for better or for worse, to accept the same facts about the world. It is wrecking the institution of public interest journalism—both by annihilating its traditional business model and by providing a platform for propaganda masquerading as journalism. And it enables more effective political campaigning of ever more hollow political parties that aim to reflect back at us the profiles they've carefully compiled on us.

Each of these dislocations would be immensely disruptive by itself, but the interaction of these three phenomena multiplies the havoc wreaked by each, three waves of disruption peaking together—or perhaps troughing? The result can be seen in the election of Trump: the wave of white working-class disaffection and sense of disempowerment created by neoliberalism, the role of fake news and propaganda in the election cycle and the inability of an inept, Establishment, business-as-usual politician to defeat him despite a wealth of opportunities to do so. Or Pauline Hanson and a clutch of her fellow senators being ushered back into federal politics by Malcolm Turnbull's insipid campaign, representing a part of Australia that feels unserved and left behind by the economy, overwhelmed by modernity and that speaks to itself in paranoid conspiracy theories online.

Three long-term, epochal challenges combining to inflict even greater damage than each could by itself. What do we do? Is there anything we *can* do?

PART 5

REPAIRING THE
PRECARIOUS CRUST

There was much delight in corners of the far Left when Donald Trump defeated Hillary Clinton. Clinton was seen as a hawkish neoconservative, likely to continue the US tradition of foreign military intervention. Her husband was, along with Tony Blair, regarded as the exemplar of the tainted 'Third Way'. Her embrace of identity politics illustrated her refusal to accept the realities of market economics and its impact on the working class. She was the ultimate Establishment candidate, representing the Democratic branch of the oligarchy that rules America, with the help of Wall Street and the military-industrial complex.

How, then, to regard Donald Trump, a lying fascist and misogynist who boasted of using his celebrity to rape women? Among the far Left, Trump's personality was to be disregarded; it was more important to understand what he *represented*. To them, Trump was either some sort of working-class id erupted into politics, the first authentic presidential candidate for decades, who had tapped into the ferocious anger at neoliberalism. Or—better yet—he was an opportunity for genuine revolutionary change, which he would provoke, if not carry out himself.

Someone, somewhere, on the internet invented the term 'purity Left' for these left-wing opponents of Clinton—people who regarded Clinton as essentially as bad as Trump, if not as personally objectionable. These were people who far preferred the more economically progressive Bernie Sanders. Most of Sanders' policies, centring on a more progressive tax system, more welfare and an increase in America's pitiful minimum wage, are in fact fairly mainstream policies in most developed countries, but he was wrongly portrayed by friend and foe alike as little short of a socialist.

But viewing a government purely through the lens of whether it will be bad enough to provoke alienation or cause 'real change' is a luxury beyond the means of many. For people in the bottom decile of income earners, government policies have dramatic consequences, even in a relatively economically secure country like Australia. In a country like the United States, with a minimal safety net, no employment protections and poor public infrastructure, a country that refuses to even look after the veterans of its many wars let alone anyone else, government policies can literally mean life or death. For such people, a less worse government, even if it fails to deliver a radical redistribution of income or overthrow market economics, makes a difference that most of us are unlikely to notice but which is crucial nonetheless. For comfortable, securely employed left-wingers, how to feed their kids, how to afford a sick day, how to access an abortion when reproductive health services have been withdrawn and attacked, are issues to tweet about, not to experience.

That, of course, is one of the annoying things about democracy—it's always a contest to determine the least-worst option. Hillary Clinton might have been a neocon offering economic business-as-usual with some tweaks to make it less repulsive to people. But for the millions of Americans—including many who refused to vote for Clinton, of course—who'll lose access to health services if Trump and the GOP get their way, for the millions of women who are seeing a steady erosion of their basic reproductive rights, the difference is important.

There's a broader point to all this: when an economic and political system is failing in the way that our own has failed in recent years, is the answer reform (actual reform, not 'economic reform') or revolution? Revolution needn't involve storming parliament and overthrowing the existing political system—it can be the adoption of radically different economic policies that reassert the centrality of government in the economy, rather than markets.

The question that vexed Keynes and other economic thinkers as the 1930s unravelled around them was how best to preserve the achievements, however limited, of civilisation when the economic structures underpinning that civilisation were driving large sections of the population into misery through no fault of their own. Or, as it was occasionally rephrased, how to save capitalism from itself, and thereby preserve the material benefits it had yielded, while limiting its tendency to ever greater exploitation of people by powerful economic interests.

But there's a trickier question arising from this (one that Keynes and his peers wouldn't have thought to grapple with because they had the mindset of a nation enjoying the last stages of empire). Given the relative success of neoliberalism—at least over other economic systems—at lifting so many people in developing countries out of poverty, to what extent are we justified in halting the entire project because people in Western countries, and especially white males in Western countries, feel threatened, alienated and angered by it? If neoliberalism is going to reduce the level of absolute poverty in the world, but also make Western people a little poorer, what are we to do? What would the Purity Left do?

There are, fortunately, common interests on this question. Compelling multinational corporations to pay a greater proportion of tax is good both for developed countries like Australia and developing countries that struggle to prevent the massive tax minimisation efforts of global companies. And efforts to improve labour conditions and wages in developing countries directly serve the interests of Western workers and businesses, which become less vulnerable to outsourcing to developing countries, and which have more opportunities for exports to developing countries where living standards and consumer demand have increased. But there's no getting away from the fact that neoliberalism and open borders are conducive to both rising incomes in developing countries, and conducive to falling incomes and growing inequality in developed countries.

The reality in any Western democracy is that households won't tolerate stagnant or falling incomes, regardless of what's happening in developing countries. While it might not be ethical, the first responsibility of politicians in Western countries is to their own voters, not to the welfare of people in developing countries. And people in Western countries are more inclined to generosity to developing countries if they feel economically secure themselves, and that their interests are represented.

Economic orthodoxies have failed us before. We've lived through major technological change. Democracies have suffered crises of confidence and internal and external challenges. In the 1930s there were two out of those three, and the result was a depression and a world war. That's not to say the same fate awaits us, but just that the stakes are considerable if we fail to address the alienation, disempowerment and resentment created by the combination of neoliberalism, internet disruption and hollowed-out governments. For those of us who prefer reform over revolution, who think we should give overhauling capitalism a crack before resorting to Venezuelan-style chaos, the challenge is to devise genuinely effective policies that not merely mitigate but *reverse* the noxious effects of neoliberalism in the West, while trying to preserve its economic benefits. Policies that don't merely stave off the kinds of election results we've seen in recent years, but actually give voters reason to support political and economic systems. Stopping revolution isn't an end in itself—giving people a valid reason to support existing institutions must be.

This is a complex challenge and necessarily there are trade-offs. Net economic growth might be marginally lower (or it may not be), but it will be more sustainable for having wider political support. The net benefits for developing countries might be lower, but still better than if a full-scale trade war broke out, and immigration to Western countries was shut down, as a result of populist governments.

In putting together some solutions, I'm going to show my working. That is, I'm going to provide the philosophical, logical (hopefully) and evidential building blocks for why the ten ideas I'm advancing will address the problems generated by this historical moment of dislocation. And that starts with some first principles.

While it's convenient to blame individuals for some of the problems described in preceding chapters, that obscures how their actions are systemic. That is, it is more useful to understand their actions as those of a system operating in what it 'understands' are its own interests. A corporate lobbyist may successfully lobby against legislation that would protect workers' safety, and people die as a consequence. An auditor may advise a large company on how to avoid tax, depriving states of much-needed revenue, which means fewer services for citizens. A senior bureaucrat may lament that Freedom of Information laws are an impediment to good government. A politician may introduce a corporate tax cut that benefits companies that have made generous donations to her party. All are functioning as parts of a system: corporations seeking to maximise returns to shareholders, bureaucrats following instructions, politicians implementing policies that reflect both ideology and self-interest. Any persistent, functional system will have within it the means to preserve and replicate itself, even in the face of threats. That's why bureaucratic organisations of any kind will clone themselves in recruitment, and devise ways to protect themselves from scrutiny, complete with carefully devised rationalisations for why scrutiny is a bad thing. It's why they will work eternally to extend their powers and resources.

Any 'solutions' that target individuals, or focus on specific policy issues, will thus risk treating only the symptoms rather than the systemic challenges created by the three forces of disruption.

It's also clear that however much we want to reverse some aspects of these disruptions, there can be no going back in many areas. Indeed, the impacts of digitisation and the internet still have decades to play out, as disintermediation, automation and outsourcing dislocate economies and disrupt new industries, this time further up the pay scale than manufacturing jobs. Nor are we likely to return to an era of mass political participation. Privatisation, in most cases, is likely to be too costly to reverse. But, again, these are symptoms, not causes. Effective changes must address the drivers of a widespread perception that the economic and political system serves the powerful, not ordinary people.

Solutions

1. Radical transparency

Political donations are one of the key mechanisms of access to, and influence over, politicians. Any serious effort to curb the influence of powerful economic interests such as large corporations and industries must deal with their ability to buy influence and access. But the regulation of political donations has proven extraordinarily difficult in Australia, because politicians have a vested interest in keeping them unreformed. The Coalition has been particularly hostile to reform, but Labor hasn't always come to the issue with good will—in particular, it is keen to ensure that its massive flow of funding from trade unions is maintained. But even if you dramatically tightened the rules around donations, or even banned donations to political parties outright, there'd still be the problem of third-party groups such as GetUp, or industry bodies. Better to remove the need for election war chests by banning any kind of political advertising. Then it becomes much easier to ban problematic donations—from businesses, from unions, from foreigners—because they're no longer necessary. Curbs on political advertising would also require parties to run better on-the-ground campaigns within electorates, providing an incentive to find ways to recruit more members.

Alas, the High Court, magically inventing an implied right to political communication at the behest of the television networks in 1992 in the ACTV case, struck down this exact approach under the Hawke–Keating government. That disastrous decision did nothing for free speech in Australia but did do an awful lot for the advertising revenues of media moguls and the political influence of unions, corporations and foreign donors.

A way through the mess created by the High Court is to dramatically limit donations to political parties and political candidates to a small sum, no more than several thousand dollars, and make that a global limit—donations to different branches of the same party would not be separately counted. This would severely limit the amount of money political parties would have to advertise, but within the bounds set out by the High Court's interpretation of the constitution. Parties should also be required to report all donations above one hundred dollars, within 24 hours of receipt, online (uploaded to an Electoral Commission public database), with an appropriate penalty for non-disclosure—say, a fine of 20 per cent of the amount of the donation for every day it hasn't been posted. Donors themselves would not have to report publicly—they would only be required to advise the Electoral Commission of their donation within some set period—a week, a month, a quarter—to act as a check on the political parties.

The definition of donations should also be amended to require the reporting of any amount of money paid to a political party, regardless of whether it was for a good or service or a simple donation, in cash or in kind. This would end what political parties have been doing for some years—shifting their donors over to a subscription basis, which doesn't require reporting.

Banning, or severely curtailing, donations to third-party groups—groups whose primary role may not even be political advocacy—has more serious implications for both free speech and other basic rights. It's also problematic to ban or strongly regulate advertising by such groups. However, there's a way to reconcile the problem. If third-party groups wish to advertise on political matters, then let them be subject to the same political donation limits, and disclosure requirements, that political parties are subject to. People can still donate. Parties and non-parties can still advertise. But the capacity for external groups to purchase influence via donations will be drastically diminished.

It's also time for a fundamental change of approach in relation to government transparency. I'm suggesting a series of arcane-sounding but powerful changes that would bring the exercise of influence over government out into the open, and undermine the culture of government and bureaucratic secrecy, based on a threshold question: 'Is there a compelling case for not making all information publicly available?'

- Mere assertion that information is 'national security' or 'commercial in confidence' should not be grounds for being withheld from release through Freedom of Information laws or via parliamentary inquiries. There needs to be an independent body within government, a Transparency Commissioner, who would have power to order the release of information subject to a test that a reasonable person would believe there were strong public interest grounds for not releasing it. And the process should operate with minimal cost to applicants.

- All politicians should be required to release detailed meeting diaries with the identities of all meeting participants, except the constituents of House of Representative MPs, with an exemption for whistleblowers. Cabinet agendas should be made available and cabinet submissions should be released after the end of the current parliamentary term. 'Cabinet in Confidence' has taken on a Holy Grail status in Canberra, wholly unjustified by the realities of government. Governments are entitled to consider, and debate, policy issues in confidence. But the tradition of waiting many years before the public sees an expurgated account of what decisions were made is a twentieth-century relic that needs to be binned.

- There should be only two, not three, senate estimates hearings a year but the second should, like budget estimates, be two weeks long to make it more difficult for bureaucrats to evade questioning. Estimates committees should be classed as references committees, not legislative committees—that is, a non-government senator would chair hearings, to prevent chairs from running interference on behalf of the executive. And there should be considerably greater use of committees' powers to conduct in-camera hearings to thwart public servants' use of excuses such as commercial confidentiality to avoid answering questions. If public servants know that an invocation of commercial confidentiality would lead not to successfully evading a question but a referral to an in-camera hearing (perhaps after the committee suspends its ordinary hearings at 11 p.m. that night), it's likely the use of that particular excuse would diminish. The practice of bureaucrats taking estimates questions 'on notice'—whereby they can evade giving answers under the pretence they don't have the answer in front of them, and undertake to provide answers in writing, usually many months later—should also be curtailed. One of the pleasures of watching the banking royal commission has been seeing banking executives respond to difficult questions with 'I'll need to take that on notice' only to be told that they can't do that and must answer. The easiest fix would be to have a recall day after every estimates committee hearing in which departments would be required to appear again and present answers to questions taken on notice or be found in contempt of the Senate.

- Ministers and their offices, and shadow ministers, should be required to publish a log of contacts with media organisations. Want to plant a report with a friendly journalist? Want to background the press anonymously? Want to co-ordinate a campaign against a particular target? All good. You just have to show how often, when and for how long you spoke to journalists.

But why should politicians have all the fun? Radical transparency should be extended to all other bodies that collect personal information. All public-service agencies, corporations, government business enterprises, political parties, trade unions, charities and NGOs should be required to provide—for free—all the information they have on any individual on the request of that individual, within ten working days (backed by large fines per day, which would be split between the individual and government, to encourage compliance). This will impose a significant cost burden on those bodies, which is partly the point. Want to collect information on people? Then have ready the systems that will enable you to tell them what you've collected. Moreover, individuals should be able to give permission to third parties, such as civil-rights organisations, to inquire on their behalf. The purpose would be partly to provide greater transparency around the data agencies and corporations collect on us, and partly to provide a mechanism for people, and bodies that represent them, to place significant financial pressure on them.

But you don't have to wait for governments to pass laws to protect your privacy. If you feel overwhelmed by the relentless accumulation of your personal data that governments and companies engage in, that's exactly how they *want* you to feel—powerless and without the ability to protect yourself. But there are some simple ways to protect your privacy:

- Install a Virtual Private Network on your computers—and pay for one, because the ones you can access for free are worth what you pay for them. If you do nothing else, do this.
- If you use Google, install an add-on like Trackmenot, which silently floods Google with a constant stream of random queries from your browser, making it very difficult to compile an accurate portrait of you from your search history.
- Facebook is a vast privacy destruction machine that sells your most personal information to terrible companies hell-bent on manipulating you. If you use Facebook, only use it in a special browser you don't use for anything else

(Facebook tracks your browsing and sells that information too). Falsify as many as possible of your personal details in Facebook, especially where you live and what you do. And do not, under any circumstances, put Facebook Messenger on your phone.

- Use the security features of your devices and apps—companies like Apple and Google have taken privacy much more seriously post Snowden, and are giving users more options, and more user-friendly options, to protect their privacy, as well as embedding greater security in their products.
- Use IP-based communications applications, rather than telephony-based applications, as much as possible—so use Signal instead of texting, use Facetime instead of calling someone.

None of these will make you safe from prying eyes. But they make the cost of surveilling you significantly greater, and reduce the capacity of companies you don't even know exist to compile a profile about you that they will use to manipulate you.

2. A significantly more progressive tax system

This would encompass not merely a higher top income tax bracket—and perhaps a new top 60 per cent bracket for incomes over one million dollars per annum—but a serious attack on capital gains as a primary source of income for the super-rich. Cutting the capital gains tax discount from 50 per cent to 25 per cent or even lower, perhaps over several years, would be a good start, and reduce the taxpayer subsidy to housing investors. Further changes to curtail superannuation tax concessions for the rich are also needed—perhaps reducing the level of tax-free super contributions from the current level

of $30,000 to $11,000, as suggested by the Grattan Institute. The new cap on annual non-concessional contributions
should also be cut further from $100,000 per year.

In line with radically greater transparency within government, the tax affairs of large companies should also be subject
to much greater scrutiny. Labor has proposed using Commonwealth procurement processes to achieve this: if large companies
want to participate in Commonwealth tenders, they should
provide detailed accounting of their tax practices for revenue
earned in Australia and their use of tax havens around the world.
A failure to provide sufficient detail of tax behaviour would rule
the tenderer out. Apple and Google, which make relatively little
money from federal government tendering, might be happy to
forgo the limited revenue they obtain from Commonwealth
contracts, but it would be a significant impact for Amazon and
Microsoft via the former's web services and the latter's widely
used software. And if all state governments applied a similar
requirement, the incentive to comply would be greater.

Increases in the taxation rates for higher-income earners,
and even a super–income tax on the very rich, are unlikely
to generate significant additional revenue, but the point is to
engender greater confidence among voters in the fairness of
the tax system, which has taken a battering in recent years:
what irks voters about Australia's tax system isn't the amount
of tax they pay (no one likes paying tax) but the sense that
some people don't pay their fair share. That plays directly
into the sense that our current economic and governmental system works to the advantage of the few, not the many.
Addressing that sense is a relatively painless way of strength-
ening support for that system. Reduction in the capital gains
tax discount, however, will generate significant revenue, while

superannuation concession changes will also provide a tidy sum that will grow in coming decades. What to do with this additional revenue? While there's a budget deficit or substantial net debt left, it should be banked. Why this application of 'austerity' budgeting? In the event of a recession or international downturn of some kind—perhaps the long-feared/hyped China crash—Australian leaders will need substantial fiscal stimulus to stave off high unemployment, as Labor did in response to the 2008 financial crisis. Having a sound fiscal position from which to do so will be particularly important, given it is unlikely that there will be similar levels of monetary policy stimulus available to the Reserve Bank: the current low level of interest rates and the unlikelihood of a medium-term return to the kinds of interest rate levels up until 2007 will mean there is limited monetary ammunition to fire at a crisis. This will also apply in other countries, meaning the overall global monetary resource for stimulus is unlikely to be as great.

There's still a lingering denialism about the role of stimulus in response to the financial crisis from neoliberals. It's understandable—hardline neoliberals want to erase any role for government in economic growth. But the Australian experience of using fiscal and monetary stimulus to keep unemployment from rising above 6 per cent and avoiding technical recession—which would have pulled the struts out from under consumer confidence—had long-term benefits that continue to this day. It is critical that we're able to do the same again, if need be.

3. A bill of rights

A bill of rights would help re-tilt the balance of power between citizen and government back toward the former, and give citizens a new mechanism for influencing policy beyond voting every three years. It's also an issue where I confess to having changed my mind. In my former life in the Australian Public Service, I took the view that, whatever I may have thought of a particular government, it had far greater legitimacy than any public servant could ever have, and it more effectively represented the 'public interest' than any bureaucrat. Accordingly, I saw my role and that of my colleagues as serving the government of the day, and not the public or the public interest.

And I extended that kind of thinking to the issue of a bill of rights: to be effective, it would have to curb the power of parliaments and legislators by allowing judges to subjectively interpret both that rights framework and a piece of contested legislation in a way that bound the legislature. Far better, in my view, to allow the public, via its representatives, to perform the role of protecting our rights.

What changed my mind was watching how differently the debates triggered by the Snowden revelations unfolded in the United States and Australia.

In the United States, while Snowden was certainly demonised, he was also seen by some legislators, including Republicans, as an important whistleblower. In Australia, Snowden was repeatedly condemned by Labor and Coalition figures alike. George Brandis called Snowden a 'traitor', despite even the Obama administration, with its war on whistleblowers well underway, not doing so. Brandis also said that Snowden had placed Australian lives at risk, but was unable to produce evidence to substantiate the claim.

Snowden's revelations also prompted a number of court actions in the United States, leading to the US Court of Appeals ruling that bulk metadata collection by the NSA was illegal, and confirmed that the Director of National Intelligence, James Clapper, had lied to Congress. But above all, Snowden ignited an extensive debate in the United States about mass surveillance and the overreach of intelligence agencies. Barack Obama at one stage even claimed that he had been intending to commence just such a debate himself, but hadn't got around to it. Obama was forced to establish a review on the intelligence community's mass-surveillance powers, which famously concluded that they hadn't been required to prevent terror attacks.

As a result of that debate, Congress curbed the generous legislative remit under which the NSA operated, preventing it from collecting and storing metadata on American citizens, and improving the transparency relating to the ways in which US agencies could force the cooperation of communications companies. The legislative changes agreed by Congress did not represent a major change in the powers of the NSA or other intelligence community agencies, but they were almost unique in that they represented a curtailment of national security powers. It is a key characteristic of the War on Terror that governments have always given themselves ever-greater powers to surveil, detain and investigate—invariably justifying each extension by saying it 'gets the balance right' between freedom and security, despite the balance only ever tilting one way. Here, remarkably, was a parliament deciding to reduce those powers in the name of balance. It was all down to Edward Snowden.

In contrast, in Australia, there was ... nothing. While US politicians felt confident arguing the pros and cons of mass surveillance and the powers of electronic intelligence gathering agencies, in Australia the major parties collaborated to silence such debate. All efforts to discuss, confirm or find out more about the activities of the Australian agency most closely involved with the NSA and other 'Five Eyes' powers, the Australian Signals Directorate, were stymied by a conspiracy of silence between Labor and the Coalition to shield our intelligence agencies from scrutiny. Only the Greens, and then-South Australian senator Nick Xenophon, were not content to accept this. But there was even little interest within our media about the immense problems raised by what Snowden had revealed about Australia.

Nor has there been any legal action undertaken in response to ASD's handling of bulk metadata on Australians to the NSA, or any other aspect of the ASD's activities, given both the lack of a legal framework for such litigation and the dearth of well-resourced civil society groups to undertake it. Indeed, the ASD appears beyond any criticism or reproach from both the mainstream media and policymakers, despite serious lapses in its performance.

Australia also lacks an effective system of parliamentary oversight of intelligence and counter-terrorism. The United States has two intelligence committees—one in the House, one in the Senate—and they aren't controlled by the executive. Here, there is a parliamentary committee with a legislated responsibility to oversee the budgets of intelligence agencies and the listing of terror groups, but it is controlled by the executive and limited in what it can do anyway. Compared to its US counterparts, the Parliamentary Joint Committee on Intelligence and Security is weak. The conflict between the US Senate intelligence committee and the CIA over the committee's torture report—which prompted the CIA to spy on the committee, then publicly apologise for having done so—is unthinkable here: such an inquiry would never be undertaken by the PJCIS—it has no power to even initiate its own inquiries.

Clearly our politicians won't—and in some cases can't, even if they wanted to—provide the kind of protections of basic freedoms that Americans have via their Bill of Rights and that Europeans have through the European Court of Justice (and a good template for an Australian bill of rights would be the first eighteen articles of the European Convention on Human Rights). If the United States can cope with a bill of rights—complaints about activist judges notwithstanding—it is hard to believe Australia couldn't also do so.

4. More power for unions

While economists, treasuries and central bankers have racked their brains trying to explain why wages growth has been so stubbornly low in recent years in so many countries, some experts have been making the point over and over again that it's no coincidence wages have stopped growing at the same time as union membership and power have reached historical nadirs.

Despite claims advanced by people like Malcolm Turnbull when it was passed, and incessantly by employer groups ever since, the *Fair Work Act* has been a huge success for Australian business. It has delivered everything that employers have traditionally claimed to have wanted—productivity growth, low levels of industrial disputation, low wages growth. Despite continuing efforts by business groups to argue that there is some missing 'flexibility' in industrial relations—independent arbiters such as the Productivity Commission and the Reserve Bank notwithstanding—it is clear that, if anything, the system is biased in favour of employers rather than unions.

Unions are the best—or, perhaps, least worst—way of protecting workers' conditions and negotiating higher pay rises than individuals themselves could manage. The experience of recent years in Australia, where a number of the country's major retailers have been found to have routinely broken the law in failing to pay their staff award wages, with apparent impunity, illustrates that Australians can't trust industrial relations regulators to protect workers. The *Fair Work Act* currently limits the range of matters on which unions can lawfully enter workplaces in relation to the protection of workers' pay and conditions, limits the matters on which they can take protected industrial action (not enough, according to employers, who want to confine all industrial relations negotiations to a tiny group of issues) and limits their capacity to take industrial action—the Fair Work Commission decided in early 2018 that any industrial action inconveniencing people—such as strikes by train drivers—is in breach of the *Fair Work Act*, even if numerous other legal hurdles to strikes have been cleared.

In each of these areas, unions should be given greater power, to enhance their bargaining power and prevent the undermining of existing protections. They should have greater workplace access, the range of matters on which industrial action can be taken should be expanded and the ban on striking in several industries that the Fair Work Commission confected should be rolled back to emergency services only.

Will this lead to more work days lost to industrial disputes? Indeed. But that's the price of more effective bargaining. Will greater rights and powers for trade unions be abused by some unionists? Absolutely. But someone can *always* be found who abuses power, no matter what the environment. At this point, the greater danger to Australians—both individually within the

workplace and for overall wages growth across the economy—
is employers abusing *their* power. In that context, the risk that
unionists will abuse their power is one worth taking.

5. More independent institutions

Australia, like a number of other countries, has an independent
central bank that has managed monetary policy very effectively
since the 1990s recession. Australia also has, in the Productivity
Commission, a highly respected independent policy arm that
delivers the kind of 'frank and fearless advice' that Australian
public service bureaucrats insist they still deliver but which
hasn't been heard in many ministerial offices for decades. The
Australian National Audit Office is one of the most ferocious
critics of incompetence within government. The ABC is one
of Australia's most respected and trusted institutions, valued
for its independence from government. We need more independent government agencies.

You need to be careful about establishing independent institutions. We live in a democracy, and by and large politicians
should be responsible for the important decisions. And the issue
is entangled in ideology. The Right likes to portray the Left
as inherently undemocratic, as favouring the rule of unelected
elitist technocrats over tribunes of the people, as believing that
ordinary people can't be trusted to know what is best for them.
Yet the concept of central banks being freed from political
pressure came from the Right. In Australia, the idea had particular resonance for the Coalition because of Paul Keating's poorly
chosen phrase that he 'had the Reserve Bank in my pocket'.
Necessarily, one's ideological view of whether the masses can
be trusted will vary depending on whether you're in power or
your opponent is.

But with the dominance of the executive branch over the parliamentary branch in Australia and the tendency of governments of both sides to shut down independent advice from the public service, more independent bodies that can publicly contest policy and administration is a good thing. An infrastructure equivalent of the Reserve Bank would be a good start—giving a body like Infrastructure Australia greater independence and its own infrastructure investment budget. Part of the mandate of a genuinely independent Infrastructure Bank could be to develop, and help fund, what the Reserve Bank and the International Monetary Fund have called for in Australia: a 'pipeline' of infrastructure projects that smoothes out the traditionally lumpy nature of infrastructure investment. By establishing a queue of projects, there would be less pressure on sector resources of the kind that arises when major projects clump together (as happened during the mining investment boom, when mining companies bid against each other to hire engineers and other talent) and, when economic growth is lower, a steady supply of major projects to keep the economy ticking over. It would also reduce costs by keeping construction plant and personnel in a smoother track of continuous work rather than allowing downtime between major projects. And it would increase the overall efficiency of infrastructure spending in Australia by reducing the proportion of projects selected for funding based on political considerations rather than the balance of benefits to costs involved.

Giving greater independence to, and more certain funding for, key business regulators, and especially the Australian Securities and Investment Commission, would also go some way to addressing the perception that corporations get off lightly when they break the law, although the problem with corporate regulators traditionally isn't politicisation, but industry capture.

Having a more independent Treasury would also instil greater confidence about the direction of economic and fiscal policy. Problematically, however, Treasury, along with other public service agencies, has become less independent and more overtly political in recent years; the tacit recognition of this has been in the bipartisan support for the establishment of a Parliamentary Budget Office, which provides, *inter alia*, independent assurance of tasks that once could have been regarded as safe in the hands of public service agencies— preparing budget forecasts and costing policies. Probably best to increase the resourcing for the PBO, and write Treasury off as an independent institution.

6. Significantly increase public funding for universities and vocational education

Workers better able to respond to the changes wrought by technology, maximise their incomes and use their skills and entrepreneurial nous to participate fully in the economy. Better informed citizens capable of critical thinking and civic participation. Those should be the goals, surely, of any tertiary education system. Some economists question the point of higher education, arguing it's simply a means for filtering people that employers will find useful. That completely ignores the capacity of tertiary education, particularly universities, to teach critical thinking skills, which are the basis both of being a useful employee and a worthwhile citizen. Being able to call bullshit on something impractical or damaging is a valuable life skill. But the story of Australia's universities since the 1980s has been a demonstration of the cliché of understanding the price of everything and the value of nothing. Heavily dependent on uncapped numbers of domestic students, and the 'export' of degrees to foreign students, Australia's universities have declined in quality as they've sought to maximise revenue and minimise costs. Australian students—who as citizens share in the communal ownership of our academic institutions—are collateral damage: governments have cut tertiary funding, confident the market will replace lost money, at the same time making universities more 'commercial', without any regard to the decline in academic standards that has ill-served those studying in them.

This decline also reduces the long-term productivity and capacity for innovation of the Australian economy. A significant cash injection that would enable universities to lift academic standards, and rely less on acting as degree factories for both foreign and domestic students, would not have immediately obvious economic benefits, but would better enable Australian students to enter the workforce highly skilled, flexible and capable of critical thinking. It would also improve us as a community and a polity in creating more engaged citizens capable of informed scepticism of powerful institutions.

But the biggest education policy disaster, primarily under Labor governments, was opening vocational education to private providers, and then providing them with public funding. The vocational education industry in Australia should at least have some value left as a how-not-to for future policymakers, a sad display of an ill-conceived neoliberal policy badly implemented. Some welcome Coalition government reforms have since driven the worst private-sector operators out of business, but what was once a successful public-sector vocational education system has become, in recent years, a scandal-plagued industry overrun by spivs. Like all public education, vocational education institutions tend to become dominated by education unions, but if featherbedding and constant demands for more funding are the worst unions ever do, that'll still be better by a long shot than the colossal disaster created by opening vocational education up to competition.

7. A treaty with, and constitutionally recognised voice for, First Australians

The 2017 Uluru Statement, calling for 'the establishment of a First Nations Voice enshrined in the constitution' and a 'Makarrata Commission to supervise a process of agreement-making between governments and First Nations and truth telling about our history', was the subject of wilful and malicious mischaracterisation and attack, by Malcolm Turnbull among others. As one reactionary said in response to the statement, it was 'just as offensive as to give people a special say due to their religion, or gender or anything else'.

The same types reject the idea of a treaty, insisting without any regard for legal doctrine that 'a country cannot have a treaty with itself', ignoring the long history of other colonial settler societies such as the United States and New Zealand, where treaties with Indigenous peoples are a core part of the law of the land. This position also, even more bizarrely, ignores the fact that in Australia, sovereignty is already split via a federation and we are only a matter of decades on from the Hawke government's deletion of the last vestiges of British sovereignty from Australian legislation. If Australians want a treaty with Indigenous Australians, they can readily have one. To assert otherwise is, bizarrely, to limit the popular sovereignty of Australia apparently so treasured by racists and reactionaries.

And there is a compelling case for a treaty with Indigenous Australians, recognition of them in the constitution and a voice for them integrated into the Australian government (which can be accomplished in any number of ways). The right-wing argument that Aboriginal and Torres Strait Islander people are just another group of Australians is a re-versioning of the lie of *terra nullius*. As the Uluru Statement notes, Aboriginal and Torres Strait Islanders are our First Nations. They must necessarily occupy a 'special' place in the Australian polity, different from all others, because they held sovereignty over this land prior to invasion. Australia remains an occupied country, where even the nation's highest court has ruled that white settlement has not obliterated forms of Aboriginal sovereignty, until a treaty is negotiated between the first peoples of the country and the nation that has been built over the top of them.

Even John Howard, notorious for his hostile attitude to reconciliation, recognised this. 'As a nation, we recognise and celebrate Indigenous people's special place as the first Australians,' his government said in 2002. Tony Abbott, who can be faulted for many things but not on his interest in and engagement with Indigenous communities, went further when leader of his party. 'We have to acknowledge that pre 1788 this land was as Aboriginal then as it is Australian now. Until we have acknowledged that we will be an incomplete nation and a torn people. We only have to look across the Tasman to see how it could have been done so much better. Thanks to the Treaty of Waitangi in New Zealand two peoples became one nation.' For once, Abbott summed an issue up perfectly— Australia remains an incomplete nation.

And a voice for Indigenous Australians is crucial not merely for symbolism but to provide greater agency to Aboriginal and Torres Strait Islander people in the way they are governed and thus to end one of the worst examples of government incompetence in Australian history. There is hard evidence, and near-unanimous agreement, that the more control Indigenous communities have over health programs, the more successful they are. The most effective way of 'closing the gap' on the extraordinary and shameful difference in health and mortality in Indigenous communities is to give those communities greater control over the prevention, diagnostic and treatment programs that will prevent Aboriginal and Torres Strait Islander peoples dying at far higher rates than the rest of us from highly preventable diseases such as heart disease, diabetes and smoking-related illnesses. Actually closing the gap, while bringing to an end white Australia's history as an occupier of stolen land, would represent a new start for a nation that has refused to accept its true nature for 230 years.

8. Don't protect industries

There are ideological reasons why neoliberals oppose protectionism. It interferes with the operation of the divinely appointed market. It increases the size of government. It arbitrarily benefits some industries at the expense of others. But the best reason to oppose protectionism is that it doesn't work. There are better ways for governments to support industries.

We've already covered how protectionism punishes consumers and other businesses, who have to pay more for products, often to protect a relatively small number of jobs. And we've seen how arbitrary protectionism tends to be—usually flowing into heavily unionised, heavily male manufacturing industries. With the decline of overt tariff-based protectionism, we're once again spending taxpayer money to prop up or expand industries that aren't competitive. In the case of the bipartisan decision to invest heavily in local naval construction capacity, this means the expenditure of millions of dollars per job. Far more jobs could be supported by taxpayers through greater infrastructure investment, which would not merely generate additional employment but provide an economically bene-ficial asset. This is in contrast to a submarine or warship that could be purchased far more cheaply offshore from countries that make them more efficiently than we ever will. Indeed, it's possible that more employment would be created by using all the government funding being poured into propping up uncompetitive sectors to give taxpayers a tax cut instead, which will increase overall demand.

Remember, also, that Australia faces the long-term problem of finding *workers*, not finding jobs, particularly in industries that we know will continue to expand in coming years, such as health and social care. Rather than protecting manufacturing industries, we should be aiming to ensure workers can shift to industries where jobs are growing. Ensuring workers have access to the kind of training opportunities that will enable them to move to growing industries is far more important than propping up, say, a local steel industry when other coun-tries produce high-quality steel much more cheaply.

9. Avoid UBI at all costs

A hardy perennial of the social welfare debate, Universal Basic Income has gained a new lease of life in the last couple of years thanks to Silicon Valley billionaires calling for it because of, they argue, the looming automation crisis. Give everyone a basic income, the tech billionaires say, and we need not be worried about mass unemployment. We can do away with the vast welfare bureaucracy, saving billions. Backers point to Milton Friedman's support for what he called a 'guaranteed income' or 'reverse income tax', as evidence of its intellectual legitimacy. And there are plenty on the Left who back the idea as well.

Earlier, we looked at the 'We'll all be rooned' automation argument and found it a little wanting, given what appears to be a growing dearth of workers in the West and, soon, in China, rather than a frightening rise in joblessness. Let's park that for a moment because there are other reasons why UBI is a terrible idea.

First, it's unaffordable. If we decided to give, say, the poorest 40 per cent of Australians (as in, not even close to everyone) the current Newstart allowance permanently, that's around $140 billion a year. The total welfare bill in Australia is only around $118 billion. Nor would you save much from sacking the 1900 bureaucrats of the Department of Social Services— around $6 billion a year.

But say you found an extra few tens of billions and decided to go ahead. What about disabled people who face higher costs and greater impediments to paid employment? We spend around $16 billion a year in additional income support to people with disabilities (despite Rupert Murdoch's papers claiming every single one is some sort of lying bludger). What about carers for people with disabilities? That's another $7 billion. Except, you sacked all the bureaucrats, so there's no one to assess these claims. So either you give *everyone* the extra income, which makes UBI even less affordable, or people with disabilities and their carers miss out. What about people living in Sydney and Melbourne versus those living in regional centres—the former face much higher housing costs than the latter. Does everyone get extra income, or do you re-employ some bureaucrats to assess housing costs as well as disability claims?

Fairly soon your UBI system either starts to resemble a targeted welfare system—or it remains grossly unfair.

Friedman thought UBI would encourage people to work, because they wouldn't lose any welfare payments even if they worked. It's true that UBI would remove the disincentive of high effective marginal tax rates, but it would also remove current incentives to enter the workforce at all. The evidence is mixed from UBI trials and longitudinal studies of welfare recipients about whether income support deters people from working, but it's hard to imagine how UBI would not encourage at least some people to give up looking for work altogether, entrenching long-term unemployment, reducing the economy's productivity and skill base and lowering participation—not to mention the long-term psychological and social costs of joblessness.

Nor is UBI a particularly good tool for addressing poverty, which is far more than a lack of cash. Those extra tens of billions you need for UBI might be more effectively directed at providing better education, better training, better childcare and early childhood education or health services, or social housing, than as income support—particularly if we think that education is the vector by which the inequality of neoliberalism impedes economic growth. In this sense, UBI is a market economics solution—simply give people on low incomes more money and let the market decide how to use it. But it's not clear that this won't simply perpetuate poverty rather than reduce it.

The real reason that many super-wealthy business people like UBI is that it would give them an excuse to pay lower and lower wages, confident that, first, people won't starve while working for them, and second, that there'll still be some basic level of demand for their products within the economy even if they slash wages. The fact that billionaires from the tech sector, which has a terrible reputation for being anti-union and paying low wages in the United States, are the most enthusiastic advocates of UBI should serve as warning about the real agenda behind it. And if, as some of them claim, the future will be one of widespread joblessness due to automation, then the arguments for UBI may change dramatically. Until then, it's a lazy policy option for people who think markets can fix everything.

10. Stop perpetuating the endless War on Terror

In 2017, Donald Trump, who had campaigned on withdrawing US troops from Afghanistan and ending America's long history of offshore military intervention, reversed himself and decided America needed to dramatically *escalate* its military involvement in Afghanistan. Trump's justification was that it was important that Afghanistan not become a base from which terrorists could attack the United States—which was the reason for the initial US invasion and occupation of Afghanistan in 2001 in the wake of 9/11.

The rationale, of course, is self-perpetuating—there will *always* be a need to ensure Afghanistan is not unstable enough to harbour terrorists, because Western military interventions and occupations, such as in Afghanistan, will always *generate* terrorists. And it's not merely Western troops: our air strikes that kill civilians, our drone strikes that incinerate children, Western-backed forces that commit war crimes (like the Saudi regime in Yemen), all radicalise people in the region and further afield—people who see Muslims being endlessly killed by the West or its proxies.

Western interventionism is not the sole reason for radicalisation—there are many others—but it's a primary reason, as some of the most senior intelligence officials in the West have repeatedly told us. Continuing military interventions in Middle Eastern countries guarantee that there will be a continuing 'need' for intervention for decades to come.[36] That's why neoconservatives like to talk about the 'decades-long' and 'century-long' War on Terror. And from their point of view, that's perfectly fine, because they, and the defence companies on whose boards they sit, and the policy think tanks they reside in, and the media that employs them as 'terrorism experts', and the governments that use terrorism to endlessly increase the powers and funding of security agencies, all benefit from it. For anyone genuinely interested in winning the War on Terror, the first step is to stop perpetuating it by sending Western soldiers, sailors, airmen and women and drone operators into the fray. The West should limit its role in Middle Eastern conflicts to humanitarian aide, and withdraw all military forces.

But surely, some will say, this will allow terrorists and monstrous regimes to prosper? The problem is, they're prospering *now*. The invasion of Iraq and the defeat of Saddam Hussein's monstrous regime led to the creation of ISIS. And the defeat of ISIS has allowed the Iranian mullahs—noted human-rights abusers and patrons of terrorists—to move into

---

36 In 2010, terrorist Faisal Shahzad tried to detonate a bomb in Times Square, and said he did so in revenge for the US war in Afghanistan. In 2017, US Defense Secretary James Mattis convinced Trump to re-expand the US presence in Afghanistan 'to prevent a bomb from going off in Times Square'.

Syria, along with Vladimir Putin's brutal thugocracy. All thanks to Western intervention.

The second step is to stop backing brutal Middle Eastern regimes because we think they're better for our own interests than governments that might be selected by their own people. That includes Israel, where our support for the corrupt apartheid regime of Benjamin Netanyahu has guaranteed there will be no resolution to the ongoing occupation of Palestinian territories and the maltreatment of Palestinians.

We might be amazed to discover they no longer 'Hate us for our freedom' if we respect theirs a bit more.

Vade in pace

It's said that the basic difference between progressives and conservatives is that the latter have a fundamentally pessimistic view of human nature, while the former take a more positive view. Annoyingly, both are justifiable positions. Sartre was right. Other people are hell, as any air traveller can tell you. Once you get to know them, though, people can be okay—good, even.

As a confirmed grump, a person whose curmudgeon-liness—curmudgeoneity?—is a matter of public record, I bow to no one in my willingness to assume the worst of the world and the people who inhabit it. But as someone with an interest in history, I also know this is the least worst time to be alive, and that history has shown us how that has been achieved. That democracy is the least worst way of governing ourselves. That capitalism, appropriately regulated, is the least worst way of running an economy, but in many areas we need governments to not merely regulate and nudge and prod, but *do* things, and do them competently, because the market screws up far more often than its dogged advocates will admit. That inequality is dangerous, and destabilising, and the innate tendency of capitalism to generate it must be constrained. That diversity and tolerance not merely make society more pleasant for anyone who isn't a heterosexual white male, but make it more productive and more efficient and wealthier. That bureaucracies of any kind always need to be strongly fenced in, with their powers limited and their workings made transparent, otherwise they'll expand and start to control us for, they'll insist, our own benefit. And that Australia will never resolve its identity as a colonial settler society properly without recognising, and negotiating a treaty with, its First Peoples.

But in the West, a lot of the social and economic progress we've made in recent decades is in serious danger. Dark forces that we thought we'd vanquished in the 1940s are, literally, on the march again. To see actual Nazis proudly protesting in the streets of an American city without rebuke from that country's president, to see Pauline Hanson don a burqa to mock Islam in Australia's Senate, is to be reminded that the politicisation of hate is only ever suppressed, not vanquished, and that the crust of civilisation can be precarious indeed.

All this, doubtless, will strike some readers as a bunch of centrist apologia, perhaps even more of the nonsense that got us to this awful moment in history in the first place. But I think Keynes was right: our civilisation relies on those 'rules and conventions skilfully put across and guilefully preserved'. It is the trashing of those rules and conventions, and their undermining by historical forces, that has given us the chaos of the last few years. The unglamorous and unexciting work of repairing and upgrading them, and getting our key institutions functioning more effectively than they have in recent decades, is the best way to bring this depressing chapter of Western history to a close.

ABOUT THE AUTHOR

Bernard Keane has been Crikey's correspondent in Canberra since 2008, writing on politics, media and economics. He was educated at the University of Sydney, where he studied history. Before joining Crikey he was a public servant and speech-writer in transport and communications. He is the author of the ebook *War on the Internet* and co-author of the bestseller *A Short History of Stupid*, with Helen Razer. He is also the author of *Surveillance*, his first novel.